Problem Solving with Prolog

Problem Solving with Prolog

John Stobo

School of Information Sciences
Hatfield Polytechnic

Pitman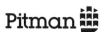

PITMAN PUBLISHING
128 Long Acre, London WC2E 9AN

A Division of Longman Group UK Limited

© John Stobo 1989

First published in Great Britain 1989

British Library Cataloguing in Publication Data
Stobo, John
  Problem solving with prolog.
  1. Computer systems. Programming languages :
  Prolog
  I. Title
  005.13'3

ISBN 0 273 02933 9

Reproduced and printed by photolithography
in Great Britain by Biddles Ltd, Guildford

Contents

Preface

Prolog is a programming language in which solutions to computing problems are expressed as facts representing relationships between objects and as rules specifying consequences which derive from facts. In Prolog, the mechanisms for representing knowledge about objects and relationships are both high-level and general-purpose. This brings two substantial benefits to the programmer. The first is that, to a very large extent, he or she is freed from concern about the organisation of physical storage for the data which a program is to manipulate. The second is the ease with which concepts and relationships from many areas of human activity can be expressed in the language. You will be able to use Prolog to tackle problems from outside the familiar scope of traditional computing, and you will be able to describe them in a concise and powerful notation. Many of these problems are in the exciting and growing area of Artificial Intelligence, where the ground rules for tasks are often uncertain or scarcely articulated, the tasks themselves so open-ended as to have no identifiable conclusion. Such tasks as general problem-solving, understanding natural language and acquiring and using expertise have been the province of human intellectual endeavour. Programming a computer to carry out these tasks is a challenge indeed.

When we consider applications such as these, we have to recognise that the traditional disciplines of systems design are not wholly appropriate. We cannot establish a full statement of requirements as a starting point, for these are ill-defined and come into focus only as system development proceeds. Instead, we develop systems incrementally. Prolog is a very valuable tool in this context because of its tremendous flexibility. It is normal to develop, test and refine parts of a large Prolog program separately and to extend the capabilities of the whole progressively.

Recognising that the need for an incremental approach to system development is inescapable, I teach in this book a method of program design and implementation which ensures the soundness of it. It is based on a collection of programming techniques that I call "The Programmers' Toolkit". Each technique comprises a description of what it is used for, and a step-by-step guide to how to use it. Program development consists in choosing the right tools from the kit and following carefully the instructions for their use.

I do not wish to foster the impression that Prolog is an esoteric language, of interest only to specialists in Artificial Intelligence. On the contrary, I consider that it has a great deal to offer to systems developers in more traditional areas, such as text processing, databases and networking. In this belief, the emphasis throughout is on the application of the toolkit to practical programming problems, and not to examples contrived just to illustrate features of the language.

Part 1 of the book begins with a description of the building blocks out of which Prolog programs are constructed; this is Chapter 1. Chapter 2 describes how a Prolog program is executed. I hope this book will be of value to experienced Prolog programmers as well as to novices, but the expert may well wish to skip these chapters.

Chapter 3 introduces the crucial topic of recursion, and it focuses on the inter-dependence of recursive programs and data types. In Chapters 4 to 6, I describe the built-in predicates of Prolog, which provide useful operations that are essential for serious programming. In Chapter 7, I investigate the scope for meta-programming in Prolog, and in Chapter 8, I look at the use of Prolog for writing grammars, either of natural languages or artificial ones.

Prolog offers a great opportunity for accuracy and clarity of expression in programs, but the programmer has to learn how to use this opportunity. So, Chapter 9 covers the testing, debugging and documentation of Prolog programs, topics which I consider have not been adequately treated in most textbooks on the language.

Part 2 illustrates the application to large-scale programming of the lessons taught in Part 1. The techniques in the toolkit, introduced at intervals through Part 1, are applied in two case studies: the development of a general problem-solving system and of an intelligent electronic diary. Of course, each of these is an open-ended exercise. I hope readers will be enthused by what they learn in this book of the scope for exciting and challenging programming that Prolog offers, and for them I suggest ambitious routes for the further development of each system.

Prolog is a language that is still evolving. As it is applied to an ever-increasing range of applications, so suppliers of Prolog systems add new features to meet the needs of users of their products. I describe a core of Prolog that is common to most implementations. I also include a brief account of the work on a standard for the language at present being done by the British Standards Institute, and I comment on aspects of the language where the BSI is likely to propose departures from the current core Prolog.

A note about style is appropriate here. I have avoided formations of contemporary English such as "s/he" and "him/her", and I have used the masculine pronouns throughout. It should not need saying, but perhaps it does, that this usage does not imply that I am addressing the book to a male readership only.

Acknowledgements

I am pleased to thank Pete Brown of Pitman Publishing, Tony Dodd of Expert Systems International and Cliff Hunter and Paul Skuce of Hatfield Polytechnic for the help they have given me in the preparation of this book.

John Stobo
Hatfield,
December 1988

Part 1

The Prolog Language

Chapter 1

Programming with Facts

In this chapter, we describe the components of Prolog programs, and we use them in a small but complete program. The program is a database about people, and we show how to retrieve information from it. The same information may be represented in many different ways; we illustrate how a good representation makes the information retrieved easier to interpret.

1.1 Data Objects: the Term

Prolog provides only one data type, called a *term*. All the objects in the problem being represented, and all the relationships between objects, are represented using types of term. For instance, we might represent a date by the following term:

date(thursday, 22, march, 1989)

This is an example of a *structured term*, usually called simply a *structure*. A structure consists of a *functor*, which is the name of the relationship, and a sequence of *components*, which are the objects in the relationship. The number of components in a structure is called the *arity* of the structure In the example given:

date   is the functor of the structure, and

thursday
22
march
1989 are the components of the structure.

The arity of the structure is four. The syntax of Prolog requires that:

• The components of a structure are enclosed in brackets.

• The components are separated by commas ",".

- There is no space between the functor and the opening bracket which introduces the components.

It is important to realise that the names we choose for the functor and the components of a structure are arbitrary and have no special significance within the language.   When we use a structure to represent a relationship, we must state how the structure is to be interpreted, and we must be consistent in interpreting all structures having the same functor and the same arity in the same way within a program.   In this case, our interpretation of the structure is:

> "The structure represents a date.   The four components represent the day on which the date falls, the date in the month, the month and the year."

It is good programming practice to choose, for the functor and components of a structure, names which remind a program's reader of how to interpret the structure.

In this example, the first and third components of the structure are *atomic constants*, usually called simply *atoms*.   An atom is another type of term.   An atom may include any character, but one which includes anything other than alphanumeric characters and the underline character "_" must be enclosed in single quote marks.   Also, an atom which begins with a capital letter, a digit or "_" must be quoted.   So:

'my mother'   'george,and,gertie'   '205'   '_first'   'George'

are all examples which would not be atoms without the quote marks.

The other type of constant is a *numeric constant*, usually called simply a *number*.   Examples of numbers are:

205   -10   3.75

The first two are *integers*, the third a *real*.   The second and fourth components of the structure representing the date are integers.

Exercises 1.1

(a)   Which of the following are valid atoms:

  (i)   b
  (ii)   B
  (iii)   an_extremely_long_sequence_of_characters
  (iv)   7
  (v)   man(george)
  (vi)   'man(george)'

1.2   A Complete Program

Our first Prolog program records information about the soldiers of an army and their ranks, such as:

> "Peckem is a general."
> "Cathcart is a colonel."
> "Moodus is a colonel."

In the program, we represent each soldier by a structure with functor soldier and arity 2. Each component is an atom, the first representing the name of a soldier in the army and the second his rank. In writing our program, we wish to assert that relationships of this type do indeed hold for soldiers in the army. To make an assertion, we write the structure which expresses the relationship as a *fact* in our program. Each fact is followed by a full-stop ".":

```
soldier(peckem, general).
soldier(cathcart, colonel).
soldier(moodus, colonel).
```

A fact is one way in which a structure can be used in Prolog. A simple program consists of a series of facts.

In most implementations of Prolog, a program is created externally to the Prolog system, using a text-editor provided as part of the computer system. A command is then given to run the Prolog system, followed by a command to Prolog to load the previously-created program. The details of this process differ somewhat between systems. The typical sequence is described in section 2.5.

In the rest of this section, we illustrate the operation of Prolog by reference to the following program, which describes part of the army:

```
soldier(peckem, general).
soldier(cathcart, colonel).
soldier(moodus, colonel).
soldier(towser, sergeant).
soldier(knight, sergeant).
soldier(aardvark, captain).
soldier(dunbar, lieutenant).
soldier(flume, captain).
soldier(danby, major).
```

When the program has been loaded, we can ask questions about the relationships described in the program.

A question has the form of a structure, preceded by the symbol ?- and terminated by a full-stop.[1] An example of a question is:

?- soldier(towser, sergeant).

Under our interpretation of the meaning of structures with functor soldier and arity 2, this question is asking:

"Is there a soldier Towser with the rank of sergeant?"

A structure used as a question is a *goal*, which the user is asking Prolog to *satisfy*. One way in which a goal is satisfied is when the structure which is the goal *matches* a structure which is a fact in the program. The second way in which a goal is satisfied involves the use of *rules*. Programs with rules are introduced in chapter 2. Prolog recognises any match between a goal and a fact in the program. If a match is found, Prolog responds with:

yes

to indicate that the goal has been satisfied. If no match is found, the response is:

no

which indicates that the goal has failed to be satisfied. So the response to our first question:

?- soldier(towser, sergeant).

is:

yes

However, if we ask:

?- soldier(cathcart, captain).

the response is:

no

---

[1] In most Prolog systems, the system's prompt to the user is ?-, and the user does not have to type this symbol to introduce a question. All terms input in response to this prompt are assumed to be questions. However, throughout this book we preface every question with the ?- symbol, to distinguish questions from structures used in other contexts.

The goal does not match any fact in the program. Cathcart is not a captain. In the same way, the response to:

    ?- soldier(dreedle, general).

is:

    no

because we have no fact in the program about a soldier called Dreedle.

A goal may include *variables* as components of a structure. A variable is a place-holder, denoting an unspecified value which we wish Prolog to fill in. A variable begins with an upper-case letter or with the underline character. An example of a goal which includes a variable is:

    ?- soldier(aardvark, R).

This goal is to be interpreted as asking the question:

> "For what value of R is it true that Aardvark is a soldier of rank R?"

Phrased in everyday English, the question is:

> "What is Aardvark's rank?"

When a goal which includes variables is satisfied, Prolog displays the value which it has substituted for each variable in the goal. So, the answer to the question would be:

    R = captain

We can ask Prolog to list all possible values for the variables in a goal. In most Prolog systems the user does this by typing a semi-colon ";" after the first answer. If other answers exist, Prolog displays the values of variables in them. If there is no alternative, the response is: no, as for a goal that fails to be satisfied. For example, we might want to know:

> "What soldiers hold the rank of colonel?"

The question is formulated as:

    ?- soldier(S, colonel).

and the answers are listed:

S = cathcart;

S = moodus;
no

Our program can be used to answer more complicated questions, for example:

"Do Aardvark and Flume hold the same rank?"

We can re-phrase this question in a way which makes clear that it can be answered by using two goals in succession, the result of the second depending on that of the first:

"What is the rank that Aardvark holds, and, denoting Aardvark's rank by R, does Flume also hold the rank R?"

To express that a succession of goals are to be satisfied together, we separate the goal structures by a comma. Our question becomes:

?- soldier(aardvark, R), soldier(flume, R).

and the answer is:

R = captain

1.3   Recursion in Structures

The functor of a structure must be an atom, but the components can be terms of any kind. The definition of a structure reveals that an atom is just a special kind of structure: one with arity 0. It says:

A structure comprises a functor, which must be an atom, and zero or more components, each of which is a constant, a variable or a structure.

This definition is interesting because we have defined what a structure is partly by reference to a structure. A definition which uses the thing being defined within the definition itself is called a *recursive* definition. A structure is a recursive data type. The significance of this becomes apparent in chapter 3, where we write recursive programs to process recursive structures. At this stage, we simply give one illustration of how the meaning of facts in a program can be captured very precisely by the mechanism of a recursive data type.

Consider the problem of Sergeant Major. In our chosen representation, his existence would be recorded in our program by the fact:

soldier(major, sergeant).

If we wanted to ask the question:

"Who is in the army, and what ranks do they hold?"

we would formulate the question as the goal:

?- soldier(A, B).

For Sergeant Major, the answer would be:

A = major
B = sergeant

The problem with this answer is that is does not make clear which is the name of the soldier and which his rank. The user who asks the question must remember the meaning of the two components of structures with functor soldier and arity 2 and the order of the components. We can prevent this difficulty arising by representing name and rank not by atoms but by structures whose functors suggest the meaning of the component. Using a structure with functor name and arity 1 to represent the soldier's name and a structure with functor rank and arity 1 for his rank, the existence of Sergeant Major would be denoted by the fact:

soldier(name(major), rank(sergeant)).

Even if the army also included a Major Sergeant, denoted by the fact:

soldier(name(sergeant), rank(major)).

there would be no confusion in the answers when the user asks the question:

?- soldier(A, B).

Among the answers would be:

A = name(major)   This is Sergeant Major.
B = rank(sergeant);

A = name(sergeant)   This is Major Sergeant.
B = rank(major)

It is the simplicity and flexibility of the data type term that is the source of Prolog's power in representing the many complex objects and relationships which the programmer recognises in the problem he is addressing.   An important skill of the programmer is the ability to use this power to construct terms which represent in a meaningful way the objects and relationships in a real-world problem. As the examples in this section have shown a more meaningful way of representing the soldiers and their ranks, we shall re-write our first program in this improved representation. The program becomes:

```
soldier(name(peckem),  rank(general)).
soldier(name(cathcart),  rank(colonel)).
soldier(name(moodus),  rank(colonel)).
soldier(name(towser),  rank(sergeant)).
soldier(name(knight),  rank(sergeant)).
soldier(name(aardvark),  rank(captain)).
soldier(name(dunbar),  rank(lieutenant)).
soldier(name(flume),  rank(captain)).
soldier(name(danby),  rank(major)).
```

For the beginner, the different types of term can be confusing. It is helpful to keep in mind the hierarchy shown in Figure 1.1.

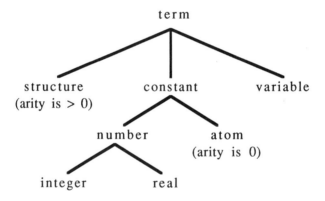

Figure 1.1 Hierarchy of terms

Exercises 1.3

(a) Identify which of the following are valid structures and, for those which are valid, identify the arity of the structure and the arity of each component:

(i) 22nd(street)
(ii) street(22)
(iii) orchestra
(iv) orchestra(strings, brass, woodwind, percussion)
(v) string_orchestra(strings(violins, violas, cellos, basses))
(vi) quartet(string(violin(first), violin(second), cello, bass))

     (vii) string_quartet(violin(first), violin(second), cello, bass)
    (viii) jazz_ensemble(trumpet trombone fiddle clarinet drums)
     (ix) jazz_ensemble('trumpet trombone fiddle clarinet drums')
     (x) jazz_ensemble(trumpet, trombone, fiddle, clarinet, drums)

(b)   Re-formulate each of the questions about the army in section 1.2 to take account of the revised representation for a soldier.

(c)   Musical instruments are of various types. For instance, the violin and the viola are string instruments, the clarinet and the bassoon are woodwind instruments and the trumpet, trombone and horn are brass instruments. Using the structure instrument(instrument(A), type(B)) to represent that instrument A is of type B, write a program, consisting of a series of facts, to represent some of the instruments that might be found in a symphony orchestra and their types.

1.4   Matching between Structures

To understand when a goal matches a fact, you must master the rule which determines when two structures match. The rule is as follows:

Two structures match if:

- they have the same functor, and
- they have the same arity, and
- components in corresponding positions in the two structures match.

Two components match if:

- both are variables (the two variables *share*), or
- one of them is a variable (a variable matches any term and the term is substituted for every occurrence of the variable), or
- each is a structure and the two structures match.

Notice that here also we have used a recursive definition: within a rule which defines when structures match, we refer to a requirement for components which are structures to match.

To see the effect of this rule in practice, consider the following examples.

Example 1

Do the structures: orchestra(strings, B, C, D)
and: orchestra(strings, wind, percussion, keyboard)
match?

We test each of three requirements for matching in turn. The two have the same functor: orchestra and the same arity: 4, so we must compare components in corresponding positions in the two structures. The first components of each, strings and strings, are matching structures. (Remember that atoms are simply structures with arity 0.) In the case of the second components, the variable B matches the atom wind, and the value wind is substituted for the variable B in the first structure. The same type of match between a variable and an atom occurs with the third and fourth components of the structures, resulting in the substitution of percussion for C and keyboard for D. The answer, therefore, is that the two structures do match.

Example 2

Do the structures: pets(dog(fangs), cat(paws))
and: pets(Animal, Animal)
match?

Again, we readily note that the two have the same functor: pets and the same arity: 2, so the question is whether components in corresponding positions match. For the first components, the structure dog(fangs) would match the variable Animal, with the value dog(fangs) being substituted for the variable. For the second components, the structure cat(paws) would match the variable Animal, with the value cat(paws) being substituted for the variable. However, in Prolog a variable in a structure can only take a single value. It is not possible for different substitutions to be made for the same variable in a single structure. Hence, the two structures do not match.

Exercises 1.4

(a) Determine whether each of the following pairs of structures match. If a pair does match, identify the values which are substituted for variables in the structures. If a pair does not match, say why not.

(i)   book(title('animal farm'), author('george orwell'))
       and
       book(title(T),   Author)

(ii)   date(day(wednesday), date(21), month(M), year(1986))
       and
       date(Day, Date, Month, Year)

(iii) holiday(christmas, date(day(25), month(december), year(Y)))
       and
       holiday(H, date(Day, Month, year(1986)))

(iv) holiday(mayday(1, may))
and
holiday(mayday, 1, may)

1.5   Summary

In this chapter, we have introduced the following ideas:

* Every object in a Prolog program is a term.

* The types of term form a hierarchy.

* A structure is identified by its functor and its arity.

* A fact is a structure which is used in a program to represent an object or a relationship in a real-world problem.

* We ask questions by using structures as goals.

* A goal is satisfied if it matches a fact in the program.

* The structure is a recursive data type.

* A variable is a place-holder. Any term may be substituted for a variable, but the same substitution must be made for every occurrence of a variable in a structure.

* When two terms match, values are substituted for the variables in them.

Chapter 2

Programming with Rules

In Chapter 1, we saw how to construct a program from facts, and we wrote a program in which each fact identified one soldier in an army. In this chapter, we add rules to the program. We then introduce some terminology and explain how Prolog sets about satisfying the goals which the user types in. In the final section, we show what a typical interactive session with Prolog ` looks like, though the details do vary somewhat between implementations of the language. We describe some of the proposals for a standard for the language in Appendix 3. After reading this chapter, you will have a sufficient understanding of the workings of Prolog to write simple programs of your own and run them on your Prolog system.

2.1 Rules

The advantage of using a rule is that the programmer can express a general principle governing the relationship between objects, rather than just listing specific instances of a relationship. For example, we expressed the question:

"Do Aardvark and Flume hold the same rank?"

as a conjunction of the two goals:

```
?- soldier(name(aardvark), R), soldier(name(flume), R).
```

In fact, it is true of any two soldiers that if each is of some rank R, then the two are of the same rank. We can express this principle in the following rule:

```
same_rank(A, B) :-
    soldier(A, R),
    soldier(B, R).
```

A rule has a *head* and a *body*, separated by the special symbol :-, which is pronounced "if". The body consists of one or more *sub-goals*, separated by commas. Each sub-goal must be a structure or an atom. The whole rule is terminated by a full-stop. In the example given:

same_rank(A, B)   is the head of the rule,

soldier(A, R), soldier(B, R).   is the body of the rule,

soldier(A, R)   is the first sub-goal,

soldier(B, R)   is the second sub-goal.

A rule states that the relationship in the head holds if each relationship in the body holds. So, the meaning of our example rule is:

"It is true that: soldier A holds the same rank as soldier B
    if it is true that: soldier A holds rank R
    and it is true that: soldier B holds rank R."

If we add this rule to our program, the form of the question which previously comprised two goals is now:

?- same_rank(name(aardvark), name(flume)).

and the answer is:

yes

There are other ways in which we might use our rule. For instance, if we want to know:

"Which soldiers hold the same rank as Moodus?"

we use the goal:

?- same_rank(Soldier, name(moodus)).

and we get the answers:

Soldier = name(cathcart);

Soldier = name(moodus);
no

The question could equally be asked as:

13

?- same_rank(name(moodus), Soldier).

with answers as before.

Does the second answer come as a surprise to you?   Probably so, though
if you had thought carefully about the rule you might have noticed that
there is nothing in it which says that soldiers A and B have to be different;
and indeed it is true that every soldier holds the same rank as himself.   But,
perhaps it is not a very useful truth, one which we might have preferred
our program not to remind us of.

We could equally ask:

"Which pairs of soldiers hold the same rank?"

The question is formulated as:

?- same_rank(X, Y).

Many substitutions of values for X and Y are possible.   The first few are:

X = name(peckem)
Y = name(peckem);

X = name(cathcart)
Y = name(cathcart);

X = name(cathcart)
Y = name(moodus);

X = name(moodus)
Y = name(cathcart)

As these answers are produced, it becomes apparent that Prolog is not
only enumerating identical pairs: X = name(peckem) Y = name(peckem), which
by now you should be expecting, but it is also giving answers which are
duplicates, save for the substitutions being reversed: X = name(cathcart) Y =
name(moodus), followed shortly by: X = name(moodus) Y = name(cathcart).
Here also, we have to acknowledge that as the same_rank relationship is
reflexive, the responses are strictly correct, though once again they are
probably not what we would want.

Whether or not we wish to prevent this program from exhibiting this
behaviour, we do need to understand how Prolog produces its answers.
Before we can progress to writing more complex programs, we have to learn
how a program is executed, not just what a program comprises and what it
means.   That is, we have to learn about the program's procedural behaviour,
rather than just understanding it as a declarative description of objects and
relationships between objects.   Prolog's procedural behaviour is the subject
of section 2.3.

Exercises 2.1

(a) When the user formulates the question: "Do Aardvark and Flume hold the same rank?" by the succession of goals:

?- soldier(name(aardvark), R), soldier(name(flume), R).

Prolog gives the value which has been substituted for the variable in the goal:

R = rank(captain)

When he formulates the question as:

?- same_rank(name(aardvark), name(flume)).

the answer is just:

yes

Write a version of the same_rank rule which does give the rank of the two soldiers, if they are of the same rank.

(b) Hermann, Klaus, Charlotte and Wilfrid are musicians. Hermann plays the violin, and Charlotte plays the horn and the trombone. Klaus plays any string instrument, and Wilfrid plays any musical instrument at all. Using the structure plays(player(A), instrument(B)) to represent that person A plays instrument B, write a series of facts and rules to describe the musical talents of the quartet. Use the program describing the instruments of a symphony orchestra that you wrote for exercise 1.3(c).

2.2 Terminology: Procedures, Clauses and Predicates

The declarative view of a Prolog program is that it is a collection of data items. Indeed, a complete program is called a *database*, reflecting the fact that every object in a Prolog program is a data item. Facts, rules, the head of a rule, the body of a rule, goals: all these are, at the level of syntax, simply structures. We have a range of vocabulary which enables us to distinguish the context in which structures are used: a fact is a structure used as an assertion; a goal is a structure used as a question. This section introduces you to more words in the terminology of Prolog, words which are used when talking about the procedural behaviour of a program, rather than about its declarative characteristics as a collection of structures. The terminology of any subject can be confusing for the beginner. The terminology of Prolog is particularly so because it is providing a number of different words

15

for concepts which at the level of syntax are identical.

Each fact and each rule in a program is called a *clause*. A rule is a clause which has a head and a body. A fact is a clause which has a head and an empty body. If you answered exercise 2.1(b), you probably wrote a program something like:

```
plays(player(hermann),  instrument(violin)).
plays(player(charlotte),  instrument(horn)).
plays(player(charlotte),  instrument(trombone)).
plays(player(klaus), X) :-
    instrument(X,  type(string)).
plays(player(wilfrid), X)  :-
    instrument(X,  Any_type).
```

In this program, the head of each clause is a structure of the same type: functor plays, arity 2. A collection of clauses whose heads have the same functor and the same arity is called a *procedure*. So the program comprises one procedure having five clauses. The set of clauses for a procedure defines a relationship. The relationship which is defined by a procedure is called a *predicate*, and associated with the predicate is its arity. Our program is, therefore, a definition of the predicate plays with arity 2. We use the notation plays/2 as shorthand for the phrase: "the predicate plays with arity 2".

Prolog is not at all fussy about the layout of a program. The only requirement is that there must be a <space> or <newline> character after the full-stop at the end of each clause. Throughout this book we observe the following conventions:

- Each fact is written on a new line.

- The head of a rule and the :- symbol are written on one line, and each sub-goal is written indented on a new line.

- Procedures are separated by a blank line.

The language allows comments to be used freely in a program. Any text between the pair of symbols /* and */ is treated as a comment. So:

```
/ *
This is a comment.
It continues over several lines.
Comments can appear wherever a <space> character would be legal.
* /
```

Any text after the symbol % on a line is also treated as a comment. The end of the comment is the <newline> character. So:

%   Procedure for plays/2

```
plays(player(hermann), instrument(oboe)).   % hermann plays the oboe
plays(player(charlotte), instrument(horn)).  % charlotte plays the horn
```

Once we have written a procedure for a predicate, we call that procedure as a goal by using the name of the predicate, together with the required number of *arguments*, in a question:

```
?- plays(player(charlotte),  instrument(glockenspiel)).
no
```

In this call, the arguments associated with the call to the procedure plays are the structures player(charlotte) and instrument(glockenspiel). The term "argument" is the word used for a component of a goal structure.

2.3   Procedural Behaviour: How Goals are Satisfied

Equipped with the necessary terminology, we can now describe what happens when the user types in a goal. The questions are:

- For a program which includes both facts and rules, when is a goal satisfied?

- In what order does Prolog search the clauses of a program for a match with a goal?

- What does Prolog do when a goal fails?

- How does Prolog produce alternative answers?

We consider these questions in turn.

2.3.1   Satisfying a goal

We must amplify the statement we made in section 1.2 about when a goal is satisfied, for in that chapter we were writing about programs which consisted of facts only. Taking rules into account leads us to the following:

> A goal can be satisfied if it matches the head of a clause for a procedure. If the match is with the head of a clause which has an empty body (i.e. the clause is a fact), the goal is immediately satisfied. If the match is with the head of a clause which is a rule, the goal is satisfied only if each sub-goal in the body of the rule is satisfied when called as a goal. The sub-goals are called in the order in which they are written.

2.3.2   Searching for a match

For each goal or sub-goal, Prolog searches the clauses of the program in the order they were written by the programmer, starting the search, for each goal or sub-goal, from the beginning of the database.   We illustrate this process of search with example goals and a program comprising procedures for same_rank/2 and soldier/2.   Consider first the goal:

   ?- same_rank(name(aardvark), name(flume)).

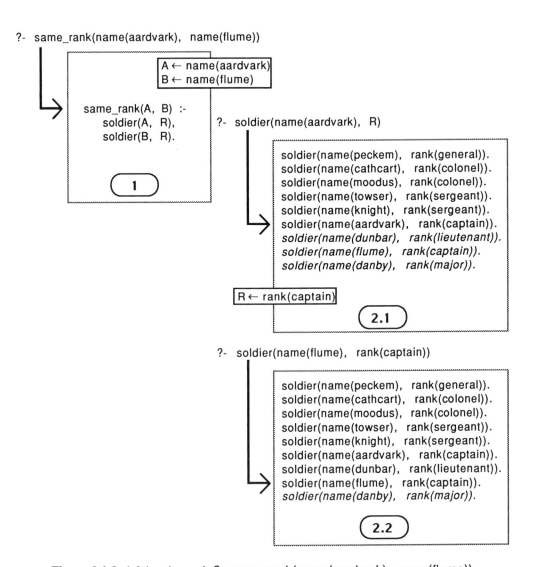

Figure 2.1 Satisfying the goal: ?- same_rank(name(aardvark), name(flume))
by satisfying two sub-goals

Figure 2.1 shows the goal and, in box **1**, part of the program text. The heavy arrow from the goal points to the clause in the program with whose head the goal matches. The match results in the substitution of values for variables A and B. The substitutions are shown in the small box and are denoted by the symbol ←. As the match is with a rule, the goal is satisfied only if the sub-goals can be satisfied. The first sub-goal, after the substitution A ← name(aardvark), is: ?-soldier(name(aardvark), R). We have drawn the relevant clauses of the program in box **2.1**, and the heavy arrow points to the place at which a matching clause is found. The match results in the substitution of the value rank(captain) for the variable R, as shown in the small box. As the matching clause has an empty body, the sub-goal is immediately satisfied.

The second sub-goal is shown beneath the first. Note that its form is now: ?-soldier(name(flume), rank(captain)), following the substitution R ← rank(captain). We have re-drawn the clauses for soldier/2 in box **2.2** to emphasise that for each sub-goal there is a separate search starting afresh from the beginning of the database. The heavy arrow from the goal to the clause in box **2.2** shows the point at which a match is found. The match is with a fact, so the goal is immediately satisfied. Now both the sub-goals in the body of the clause for same_rank/2 are satisfied. The parent goal is satisfied, and Prolog's answer is:

yes.

The answer was produced without Prolog searching the complete database for each sub-goal. Clauses for soldier/2 which were not examined in the process of satisfying the sub-goals are italicised in boxes **2.1** and **2.2**.

2.3.3   Failure of goals

We illustrate Prolog's action when a goal cannot be satisfied with the example:

?- same_rank(name(peckem), name(dunbar)).

The situation is shown in Figure 2.2.

The first sub-goal has been satisfied, with the substitution R ← rank(general). The form of the second sub-goal is then: ? - soldier(name(dunbar), rank(general)), and, as shown at box **2.2**, the end of the database is reached without the goal being satisfied. This is what we mean by saying that a goal fails. When a goal fails, Prolog backtracks to the previous goal and attempts to *re-satisfy* it. When Prolog tries to re-satisfy a goal, it undoes any substitutions of values for variables which the first match had produced and then continues its search for another matching clause from the clause in the database after that at which the previous match had been found.

?- same_rank(name(peckem), name(dunbar))

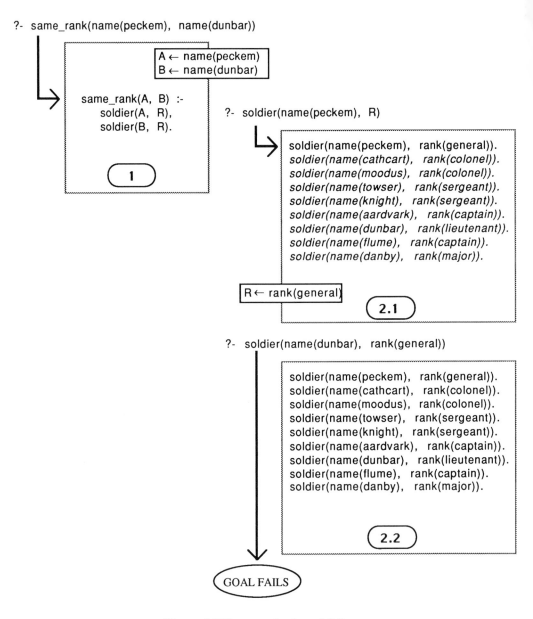

Figure 2.2 The second sub-goal fails

In our example, the goal before the failed goal is: ?-soldier(name(peckem), R). It had previously matched with the first clause for soldier/2, with the substitution R ← rank(general). That substitution is undone, restoring the goal to its original form, and the search for a match continues from the next clause after that arrowed in box **2.1** of Figure 2.2. However, there is no other matching clause in the database, and, as shown in Figure 2.3, that goal also fails.

?- soldier(name(peckem), R)

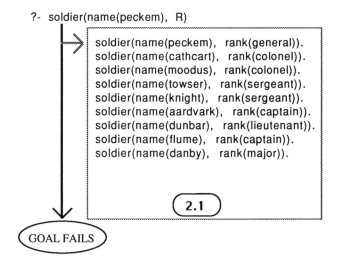

Figure 2.3 The first sub-goal fails to be re-satisfied

The goal before: ?- soldier(name(peckem), R) was: ?-same_rank(name(peckem), name(dunbar)). The attempt to re-satisfy that goal also ends in failure, as shown in Figure 2.4

?- same_rank(name(peckem), name(dunbar))

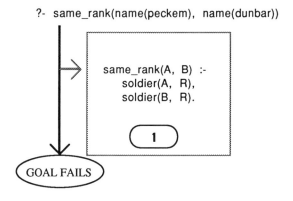

Figure 2.4 The goal: ?- same_rank(name(peckem), name(dunbar)) fails

But this was the goal typed in by the user, so there are none before it! At this point Prolog gives up, and the response to its user is the familiar: no.

2.3.4 Producing alternative answers to questions

It is by backtracking that Prolog produces alternative answers to questions which include variables. Consider the goal:

?- same_rank(S, name(knight)).

The progress of the attempt to satisfy this goal is illustrated in Figure 2.5.

?- same_rank(S, name(knight))

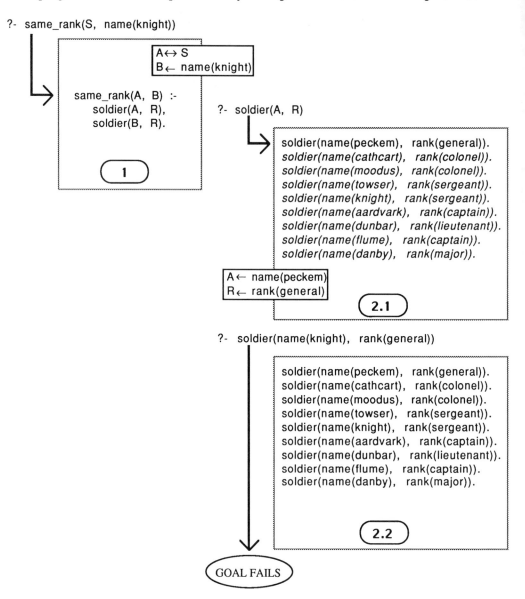

Figure 2.5 The second sub-goal fails; backtrack to the first

The match of the goal with the clause for same_rank/2 causes the variable S in the goal to share with the variable A in the clause head and results in the substitution B ← name(knight). In the figure, we denote the sharing of two variables by the symbol ↔. When two variables share, a substitution of a value for either one of them causes the same substitution to be made for the other. The first sub-goal is: ?- soldier(A, R), and this goal is immediately satisfied by a match with the first clause for soldier/2, producing substitutions as shown by box **2.1**. However, Knight is not recorded as holding the rank of general, so the second sub-goal fails. Though the goal: ?-soldier(A, R) can be re-satisfied on backtracking by matches with each clause for soldier/2, the second sub-goal fails repeatedly until the match with the fourth clause produces the alternative substitution R ← rank(sergeant). Now the second sub-goal has a form ?-soldier(name(knight), rank(sergeant)) in which it can be satisfied. Figure 2.6 illustrates the situation.

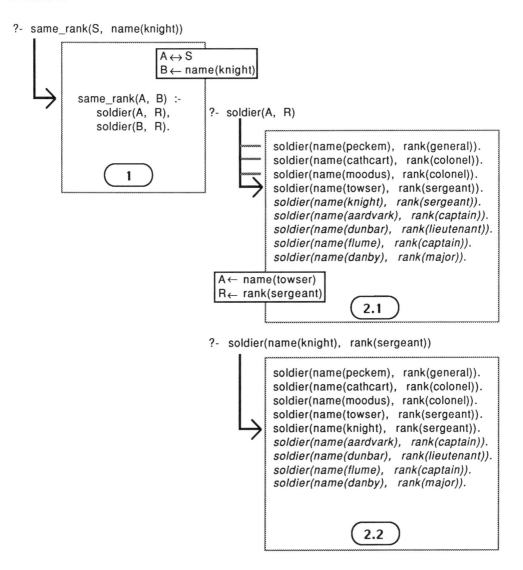

Figure 2.6 The first sub-goal is re-satisfied, and the second is now satisfied.

Notice that the goal has been satisfied without searching the entire database for each sub-goal. Because S shared with A, the substitution A ← name(towser) also caused the substitution S ← name(towser), so Prolog's response to the question is:

S = name(towser)

The user has the option of accepting this answer, by simply pressing <return>[1], or rejecting it by typing ";" and pressing <return>.

The effect of rejecting an answer is to force Prolog to attempt to re-satisfy the most recent sub-goal. This is the goal: ?- soldier(name(knight), rank(sergeant)). This goal cannot be re-satisfied, as Figure 2.7 shows, so Prolog backtracks to the previous goal.

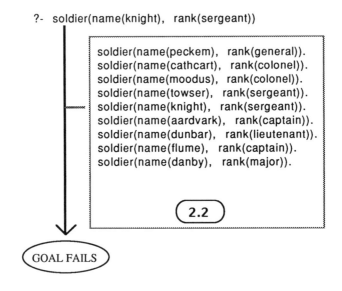

?- soldier(name(knight), rank(sergeant))

soldier(name(peckem), rank(general)).
soldier(name(cathcart), rank(colonel)).
soldier(name(moodus), rank(colonel)).
soldier(name(towser), rank(sergeant)).
soldier(name(knight), rank(sergeant)).
soldier(name(aardvark), rank(captain)).
soldier(name(dunbar), rank(lieutenant)).
soldier(name(flume), rank(captain)).
soldier(name(danby), rank(major)).

2.2

GOAL FAILS

Figure 2.7 The sub-goal: ?- soldier(name(knight), rank(sergeant)) cannot be re-satisfied on backtracking

The previous goal was: ?- soldier(A, R), last satisfied as illustrated in box **2.1** of Figure 2.6. That goal is immediately re-satisfied by matching with the next clause for soldier/2, as shown in Figure 2.8, and new substitutions for A and R result.

---

[1] In some implementations, the user has to type a character to indicate acceptance of an answer. The character is usually the full-stop.

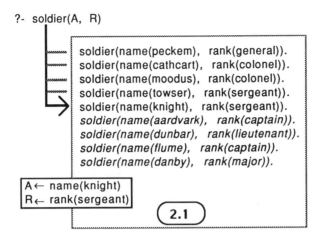

Figure 2.8 Re-satisfying the sub-goal: ?- soldier(A, R) produces
a different substitution for the variable   A

The form of the second sub-goal is again: ?- soldier(name(knight), rank(sergeant)), which is satisfied, as indicated in Figure 2.9.

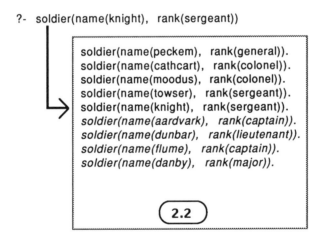

Figure 2.9 The sub-goal: ?- soldier(name(knight), rank(sergeant))   is satisfied

Prolog has now re-satisfied the original goal: ?- same_rank(S, name(knight)) with a different substitution:

S = name(knight)

If the user rejects this answer, the first sub-goal: ?- soldier(A, R) is re-satisfiable by matching in turn with each of the remaining clauses for soldier/2. However, at each match the value substituted for R denotes a rank other than sergeant, and the second sub-goal repeatedly fails. The first sub-goal fails, causing failure of the parent goal and the answer:

no.

It is essential to grasp the difference between the mechanism of backtracking to re-satisfy a goal and that of satisfying a new goal. The first sub-goal: ?- soldier(A, R) is repeatedly re-satisfied by a search which continues each time from the clause after the previously-found match. Examine Figures 2.5 (box **2.1**), 2.6 (box **2.1**) and 2.8 to be sure you recognise this. The second sub-goal is generated anew each time: ?- soldier(A, R) is satisfied. Contrast Figures 2.5 (box **2.2**), 2.6 (box **2.2**) and 2.9. The three are separate sub-goals. The attempt to satisfy each starts at the beginning of the database.

Exercises 2.3.4

(a) Using the clauses for plays/2 given in section 2.2 and those for instrument/2 given in the answer to exercise 1.3(c), show, in the notation of Figures 2.1 to 2.9, how Prolog answers the question:

?- plays(Who, instrument(violin)).

Enumerate all alternative answers to this question in the order in which Prolog would produce them.

(b) Siegfried is a musician who plays woodwind and brass instruments. His situation can be represented by the following clauses:

plays(player(siegfried), X) :-
    instrument(X, type(woodwind)).
plays(player(siegfried), X) :-
    instrument(X, type(brass)).

Assuming the same clauses for instrument/2, what answers, and in what order, would Prolog give to the question:

?- plays(player(siegfried), What).

What would be the order of the answers if the two clauses describing Siegfried's talents were reversed?

2.4   Progressive   Substitution

As a final example in this chapter of how Prolog satisfies a goal, we present a program which substitutes a complex structure for the variable in a goal. The structure represents the form of a class of very simple English sentence, and the purpose of the program is to generate, by backtracking, alternative sentences having this form.   A sentence of this class has two constituent parts: a noun phrase, which is the subject of the sentence, followed by a verb phrase, which expresses the action of the sentence.   In the program, a sentence is represented by the structure s(Subj, Vp).   The first component of the structure represents the subject of the sentence, and the second component represents the action.   The following clause for sentence/1 defines the structure of this class of sentence:

```
sentence(s(Subj, Vp)) :-
    noun_phrase(Subj),
    verb_phrase(Vp).
```

This rule says that the structure s(Subj, Vp) represents a sentence if Subj is a noun phrase and Vp is a verb phrase.   Two more rules in the program define the structure of a noun phrase and of a verb phrase:

```
noun_phrase(np(D, N)) :-
    determiner(D),
    noun(N).

verb_phrase(vp(Vb, Obj)) :-
    verb(Vb),
    noun_phrase(Obj).
```

The program is completed by some facts which assert that certain words are valid determiners, nouns or verbs:

```
determiner(d(the)).
determiner(d(a)).

noun(n(woman)).
noun(n(girl)).

verb(v(sees)).
verb(v(calls)).
```

To generate sentences consisting of these words and having the specified form, we call the goal:

```
?- sentence(S).
S = s(np(d(the),n(woman)),vp(v(sees),np(d(the),n(woman))))
```

As displayed, the form of the sentence is not easy to see. In Figure 2.10, the structure is drawn as a tree to make its form clearer.

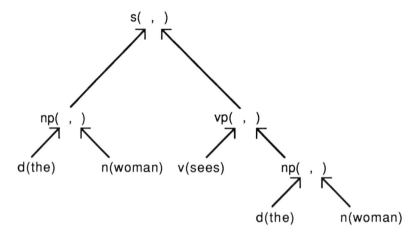

Figure 2.10   The structure s(np(d(the),n(woman)),vp(v(sees),np(d(the),n(woman))))
drawn as a tree

Figure 2.11 illustrates how Prolog satisfies the goal:

?- sentence(S).

Diagrams of this sort are familiar to you by now: in this one, we have not bothered with showing how the goal: ?- noun_phrase(Obj) is satisfied. It has an identical form to the goal: ?- noun_phrase(Subj), and is satisfied in the same way.

The important issue in this example is how the structure which is substituted for the variable in the goal is built up in the arguments to the sub-goals. The key to understanding how this is done is to recognise that at each match between a sub-goal and a clause head in the program, the value substituted for a variable in the sub-goal is a structure which itself includes variables. These new variables are then passed as arguments to further sub-goals.

In box **1**, the match of the goal with the clause for sentence/1 produces the substitution S ← s(Subj, Vp). The variables Subj and Vp are arguments to two sub-goals in which they have substituted for them other structures including variables as components: Subj ← np(D, N) and Vp ← vp(Vb, Obj). The process terminates when a sub-goal matches a fact, representing a word, and the term substituted for the variable in the goal contains no variables. A term which does not contain any variables is called a *ground term*. Because every match with a fact in the program substitutes a ground term for a variable, the final value substituted for S is a ground term.

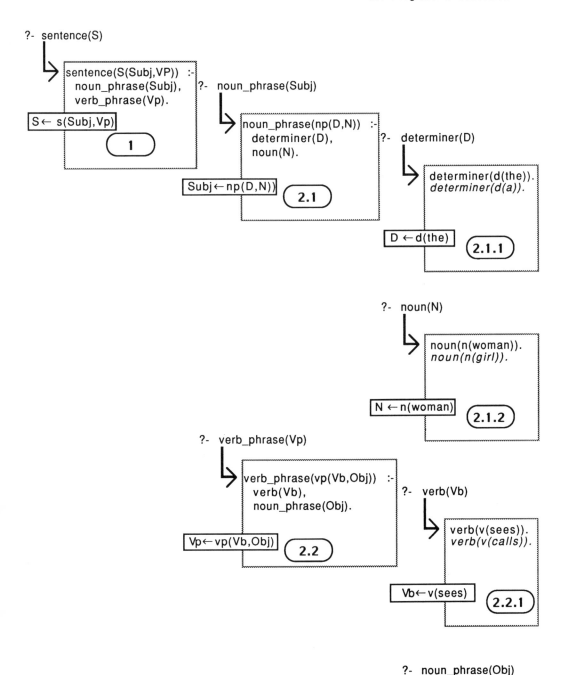

Figure 2.11 Satisfying the goal: ?- sentence(S)

As the objects and relationships in our programs become more complex, we frequently need to represent the answer to a question about those relationships by a complex structure. Building up the necessary structure in a program is a very important programming technique. The method which we have illustrated, we call *progressive substitution*. It is of such importance in Prolog programming that we encapsulate it in a concise description and include it as the first technique in our toolkit for Prolog programmers.

Progressive Substitution

The technique is used to build a recursive structure in a series of stages. It comprises the following steps:

- The functor and arity of the structure which is to be built up are defined in the head of a rule. One or more components of the structure are variables. These variables are passed as arguments to sub-goals in the body of the rule.

- A structure with several nested levels is built up in several nested sub-goals.

- The progression is terminated by specifying a ground term as the structure in the head of a clause. Such a clause is usually a fact.

The third step in applying the technique is particularly important because unless the final term substituted is ground, the whole structure which is substituted for the variable in the goal still includes variables. This can be very confusing because Prolog displays a variable as an integer preceded by "_", and this form, which is its internal representation of variables, bears no resemblance to the names which the programmer uses for variables.

Exercises 2.4

(a) List all the answers Prolog would produce in response to the goal:

?- sentence(S).

(b) In another class of English sentence, the verb phrase consists of just a verb. "The girl calls" is a sentence of this class. Write another clause for verb_phrase/1 to describe such verb phrases.

2.5   An Interactive Session

For the example in this section, we assume that the user has created a text file soldiers.plg containing the procedure for soldier/2 and a text file rank.plg containing that for same_rank/2. Also, we make use of several *built-in predicates*. A built-in predicate is a predicate which is defined as part of Prolog and for which the user does not have to write a procedure.

Every Prolog system comes with a large number of them. Some provide facilities which it is impossible to obtain in Prolog; others offer helpful facilities which save the programmer writing his own procedures.

After giving a command to run the Prolog system, the user loads the programs by typing:

```
?- consult('soldiers.plg').
soldiers.plg consulted
yes

?- consult('rank.plg').
rank.plg consulted
yes
```

consult is a built-in predicate. Its definition is:

> consult/1
> The argument in the call should be an atom. It is interpreted as the name of a file containing Prolog procedures. The clauses for the procedures are read and added to the Prolog database. For each procedure, the order of the clauses is preserved in loading the file. The goal always succeeds and is not re-satisfiable.

We enclosed the file names in single quotes to make a valid atom of each.

A series of calls to consult/1 can be abbreviated to a single command by enclosing the names of the files in square brackets, the file names being separated by commas. Our first two commands could have been entered as:

```
?- ['soldiers.plg', 'rank.plg'].
soldiers.plg consulted
rank.plg consulted
yes
```

If there are any syntactic faults in the program, they are reported to the user at this stage. The style of the error report varies between implementations of the language, but it is usual for the text of faulty clauses to be displayed at the user's terminal. When the program has been loaded without error messages, the user can begin entering questions.

Questions can also be included in a program itself. Such questions are called *directives*, and when Prolog encounters a directive, it immediately tries to satisfy the goals in the directive. One use of a directive is as a convenient way of loading several files. If we put the directive:

```
?- [first, second, third, fourth].
```

in a file called startup, we load the files: first, second, third and fourth into the Prolog database by consulting this file:

```
?- [startup].
first  consulted
second  consulted
third  consulted
fourth  consulted
startup  consulted
yes
```

Two built-in predicates enable the user to inspect the contents of the Prolog database. They are listing/0 and listing/1, defined as follows:

listing/0
The goal always succeeds. Its effect is to display at the current output stream clauses for all procedures in the database.

listing/1
The argument in the call should be an atom. The procedure behaves as listing/0, except that clauses displayed are just those with the atom as name, of whatever arity.

So, we get:

```
?- listing(soldier).
soldier(name(peckem),  rank(general)).
soldier(name(cathcart),  rank(colonel)).
soldier(name(moodus),  rank(colonel)).
soldier(name(towser),  rank(sergeant)).
soldier(name(knight),  rank(sergeant)).
soldier(name(aardvark),  rank(captain)).
soldier(name(dunbar),  rank(lieutenant)).
soldier(name(flume),  rank(captain)).
soldier(name(danby),  rank(major)).
yes
```

By default, the user's terminal is the output stream.

Often, a call to listing reveals a fault in a program. Let us suppose that there is an omission from the list of soldiers: Captain Black. It is possible to add new clauses to the database from the terminal. The terminal is treated as a special file, the default for input and output, called user. By typing:

```
?- [user].
```

the user instructs Prolog to read clauses from the terminal and store them in the Prolog database. In most implementations of the language, the prompt to the user changes to signal that input will be treated as clauses to be added and not as goals to be satisfied. The user indicates the end of input by entering the end-of-file character, which is usually <control-z>.

Assuming that the changed prompt is "|", we get:

| soldier(name(black), rank(captain)).

^z

user consulted
yes

Equally likely is that the fault in the program is an incorrect procedure for a predicate, rather than an omission from the procedure. In this case, the user will wish to replace the faulty procedure. The built-in predicate reconsult allows this. It is defined:

reconsult/1
The argument in the call should be an atom. The atom is interpreted as the name of a file containing Prolog procedures. The clauses for the procedures are read and added to the Prolog database, replacing any existing clauses for the same procedures. For each procedure, the order of the clauses is preserved in loading the file. The goal always succeeds and is not re-satisfiable.

A series of calls to reconsult/1 can be abbreviated, as for consult/1. To indicate that procedures in the files being loaded are to replace existing ones for the same predicates in the Prolog database, each file name is preceded by a minus sign "-". So, if the file soldiers2.plg contains another list of soldiers as clauses for soldier/2, the command:

?- [-'soldiers2.plg'].
soldiers.plg reconsulted
yes

reads the file and replaces the previous clauses for soldier/2 with those read.

The user leaves the Prolog system by calling halt/0, another built-in predicate.

To conclude this section, a word of warning is in order. It may appear to you very convenient to be able to extend and modify programs without leaving Prolog, but this technique is unsound as a method of correcting any but the smallest programs. Modifications entered at the terminal are made only to the Prolog database and do not affect the files, which are external to Prolog. It is all too easy for the programmer to find that, after altering a program at the terminal and leaving Prolog, he cannot remember the changes he made. The predicates which we have described in this section are not intended as a set of debugging tools. We consider the question of debugging Prolog programs in section 9.2.

2.6 Summary

In this chapter, we have introduced the following ideas:

- A rule has a head and a body.

- The meaning of a rule is that the relationship in its head holds only if the relationships in its body all hold.

- Rules and facts are both clauses. A fact is a clause with an empty body.

- A procedure is a collection of clauses together defining a predicate.

- Satisfying a goal may involve satisfying sub-goals.

- For each goal and sub-goal, Prolog searches for a matching clause starting each time from the beginning of the database.

- Prolog backtracks to re-satisfy a sub-goal if a later sub-goal fails.

- The user can force Prolog to backtrack by rejecting the answer it produces.

- When trying to re-satisfy a goal, Prolog resumes searching the database at the clause after that which had previously satisfied the goal.

- Progressive substitution is a technique for building up recursive structures in a program.

- Prolog has built-in predicates which enable the user to manage an interactive session with a Prolog system.

Chapter 3

Recursion in Rules

A recursive rule is one in which a procedure includes a call to itself as a sub-goal in the body of at least one of its clauses. For the beginner, it is hard to see how such a procedure is executed when called as a goal. So, in section 3.1, we use the graphical notation of Chapter 2 to show how a simple recursive procedure is executed. In section 3.2, we show how to use progressive substitution to build a recursive structure in a recursive procedure. In section 3.3, we introduce a very important recursive data type: the list, and we show how to represent lists in Prolog. In section 3.4, we introduce list processing predicates and develop procedures for them. The simplicity and elegance of recursive procedures masks the painstaking stages in their development. We unravel those stages, describing a program development method called *case analysis*. We conclude the chapter with some advice on how to choose the representation for a problem, emphasising when to use lists and when not to use them!

3.1   Recursive Rules

Our first example of a recursive program is a procedure for subordinate/2. When we call this procedure with the names of two soldiers as arguments, the goal is satisfied if the first soldier is subordinate to the second. The procedure retrieves from the clauses for soldier/2 the rank of each, then compares the two ranks:

```
subordinate(lower(Low), higher(High)) :-
    soldier(name(Low), rank(L)),
    soldier(name(High), rank(H)),
    lower_rank(L, H).
```

We intend that the call to lower_rank/2 succeeds if the first rank is lower than the second. The first step is to define the order of ranks. We use a series of facts for next_rank/2:

```
next_rank(private,  sergeant).
next_rank(sergeant,  lieutenant).
next_rank(lieutenant,  captain).
next_rank(captain,  major).
next_rank(major,  colonel).
next_rank(colonel,  general).
```

The interpretation of a structure of the form next_rank(R1, R2) is:

"The next higher rank to R1 is R2."

The first clause of the procedure for lower_rank/2 states that R1 is lower than R2 if R2 is the next rank to R1:

```
lower_rank(R1,  R2)  :-
    next_rank(R1,  R2).
```

The clause deals with all cases where the ranks given are adjacent in the hierarchy. Otherwise, R1 is lower than R2 if the next rank to R1 is rank R3 and R3 is itself lower than R2. This introduces the recursive element. A call to next_rank/2 identifies the rank R3 which is next up in the hierarchy from R1; to determine whether R3 is lower than R2, we call lower_rank/2 again, with R3 as its first argument in place of R1. The clause is:

```
lower_rank(R1,  R2)  :-
    next_rank(R1,  R3),
    lower_rank(R3,  R2).
```

To see how a question involving this procedure is answered, consider the goal:

```
?- subordinate(lower(towser),  higher(moodus)).
```

The first two sub-goals are satisfied by matches with clauses for soldier/2, producing the substitutions L ← sergeant and H ← colonel. The third sub-goal is then: ?- lower_rank(sergeant, colonel). Figure 3.1 illustrates how it is satisfied.

The call succeeds after four recursive calls to lower_rank/2. They are shown in boldface. At each, the first argument in the call is the next higher rank, reaching eventually the rank R for which the goal: ?- next_rank(R, colonel) is satisfied. This is the rank of major.

We have re-drawn the procedure for lower_rank/2 for each level of recursion to make clear that the process of matching is the same at each level. At each, we obtain a new set of variables R1, R2 and R3, particular to one call to lower_rank/2, and for each instance of this goal new substitutions of values for them are made.

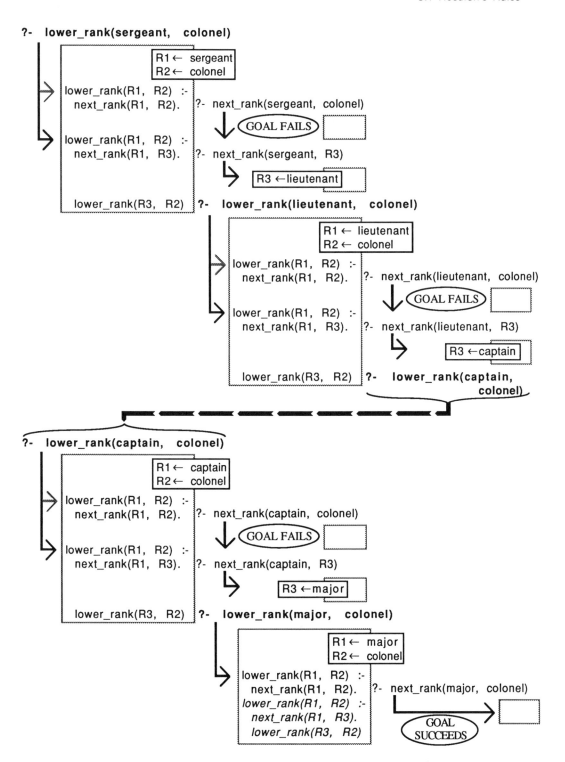

Figure 3.1 Satisfying the sub-goal: ?- lower_rank(sergeant, colonel)

The top-level goal: ?- lower_rank(sergeant, colonel) produces substitutions for the variables R1 and R2 in the head of the second clause for the rule: R1 ← sergeant, R2 ← colonel. The success of the first sub-goal yields the substitution R3 ← lieutenant. The substitutions made for R2 and R3 dictate that the form of the second sub-goal is: ?- lower_rank(lieutenant, colonel). As a variable is local to the clause in which it occurs and to one instance of the clause, this goal term matches the heads of clauses for lower_rank/2, with their variables R1 and R2, exactly as the top-level goal did. There is no connection between the discrete variables that the names R1, R2 and R3 denote at successive levels of recursion. Indeed, Prolog internally does not use the names the user gives, but generates new names for the variables that exist at each level of recursion. As we mentioned in section 2.4, these names may be made visible to the user in certain circumstances.

3.2   Building Recursive Structures

We illustrate how a recursive structure is built by a recursive procedure with the example of a program to compute the route of promotion for a soldier. In line_of_promotion/2 the first argument is the name of the soldier and the second is the sequence of ranks through which the soldier would progress to reach the highest rank in the army. The program uses next_rank/2. We represent the sequence of ranks, which is of unknown length, as a *list*. A list is a data type, defined as follows:

> A list is either empty or consists of two components, called the *head* and the *tail* of the list. The head of a list may be an element of any type, but the tail of a list must be a list.

This is another recursive data type: to know the form of the tail of a list, consult the definition of a list.

By the nature of this recursive definition, a sequence of any number of items can be represented by a single list. For a list of length n, the list of length n + 1 is obtained by replacing the empty list at its end by the list consisting of one item followed by the empty list. For this reason, the list is an appropriate data type to represent the sequence of ranks. The ranks are the elements of the list.

To represent a list as a Prolog structure, we must choose a distinguished atom to represent the empty list and a functor for the structure which represents the list with a head and a tail. The structure has arity 2, the first component representing the head and the second the tail. For the present example, we use last_rank to denote the empty list and rank as the functor for constructing a non-empty list. So, a call of the form:

?- line_of_promotion(name(dunbar), L).

produces the answer:

L = rank(captain, rank(major, rank(colonel, rank(general, last_rank))))

The call:

?- line_of_promotion(name(peckem), L).

produces the answer:

L = last_rank

Peckem is at the highest rank.
The form of the first of these structures can be more easily seen when drawn as a tree, as in Figure 3.2.

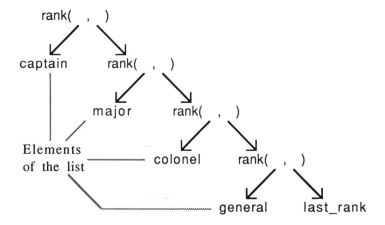

Figure 3.2 Representation as a tree of the route of promotion
for Lieutenant Dunbar

At each level of the tree, the left branch, which is the head of a list, is a list element and the right branch, the tail of a list, is another list. To build the list structure, we use the toolkit technique of progressive substitution.
The procedure first retrieves the rank of the given soldier and then calls a recursive procedure which deals with ranks, not names:

```
line_of_promotion(Soldier, Route) :-
    soldier(Soldier, rank(R)),
    progression(R, Route).
```

The simplest type of progression is that for the rank of general, because it is the last rank. The first clause expresses this fact:

```
progression(general, last_rank).
```

In this clause, we substitute for the second argument the atom which represents the empty list.

For any other rank, the progression consists of a step to the next rank, followed by a progression through other higher ranks. The clause is:

```
progression(R1, rank(R2, Route)) :-
    next_rank(R1, R2),
    progression(R2, Route).
```

In this case, we substitute for the second argument the structure which represents a non-empty list. In the head of the clause, the head and tail of the list are variables: R2 and Route. The values for the head and tail are obtained by progressive substitution of values for R2 and Route in the two sub-goals. The process is illustrated in Figure 3.3 for the goal:

```
?- progression(captain, Route).
```

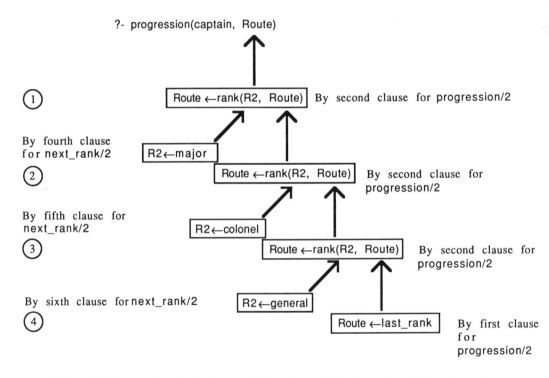

Figure 3.3 Progressive substitutions applied to the variable Route in satisfying the goal:
?- progression(captain, Route).

The circled numbers indicate the level of recursion in the calls to progression/2. The same substitution is applied to the variable Route at each level of recursion until the highest rank is reached. The substitution is completed when the ground term last_rank is substituted for Route. In this procedure, the technique of progressive substitution is applied exactly as described in section 2.4. The difference from the program sentence is that the list structure is built up by recursive calls. The number of these calls, and therefore the length of the list, is unspecified. By a recursive procedure, the programmer is able to define the form of the structure which the procedure constructs without prescribing the size of it.

Exercises 3.2

(a)   Formulate the following questions as calls to line_of_promotion/2:

"Which soldiers are at least two ranks below the highest?"

"Which soldiers are exactly two ranks below the highest?"

(b)   Write a procedure for commands/2 which takes as its first argument the name of a soldier and gives a list of the ranks he commands, in descending order.   (Moderately easy!)

(c)   Write a procedure for relative_ranks/3 which takes the names of two soldiers as its first two arguments and gives as its third argument a list of the ranks through which the first soldier would progress to reach the rank of the second.   (Harder!)

(d)   Write a different procedure for commands/2 which returns the list of ranks in ascending order. (Definitely hard!)

3.3   Notation for Lists

The list is a very useful data type with many applications in Prolog. As the examples in exercise 3.2(a) showed, we can with a single predicate answer a surprising variety of questions by specifying in a goal a list of a particular form.   However, there are some difficulties with the representation for lists that we have used so far. Firstly, the multiple brackets make it hard for a user to express the form of a list correctly and to interpret the lists which a program returns as output.   Secondly, if a programmer chooses a new name for the empty list and for the functor of a non-empty list each time he uses a list to represent a collection of objects, he is obliged to write a different predicate for each representation, even if the definitions of the predicates and the structure of the procedures for them are identical.   In section 3.4, we give a collection of very useful list-processing predicates.   It would be extremely tiresome to have to write these afresh for each new type of list element.

For these reasons, a conventional notation is defined for the representation of lists in Prolog, with a convenient abbreviation of the normal syntax of terms to eliminate the multiple brackets. Using this abbreviation, the list comprising the items a b c and d is written:

[a, b, c, d]

This is an abbreviation for the structure:

'.'(a, '.'(b, '.'c(, '.'(d, [ ]))))

Writing the list in the standard syntax of terms reveals that '.' (pronounced "dot") is the functor of the non-empty list and [ ] is the atom which denotes the empty list. These are the correlatives in the conventional notation of rank and last_rank which we used as functor and distinguished atom in the procedure for progression/2. Other examples of lists and the notation for them are shown in Figure 3.4.

Elements of the list	Standard syntax using "." and [ ]	Abbreviated syntax
major colonel general	'.'(major, '.'(colonel, '.'(general, [ ])))	[major, colonel, general]
soldier(towser)	'.'(soldier(towser), [ ])	[soldier(towser)]
[towser, peckem] [flume, knight]	'.'([towser, peckem], '.'([flume, knight, [ ]))	[[towser, peckem], [flume, knight]]
[ ]	'.'([ ], [ ])	[[ ]]
[12, 13] may [ ] 1988	'.'([12, 13], '.'(may, '.'([ ], '.'(1988, [ ]))))	[[12, 13], may, [ ], 1988]

Figure 3.4 Some lists in the standard and the abbreviated syntax

The third example shows that the items in a list can themselves be lists and the fourth makes clear that the atom [ ] can occur as an item in a list. All lists which are input to a program can be in the abbreviated syntax, and lists output by the program are displayed in the same syntax. In the text of the program itself, the list with head H and tail T is denoted by: [H|T]. In the standard syntax, this is the structure: '.'(H, T). It is important to understand how lists match. Figure 3.5 makes clear that the list whose form is [H|T] matches any non-empty list and shows what substitutions are made in various cases for the variables H and T.

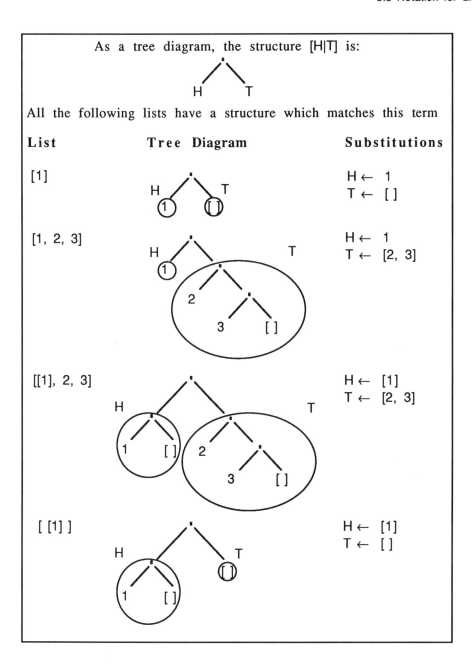

Figure 3.5 Matching between lists and the term: [H|T]

If we had used the conventional notation for lists in writing the procedure for line_of_promotion/2, the two questions in exercise 3.2(a) would
have been expressed as the goals:

?- line_of_promotion(Who, [M, N|P]).

and

?- line_of_promotion(Who, [M, N]).

Figure 3.6 illustrates the lists which the two patterns define.

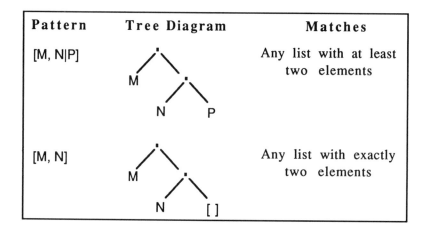

Figure 3.6 Defining types of list by a pattern

More examples of matching between lists are given as exercise 3.3(a), and we urge you to work through them before going on to the next section. If you are unsure about any of the answers, clarify the form of the lists by drawing them as trees in the manner of Figures 3.5 and 3.6.

Exercises 3.3

(a)   Identify whether each of the following pairs of terms match, and, for those that do match, the substitutions made for variables.

(i)	[[grey, green], black, blue]	and [H|T]
(ii)	[[george, millicent]]	and [H| [ ]]
(iii)	[[william, mary] |Others]	and [First, Second]
(iv)	[horse, ass, mule]	and [H, T]
(v)	[[married(george, millicent)]]	and [A]
(vi)	[[1805], 1815]	and [[A|B], C|D]
(vii)	[[1805], 1815]	and [A|B, C|D]
(viii)	[jack, jill]	and [A,B|C]
(ix)	[[jack, jill]]	and [[A],B|C]

3.4 Developing Procedures through Case Analysis

In this section, we give procedures for some useful list-processing predicates. The first is member/2, which takes as arguments an item and a list and succeeds when called as a goal if the item occurs in the list. The procedure examines successive elements of the list. If that at the head of the list is the same as the given item, the goal is satisfied immediately. To express this as a fact, we use the same variable name in the two positions. It can have only one value substituted for it:

```
member(Item, [Item|T]).
```

If the item and the first element are different, a call does not match this clause. The second clause checks whether the item occurs in the tail of the list. This is where recursion comes in: to apply the check, we have only to call member/2, giving as second argument the tail of the original list. The clause is:

```
member(Item, [H|T]) :-
    member(Item, T).
```

member/2 can be used to determine list membership:

```
?- member(dickens, [thackeray, trollope, eliot, dickens, austen]).
yes
```

or to generate through backtracking all elements of a list:

```
?- member(Author, [thackeray, trollope, eliot, dickens, austen]).
Author = thackeray;

Author = trollope;

Author = eliot;

Author = dickens;

Author = austen;
no
```

We use member/2 in the second way in the procedure for common_element/3, a predicate which succeeds when called as a goal if two lists have an element in common and the third argument is that element:

```
common_element(L1, L2, E) :-      % E is common to L1 and L2 if . .
    member(E, L1),                % it is a member of L1, and . . .
    member(E, L2).                % it is a member of L2
```

In the case of the call:

> ?- common_element([sartre, genet, beckett], [pinter, albee, beckett], E).
> E = beckett

the first sub-goal generates successive members of a list; the second tests whether they occur in another list.

Though it may appear to you that the procedure for member/2 emerged by an unfathomable intuition in its author's mind, it was, in fact, developed in a series of distinct steps about which there is no mystery. First, we identified that there were two possibilities for the given item and list. Then, we described the possibilities as patterns of arguments: Item and [Item|T] or Item and [H|T]. Finally, we specified the processing required to deal with each possibility: in the first, the goal is immediately satisfied, and in the second it is satisfied if a recursive call is satisfied. These steps are three of the stages of case analysis, a technique from the programmer's toolkit.

Case Analysis

The technique is a method of developing a procedure, given a statement of the meaning of a predicate. It comprises the following steps:

- Identify the categories, or cases, of the input arguments to the procedure. Usually, the procedure will have a clause for each case.

- Determine how each case is recognised. It may be by a pattern in the head of the clause which is to handle the case or by a sub-goal which is the first one called in the body of the clause.

- Specify the processing required for each case. This includes specifying the form of output arguments. There are two classes of case, and each procedure has a clause for at least one case of each class:

  - the *base case*
    In this case, there is no further recursion. If the output arguments are being constructed by progressive substitution, the output for each is the ground term which terminates the substitution.

  - the *recursive case*
    In this case, a clause specifies some substitution to be applied to the output argument and includes a recursive call. The recursive call must approach a base case.

- Determine the order of the clauses. Place the clauses which handle the base cases first. There will often be a *catch-all* clause. It defines the processing to be carried out when no other case applies, and it is the last clause in order.

- Determine whether the cases are *mutually exclusive*. If the predicate definition prescribes a single result, you must ensure that each possible input falls into just one of the cases you have indentified. Otherwise, Prolog may find incorrect results on backtracking.

You can check that a recursive call does approach a base case by comparing the arguments given in the head of the clause with those which you have used in the recursive call. In the second clause of the procedure for member/2, the second argument in the head is the structure [H|T] and in the recursive call it is the variable T. At each recursive call, the list is shorter by the removal of its head. Recursive calls terminate in success with a match between a sub-goal and the first clause or in failure when the empty list is reached.

Usually, the case of the empty input list is the one to consider first because it is the base case, as our next example illustrates. conc/3 is a predicate which defines the concatenation of two lists. The lists to be joined are given in the first two arguments and the result is returned in the third. The output is constructed from successive elements of the first list, followed by the whole of the second list. So, we have two cases, depending on whether the first list has the form [H|T] or is empty, and these correspond to two clauses for the procedure. These cases are recognised by patterns in the heads of the two clauses.

In the base case, the procedure simply returns the second list:

```
conc([ ], L, L).
```

In the recursive case, we begin to construct the output list by progressive substitution, having identified that H, the head of the first input list, is its first element. The tail T is passed to the recursive call to construct the tail of the output list:

```
conc([H|T], L1, [H|L2]) :-
    conc(T, L1, L2).
```

The behaviour of the predicate is:

```
?- conc([tabby, persian], [siamese], L).
L = [tabby, persian, siamese]
```

The procedure can be called with other patterns of input and output argument, for example to determine all the ways in which a list may be split in two:

```
?- conc(L1, L2, [red, white, blue]).
L1 = [ ]
L2 = [red, white, blue];

L1 = [red]
L2 = [white, blue];

L1 = [red, white]
L2 = [blue];

L1 = [red ,white, blue]
L2 = [ ];
no
```

Another useful list-processing predicate is remove/3. It is defined as a kind of extension of member/2: determining whether an item occurs in a list, but also returning as its third argument the list with that item removed. The cases are the same as for member/2, but we must also specify how the output list is constructed. In the base case, the output is the tail of the given list:

```
remove(H, [H|T], T).
```

In the recursive case, the output list is constructed by progressive substitution, with the head of the input list as its first item:

```
remove(Item, [H|T], [H|L]) :-
    remove(Item, T, L).
```

The two clauses are not mutually exclusive, as those of the procedure for member/2 were not. An item which is found at the head of a list and removed (first clause) will then be put at the head of the second list if Prolog backtracks to use the second clause. If a list contains more than one occurrence of the item to be removed, the goal is re-satisfiable on backtracking:

```
?- remove(charles, [george, charles, henry, charles, edward], L).
L = [george, henry, charles, edward];

L = [george, charles, henry, edward];
no
```

When called with its first and third arguments as variables, this procedure selects, through backtracking, successive items in a list. We use it in this way in a program to explore the possible pairings of players in a tennis match, given lists of players to be paired up. pairings/3 does this.

The procedure is:

```
pairings([ ], [ ], [ ]).
pairings([H|T], L1, [pair(H, P)|Ps]) :-
    remove(P, L1, L2),
    pairings(T, L2, Ps).
```

The results are:

```
?- pairings([beth, victoria, mary], [charles, george, edward], M).
M =   [pair(beth, charles), pair(victoria, george), pair(mary, edward)];

M =   [pair(beth, charles), pair(victoria, edward), pair(mary, george)];

M =   [pair(beth, george), pair(victoria, charles), pair(mary, edward)];

M =   [pair(beth, george), pair(victoria, edward), pair(mary, charles)];

M =   [pair(beth, edward), pair(victoria, charles), pair(mary, george)];

M =   [pair(beth, edward), pair(victoria, george), pair(mary, charles)];
no
```

Our next predicate, reverse/2, illustrates a different programming technique. As its name suggests, this predicate gives in its second argument the items of the list which was the first argument in reverse order. The procedure is:

```
reverse(L1, L2) :-
    hidden_reverse(L1, [ ], L2).

hidden_reverse([ ], L, L).
hidden_reverse([H|T], L1, L2) :-
    hidden_reverse(T, [H|L1], L2).
```

We use a sub-goal with an extra argument to perform the reversing. In the call to hidden_reverse/3, the extra argument is the empty list, and one element of the first list is put at the head of it at each level of recursion. The third argument is simply passed on at each level of recursion until the base case is reached, when the value substituted for it is the value of the second argument. The technique is illustrated in Figure 3.7.

This method of building a recursive structure is called *ingoing recursion*. We include it as a technique in our toolkit.

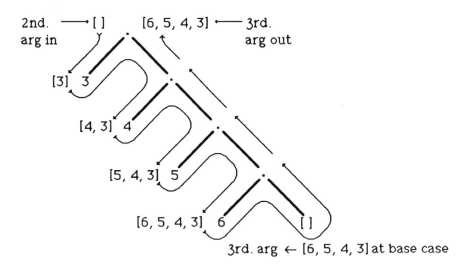

Figure 3.7 Reversing a list by ingoing recursion

Ingoing Recursion

The technique builds a recursive structure starting from the ground term which marks its end. It is used when a specific order, which cannot be obtained by progressive substitution, is prescribed for the items in the structure or when the computation in the recursive cases depends on having access to the structure built so far. The technique comprises the following steps:

- The ground term is an argument in calls to the procedure.

- At each recursive call, that argument is a new structure with the previous structure as one component.

- The variable which is to hold the final result is passed inwards, no substitutions being applied to it until the base case.

- In the base case, this variable is matched with the argument denoting the structure being built.

A procedure using ingoing recursion constructs a term in the opposite order from the familiar method of *outgoing recursion* with progressive substitution. The latter method usually results in a more natural procedure for a predicate and does not require the use of the extra argument. The solutions to exercises 3.2(b) and 3.2(d) illustrate the difference between the two methods. Look at them now if you did not do so while trying the exercises.

Our final example in this section is flatten/2. This predicate takes a list as its first argument and returns a list with nested sublists removed:

?- flatten([2, [1, 3], [4]], F).

F = [2, 1, 3, 4]

?- flatten([[2, 4], [ ], [1], 3], F).

F = [2, 4, [ ], 1 ,3]

An analysis of the forms of the input list reveals three cases:

- The list is empty: [ ].
- The head of the list is itself a list: [[H|T] | L].
- The head of the list is not a list, but an element in a list: [H|T].

This analysis identifies both the cases and how to recognise them. Our first thought might be that we could use simple outgoing recursion to define the processing appropriate to each case. In the first case, the output list would be empty:

flatten([ ], [ ]).

In the third case, the item H would belong at the head of the output list, and the tail of the output would be constructed by a recursive call:

flatten([H|T], [H|L]) :-
    flatten(T, L).

The difficulty lies in the second case, that of the list whose form is [[H|T]|L]. We cannot simply put H at the head of the output list, for it may itself be a list. Outgoing recursion alone is not an adequate method for this problem. However, if we combine ingoing recursion with our first attempt, we can overcome this difficulty. The clause is:

hidden_flatten([[H|T] | L], S, F) :-
    hidden_flatten(L, S, Lf),
    hidden_flatten([H|T], Lf, F).

The extra argument S gives the flattened list so far. It is the empty list in the call to hidden_flatten/3. The first sub-goal produces the list Lf, holding the elements of the flattened list L at the front of S. Lf is then input as the result so far to a sub-goal which flattens [H|T] to produce F.

Putting this clause together with modified versions of those for cases one and three and a top-level procedure to provide the extra input argument gives:

51

```
flatten(L, F) :-
    hidden_flatten(L, [ ], F).

hidden_flatten([ ], L, L).
hidden_flatten([ [H|T] | L], S, F) :-
    hidden_flatten(L, S, Lf),
    hidden_flatten([H|T], Lf, F).
hidden_flatten([H|T], S, [H|L]) :-
    hidden_flatten(T, S, L).
```

The behaviour of the procedure can be most easily understood by visualising the list as a binary tree which the procedure traverses in reverse order. The traversal is illustrated in Figure 3.8

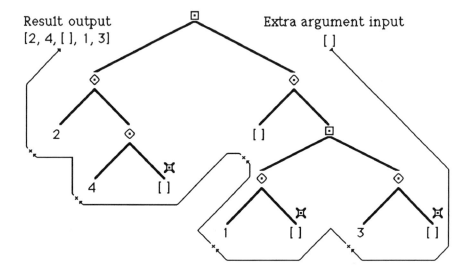

ꚍ - denotes a node at which the base case holds.

▣ - denotes a node at which the second case holds.

◈ - denotes a node at which the third case holds.

Figure 3.8 Flattening the list [[2, 4], [ ], [1], 3] viewed as a tree traversal

If left and right branches from a node are trees, the right sub-tree is traversed first, then the left (clause 2). If the left branch is a leaf node, it forms part of the output, at the head of the list formed by traversing the right sub-tree (clause 3).

Unfortunately, though the procedure does return the correct result:

```
?- flatten([ [2, 4], [ ], [1], 3], F).
F = [2, 4, [ ], 1 ,3];
```

it also generates incorrect alternatives if backtracking is forced:

F = [2, 4, [ ], [1], 3];

F = [[2, 4], [ ], 1, 3];

F = [[2,4], [ ], [1], 3];
no

These alternatives arise because our procedure does not ensure exclusion between cases, though the predicate defines just one correct answer for any given list. The case of the empty list excludes the other two, but the case of the list whose form is [H|T] does not exclude a list whose form is [[H|T] | L]. In other words, a list which matches the pattern [[H|T] | L] also matches [H|T]. We need a way of ensuring in the third clause that H is not a non-empty list. Let us assume that different/2 is defined to succeed if its two arguments do not match. Then we can add a sub-goal in the third clause:

```
hidden_flatten([H|T], S, [H|L]) :-
    different(H, [A|B]),            % Fails if H is a non-empty list
    hidden_flatten(T, S, L).
```

This is an example of a sub-goal being used to identify a case, where a pattern would not identify it exclusively. The sub-goal is called a *guard*.
We give a procedure for different/2 in section 4.5. We discuss other ways of enforcing mutual exclusion between clauses in section 6.1.2.

Exercises 3.4

(a) Use remove/3 in a procedure for permute/2, to take two lists as arguments and succeed if the elements of the second list are a permutation of the elements of the first.

(b) Write a procedure for remove_all/3 to take a list and an item and return a list from which all occurrences of the item have been removed. If the item does not occur in the list, the procedure should return the original list.

(c) Use remove_all/3 in a procedure for no_duplicates/2, to remove duplicates from a list.

3.5 Another Technique for Developing Procedures

Case analysis is a relatively easy technique for the novice Prolog programmer to master because it prescribes a clear procedure: a series of steps to follow which go some way to removing the mystique that sometimes surrounds the development of recursive programs. However, precisely because it is so overtly procedural, case analysis is not always the most suitable approach. On occasions, a higher-level approach based on identifying *logical relationships* between arguments leads to a clearer and more concise procedure.

Consider the problem of writing a procedure for sublist/2, to succeed when called as a goal if its second argument is a sublist of its first. So:

```
?- sublist([apple, orange, pear, banana], [orange, pear]).
 yes

?- sublist([apple, orange, pear, banana], [orange, banana]).
 no
```

We might develop the procedure by case anaysis. The sublist is either empty or has the form [H|T]. The two cases translate into clauses:

```
sublist(Any_list, [ ]).        % The empty list is always a sublist.
sublist(L, [H|T]) :-           % The non-empty list is a sublist of L if . . .
```

In the second clause, we would define how to find H in L and how to determine whether the elements of T were identical to the elements of L that immediately followed the occurrence of H.

However, the case analysis approach overlooks the logical relationship between a list and any sublist of it. List has Sub as a sublist if List comprises a possibly empty sequence of elements, followed by the elements of Sub, followed by another possibly empty sequence. The three sequences joined together form List. We can translate this relationship directly into Prolog using conc/3:

```
sublist(List, Sub) :-
     conc(Front, Back, List),
     conc(F, Sub, Front).
```

The logical relationship is illustrated in Figure 3.9.

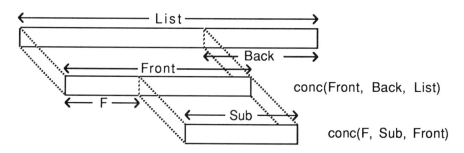

Figure 3.9 Logical relationship between List and Sub

The procedure does correctly express the logical relationship:

```
?- sublist([1, 2, 3, 4], [2, 3]).
yes
```

```
?- sublist([1, 2, 3, 4], [2, 4]).
no
```

Closer examination reveals an odd feature: when used to generate sublists of a list, the procedure produces some duplicates:

```
?- sublist([1, 2, 3], Sub).
Sub = [ ];

Sub = [1];

Sub = [ ];

Sub = [1, 2];

Sub = [2];

Sub = [ ];

Sub = [1, 2, 3];

Sub = [2, 3];

Sub = [3];

Sub = [ ];
no
```

What would happen if the sub-goals were in the other order? Evidently, the procedure would still express the logical relationship. In fact, after producing the same alternatives in a different order, it would generate a never-ending sequence of recursive sub-goals in a search for more sublists.

These oddities are not of any significance if the sole purpose of the procedure is to illustrate the nature of the sublist relation between two lists. More typically, however, we write a procedure for a predicate in order to use the predicate within a larger program. The techniques and strategies for developing large Prolog programs are the subject of Part 2 of this book. They are founded on the assumption that the programmer tests and understands every aspect of the behaviour of individual procedures. An approach to Prolog programming based on expressing logical relationships satisfies this assumption only partially. That approach can provide insights as a starting point for writing a procedure, but it must be supplemented by consideration of the procedural behaviour of the resulting program.

The first procedural issue in the execution of a declaratively correct procedure is whether a call is certain to terminate. If you apply the case analysis technique, putting clauses for base cases before those for recursive ones and ensuring that recursive cases do approach a base case, you should not experience the problem of non-termination. Consider, however, the following alternative procedure for lower_rank/2:

```
lower_rank(R1, R2) :-
    lower_rank(R3, R2),
    next_rank(R1, R3).
lower_rank(R1, R2) :-
    next_rank(R1, R2).
```

This is declaratively identical to the one we gave in section 3.1, but when it is called as a goal:

```
?- lower_rank(sergeant, colonel).
```

execution does not terminate. The first sub-goal: ?- lower_rank(R3, colonel) is generated in an identical form at each level of recursion, and the computation does not proceed to the call to next_rank/2.

A partial solution would be to reverse the order of the clauses, putting that for the base case first. Then the program would function correctly for goals which should succeed:

```
?- lower_rank(sergeant, colonel).
yes
```

but it still would not terminate if the goal ought to fail. The culprit is the clause for the recursive case, which is *left-recursive*; that is, it has a recursive call as the first sub-goal in its body. For goals which we expected to fail, the recursive sub-goal after all ranks had been checked would have an identical form to its parent goal and would not approach the base case. A complete solution to the problem demands re-ordering the clauses and the sub-goals within the recursive clause.

The second procedural issue is efficiency of execution, and we consider this in section 4.3.

Exercises 3.5

(a) Why does the procedure for sublist/2 produce duplicates of the empty list when the second argument in a call is a variable?

(b) Complete the development by case analysis of a procedure for sublist/2. What is the behaviour of the procedure when the goal is:

```
?- sublist([1, 2, 3], Sub).
```

3.6   Lists and Data Structuring

The convenience of the list notation may lead the inexperienced programmer to use it inappropriately for representing the data in a problem.
As we emphasised at the start of section 3.3, the notation is just an abbreviation for a structure constructed from the functor "dot", and, whereas the
programmer should choose functor names which are indicative of the
relationships they represent, "dot" is certainly not a meaningful name for a
structure!

Consider, for example, the problem of writing a program to store
information about countries and answer questions about them.   A user of
the program might want to know:

"What is the population of Egypt?"

"What is the capital of France and what is its population?"

"What time zone is Moscow in?"

"What is the population density of Libya?"

"Are there any languages spoken by natives of both Romania
and West Germany?"

"Are there any countries that border both Morocco and Egypt?"

The issue in this problem is how to represent the information about each
country.   The obvious choice is a series of facts, using a predicate of arity 8
if there are eight items of information:

```
country(Name, Population, Area, NameOfCapital, PopulationOfCapital,
    TimeZoneOfCapital, ListOfLanguagesSpoken,
    ListOfCountriesBordering)
```

So, for Egypt:

```
country(egypt, 42, 1000, cairo, 7500, 3, [arabic, berber, nubian, english],
    [israel, sudan, libya]).
```

This representation has several weaknesses.   The most serious is its
failure to capture the natural structure of the data stored.   The data
comprises a unique key (the name of the country) and some information
associated with the key.   That information has a structure itself: some
relates to the country as a whole, some is particular to the capital city.   A
better representation would reflect this structure.   It could be done using
lists:

```
country(egypt, [42, 1000, [cairo, 7500, 3],
        [arabic, berber, nubian, english],
        [israel, sudan, libya] ]).
```

Now the structure of the information as key and data can be reflected in the procedures which process it:

```
retrieve_and_process(Country) :-
    country(Country, Info),
    ...
```

Now process Info as required.

No procedures which process the database at this high level would need to be altered if the structure of the information stored was later changed.

The weakness now is that we are using lists for several purposes, none of which can be identified from the form of the representation alone. It is good programming practice to use lists for representing collections of items only if the collection is of variable size and if the items are of the same type. This consideration leads us to another refinement:

```
country(name(egypt),
    data(pop_in_millions(42),
        area_in_thou_sq_kms(1000),
        capital(name(cairo),
            pop_in_thousands(7500),
            time_zone_gmt(plus, 3)),
        languages([arabic, berber, nubian, english]),
        countries_bordering([israel, sudan, libya]))).
```

Besides eliminating the inappropriate use of lists, we have clarified the meaning of the integer values. The functor of a structure should recall the meaning of the information represented in the components and not itself represent information. For this reason, we prefer time_zone_gmt(plus, 3) to time_zone_gmt(plus(3)) or time_zone_gmt_plus(3).

This representation has the merit of being both well-structured and understandable. To insulate the user from the representational details, we provide predicates to pick out components of complex structures. The first of our example questions is answered by a call to population/2:

```
?- population(egypt, Pop).
Pop = pop_in_millions(42)
```

The procedure is:

```
population(Country, Population) :-
    country(name(Country), data(Population, _, _, _, _)).
```

The underline character "_" by which we denote the last four components of the structure with functor date is Prolog's *anonymous variable*. It can be used in place of any component of a structure whose value we do not wish to know, and it saves us having to think up names for variables which have no significance in the procedure. A structure may include any number of anonymous variables, and they are all distinct. We can also use the anonymous variable in questions when we are not interested in the value substituted for it. For instance, if we wanted to know the countries about which information is held, we could ask:

```
?- population(Country, _).
```

Prolog would report only the substitution made for Country.

population/2 is an example of a *selector predicate*. Selector predicates are very widely used in programs which manipulate large databases, so we include the technique in our toolkit.

Selector Predicates

A selector predicate retrieves an item from a database while concealing the structure of the database from the user of the predicate. The technique comprises the following steps:

- Identify the types of request for information which may be made. What subsets of the database would it be meaningful for a user to ask about?

- Identify how a user of the database specifies the items to be retrieved. Usually, it is by giving a key value.

- For each anticipated request, a selector predicate is needed. If the request relates to information stored as facts, the procedure for the predicate uses matching to retrieve the information from a structure. If the information is not explicitly stored, the procedure computes it. The user of the predicate is unaware of the distinction between explicitly-stored information and information derived by application of a rule.

Procedures for selector predicates to answer the other requests we gave as examples are:

```
capital_and_pop(Country, Capital, Population) :-
    country(name(Country),
        data(_, _, capital(Capital, Population, _), _, _,)).

time_zone_is(City, Zone) :-
    country(_, data(_, _, capital(name(City), _, Zone), _, _)).
```

```
languages_are(Country, Languages) :-
    country(name(Country),
        data(_, _, _, Languages, _)).

countries_bordering_are(Country, C) :-
    country(name(Country),
        data(_, _, _, _, C)).

population_density_is(Country, density(D)) :-
    country(name(Country),
        data(pop_in_millions(P), area_in_thou_sq_kms(A), _, _, _)),
        . . .
```

and now calculating P * 1000/A gives the population density in persons per square kilometre.

We do not provide selector predicates to answer the last two requests, as these are not requests for single items. A user of the database could define his own predicates using existing selector predicates and common_element/3. Though one cannot define precisely what is a single item in a database which is represented partly by rules, the principle of this design method is that a basic set of selector predicates defined for a database is extensible to support different user applications. Figure 3.10 illustrates the structure.

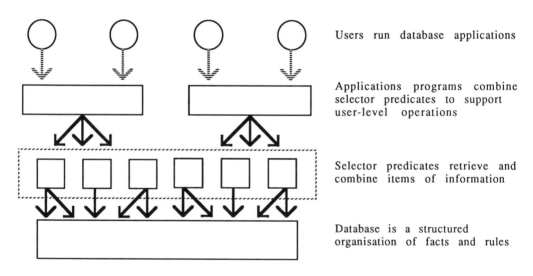

Users run database applications

Applications programs combine selector predicates to support user-level operations

Selector predicates retrieve and combine items of information

Database is a structured organisation of facts and rules

Figure 3.10 Selector predicates supporting database applications

3.7 Summary

In this chapter, we have introduced the following ideas:

- A recursive procedure is one in which the procedure itself is called as a sub-goal in the body of one or more of its own clauses.

- When the call is executed, a new set of variables is created for each level of recursion.

- The list is a recursive data type. A notation using "dot" and [ ] is used by convention for representing lists as structures. An abbreviation of the syntax of terms facilitates manipulation of lists represented in the conventional notation.

- Case analysis is a technique for developing procedures. A recursive procedure has clauses for at least one base and one recursive case.

- The programmer must enforce mutual exclusion between clauses handling cases if the predicate definition specifies just a single result for a given input.

- Ingoing recursion is an alternative method to progressive substitution for building a structure.

- Procedures can sometimes be developed by analysing logical relationships between arguments, but the procedural behaviour must always be checked.

- The procedural behaviour of a program is determined by the order of clauses and the order of sub-goals within clauses.

- Often, the list is not the best representation for data. Structures with other functors are more readily understood. Selector predicates give access to components of such structures.

- The anonymous variable can be used if we are not interested in the value substituted for it.

Chapter 4

Operations on Terms

The basic operation on terms is the test of whether two terms match. Other tests are carried out by built-in predicates. The purpose of this chapter is to introduce these predicates to you and to show how they greatly increase the power of Prolog.

4.1   Arithmetic   Operations

Arithmetic expressions are constructed using the arithmetic operators: + (addition), - (subtraction), * (multiplication), / (real division), div (integer division) and mod (remainder).   The built-in predicate is evaluates an arithmetic expression.   Its definition is:

> is/2
> The second argument should be an arithmetic expression.   The goal evaluates the expression and succeeds if the value matches the first argument; otherwise it fails.

is/2 can be written between its arguments.   Examples are:

```
?- A is 10-5-4.
A = 1

?- is(A, 10-5-4).
A = 1
```

These two are equivalent.

```
?- 35 is 5 + 10 * 3.
yes

?- 45 is 5 + 10 * 3.
no
```

A useful predicate which uses is/2 is length/2, to determine the number of elements in a list. The base case, as usual with lists, is the case of the empty list, whose length is 0. The recursive case is the case of the non-empty list, whose length is the length of its tail plus 1.

```
length([ ], 0).                    % Base case
length([_|T], N) :-                % Recursive case
    length(T, M),
    N is M + 1.
```

The procedure behaves as follows:

```
?- length([a, b, c, d], L).              How long is the list [a, b, c, d]?
L = 4
```

```
?- length([10, [11, 11], 12], 4).   Is the list [10, [11, 11], 12] of length 4?
no
```

```
?- length(L, 4).                         What list is of length 4?
L = [_66, _67, _68, _69]
```

Care is needed when using is/2. Its definition says: "The second argument should be an arithmetic expression." If it is not, a *Prolog error* results. A Prolog error is a system response when an argument in a call to a built-in predicate is not of the correct type. The response varies between implementations. Usually, it takes the form of a message printed at the screen which interrupts program execution. The possibility of Prolog errors complicates the view of a Prolog program presented in earlier chapters, in which every call simply succeeded or failed. The behaviour of programs which use those built-in predicates that impose constraints on the types of their arguments is more complex and difficult to control. For example, if we reversed the order of the sub-goals in the second clause of our length program:

```
length([_|T], N) :-
    N is M + 1,
    length(T, M).
```

the procedure's declarative interpretation would be unchanged, but a call such as:

```
?- length([a, b, c, d], L).
```

would cause a Prolog error. This is because in the expression: M + 1, M would still be a variable when is tried to evaluate the expression. A value would be substituted for this variable only when the base case was reached.

Exercises 4.1

(a) In the following call to length/2, what happens if the user rejects the first answer?

?- length(L, 3).

(b) Modify the procedure for length/2 to count the total number of elements in a list, including elements in sublists.

(c) Write a procedure for sum_of_items/2 to sum the items in a list of integers.

4.2 Relational Operations

The built-in predicates for relational operations are listed in Figure 4.1. Like the arithmetic operators, they are written between their two operands. Operands should be arithmetic expressions, and a Prolog error results if they are not. The predicates evaluate the expressions and succeed if the values stand in the stated relation.

Predicate	Relation tested
=:=	Equal to
=\=	Not equal to
>	Greater than
>=	Greater than or equal to
<	Less than
=<	Less than or equal to

Figure 4.1 Built-in predicates for relational operations

To illustrate these predicates, we give a procedure for max/3. A call of the form:

?- max(N1, N2, N3).

succeeds if the three arguments are arithmetic expressions and N3 is equal to the greater of N1 and N2. The procedure is:

```
max(N1, N2, N2) :-
    N2 >= N1.
max(N1, N2, N1) :-
    N2 < N1.
```

In calls, the third argument can be either a variable or an arithmetic expression:

    ?- max(10, 8, N).   What is the maximum of 10 and 8?
    N = 10

    ?- max(3, 7, 3).   Is 3 the maximum of 3 and 7?
    no

    ?- max(10, 10 + 3 - 4, 10).   Is 10 the maximum of 10 and
    yes   the expression 10 + 3 - 4?

A Prolog error occurs if either of the first two arguments is a variable.

We can use max/3 in a procedure for max_in_list/2 to determine the maximum value in a list of integers. In this instance, the base case is not the empty list, but the list with just one element. That element is the maximum in the list:

    max_in_list([N], N).

In the case of a list with two or more elements, we recursively determine Max_in_tail, the maximum value in the list without the head H, and we use max/3 to identify the greater of Max_in_tail and H:

    max_in_list([H, N|T], Max) :-
        max_in_list([N|T], Max_in_tail),
        max(H, Max_in_tail, Max).

This gives:

    ?- max_in_list([3, 4, 10, 5, 0], Max).
    Max = 10

    ?- max_in_list([3, 7, 7, 6], 6).
    no

For another example of relational and arithmetic operators being used in a program to manipulate lists of numbers, consider the "knapsack problem". It concerns a knapsack, which can carry a known maximum weight, and an assortment of objects of various known weights which may be carried in the knapsack. The question is: "What selection from the objects loads the knapsack exactly to its maximum weight?"

In the solution, we use lists of integers to represent the objects available and the objects included in the load and an integer to denote the maximum weight of the load. Solutions are produced by calling knapsack/3:

    ?- knapsack(Objects_available, Target_weight, Objects_carried).

65

A little thought reveals that each one of the Objects_available can be included in the Objects_carried if its weight does not exceed the Target_weight, and that if it is included, the rest of the load comprises some selection of the other objects to a total weight reduced by the weight of the object just included. This reasoning gives us the first clause:

```
knapsack([Next|Others], Target, [Next|Rest]) :-
    Next =< Target,
    Remainder is Target - Next,
    knapsack(Others, Remainder, Rest).
```

The next possibility is that an object is not included in the load, whether or not it could be. The load is then made up of a selection from the other objects. This gives the second recursive case:

```
knapsack([_|Others], Target, Load) :-
    knapsack(Others, Target, Load).
```

The base case is reached when, with every object having been considered for inclusion, the remaining weight is 0:

```
knapsack([ ], 0, [ ]).
```

The program generates all possible loads through backtracking:

```
?- knapsack([2, 7, 18, 5, 10, 3], 20, Load).
Load = [2, 18];

Load = [2, 5, 10, 3];

Load = [7, 10, 3];
no
```

Exercises 4.2

(a) What is the result of the following calls to max/3?

   (i) ?- max(4+7, 8*9, N).
   (ii) ?- max(4+7, 8*9, 72).

(b) Write a procedure for split/4 which takes a list of integers L1 and an integer N and gives lists L2 and L3 such that integers less than N are in L2 and all others in are in L3.

(c) Extend the max_in_list program to a predicate: position_of_max/3, in which the third argument gives the position in L at which N occurs.

4.3 Type Testing Operations

The programmer can prevent Prolog errors by checking that the arguments in a call are of the required type. The built-in predicates to test the type of a term are listed in Figure 4.2. Each of them succeeds when called as a goal if the argument is of the indicated type, and fails otherwise.

Predicate	Type tested
integer/1	An integer
real/1	A real number
number/1	An integer or a real number
atom/1	An atom
atomic/1	An atom or a number
compound/1	A structure
nonvar/1	An atom, a number or a structure
var/1	A variable

Figure 4.2 Built-in predicates for type testing operations

You must be careful about the order of sub-goals when using the type testing predicates. The meaning of a program may alter if sub-goals are re-ordered. For example, in the following procedure:

```
p(X) :-
    ...
    var(X),              % Is X a variable?
    substitute(X),       % If so, substitute a value for X.
    ...
```

a call to p/1 in which the argument was a variable might succeed, whereas it could not if the sub-goals were reversed:

```
p(X) :-
    ...
    substitute(X),       % Substitute a value
    var(X),              % X cannot be a variable here.
    ...
```

The type testing predicates test a term at a particular point in program execution. Thus, they have a purely procedural meaning: at a different point, the same call may produce a different result.

In Figure 4.3, we reproduce the hierarchy diagram of terms from section 1.3, with boxes to show the range of argument types for which each type testing predicate succeeds.

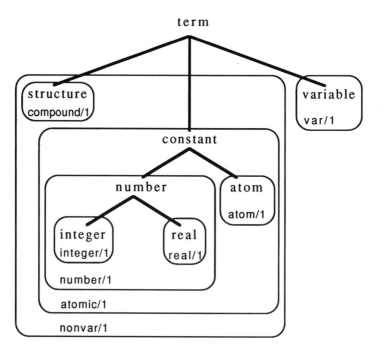

Figure 4.3 Relation of type testing predicates to types of Prolog term

A call to nonvar/1 succeeds even if the argument in the call is a structure which includes variables as components:

```
?- nonvar(reverse([ ], L, L)).
yes
```

It does not test whether the structure is ground. We give a procedure for ground/1 in the next section.

We can now write a procedure for arithmetic_expression/1 to test whether a term is a valid arithmetic expression:

```
arithmetic_expression(N)  :-
    integer(N).
arithmetic_expression(E1+E2)  :-
    arithmetic_expression(E1),
    arithmetic_expression(E2).
```

and clauses for each arithmetic operator, down to:

```
arithmetic_expression(E1 mod E2)  :-
    arithmetic_expression(E1),
    arithmetic_expression(E2).
```

To prevent any possibility of a Prolog error occurring with is/2, a call to this procedure would precede the call to is/2, as in the procedure for safe_evaluation/2:

```
safe_evaluation(Expression, Value) :-
    arithmetic_expression(Expression),
    Value is Expression.
```

The behaviour of safe_evaluation/2 is:

```
?- safe_evaluation(20+5 mod 2, V).
V = 22

?- safe_evaluation(N1 * N2 + N3, V).
no
```

The same method could be used to check the form of operands in relational operations and prevent the Prolog error which would occur if a goal such as: ?- X >= 5 were called. However, a more satisfactory outcome than the failure of the goal would be if it succeeded, substituting for X some integer for which X >= 5 is true. This cannot be done using the built-in predicate, but we can write a procedure which generates values for which the relation >= is satisfied, besides testing values given on input. The procedure is:

```
greater_or_equal(N1, N2) :-
    integer(N2),
    N2 >= N1.
greater_or_equal(N1, N2) :-
    var(N2),
    next_integer(N1, N2).

next_integer(N, N).
next_integer(N1, N2) :-
    N3 is N1 + 1,
    next_integer(N3, N2).
```

When the second argument is a variable in the call, greater_or_equal/2 is always re-satisfiable, generating progressively larger integers. A Prolog error still occurs if the first argument in the call is not an integer. We suggest an extension to overcome this limitation in the exercises.

A similar predicate is in_range_integer/3, which tests whether an integer lies between two given integers or generates integers that do satisfy this test. In the second usage, the predicate fails after generating all valid integers. The procedure is:

```
in_range_integer(N1, N2, N3) :-
    integer(N2),
    N2 >= N1,
    N2 =< N3.
in_range_integer(N1, N2, N3) :-
    var(N2),
    generate_in_range(N1, N2, N3).

generate_in_range(Base, Base, Limit) :-
    Base =< Limit.
generate_in_range(Base, N, Limit) :-
    Base < Limit,
    Next is Base + 1,
    generate_in_range(Next, N, Limit).
```

The purpose of the two clauses for in_range_integer/3 is to ensure that a call is executed in the most efficient way. If we did not distinguish between calls in which the second argument was a variable and those in which it was an integer, the call:

```
?- in_range_integer(1, 100, 100).
```

would produce 100 recursive calls to generate_in_range/3 before reaching the base case. The sub-goals: ?- integer(N2) and: ?- var(N2) are guards which ensure that the clauses which handle the two cases are mutually exclusive. We used the same method in the procedure for greater_or_equal/2 to achieve efficiency of execution, whether the procedure was testing a given value or generating values.

Notice that the conjunction:

```
?- greater_or_equal(1, N), greater_or_equal(N, 10).
```

is not equivalent to the call:

```
?- in_range_integer(1, N, 10).
```

The first sub-goal in the conjunction is always re-satisfiable, and the effect of this is that after substituting for N each of the integers from 1 to 10, the sub-goal continues generating larger integers for which the second sub-goal fails.

greater_or_equal/2 and in_range_integer/3 are *utility predicates*, and the technique which they exemplify is part of the programmer's toolkit.

Utility Predicates

The technique is used when a predicate is to form part of a larger program, and the procedure for it will be called with different patterns of arguments, either to generate values or to test values given as input. It prevents Prolog

errors and ensures that a call is executed in an efficient way. The characteristics of the technique are:

- The procedure has a clause for each pattern of arguments with which
  it may be called.

- The first sub-goals of each clause are guards, testing the type of one or
  more arguments.

- The procedure is re-satisfiable, generating all possible substitutions
  for arguments which are variables in the call.

- The behaviour of the procedure is tested for every legitimate pattern
  of arguments in a call.

- The description of the predicate states the permitted patterns of
  arguments in calls and the order in which substitutions are generated.

The value of the technique is not confined to programming problems in
which we are manipulating numbers and there is a danger of Prolog errors
if we fail to check the types of terms. Let us examine again the procedure
for subordinate/2 which we gave in section 3.1.

If we wish to know which soldiers are of higher rank than Flume, we
formulate the question as the goal:

?- subordinate(lower(flume), Who).

The process of satisfying this goal is shown in Figure 4.4. The figure shows
that the first answer to the question is:

Who = higher(peckem)

When the user rejects this answer, alternatives are produced by
backtracking to the second sub-goal: ?- soldier(name(Higher), rank(H))
shown in box 2.2. The goal can be re-satisfied by a match with each clause
for soldier/2. For those soldiers who are of higher rank than Flume, the
value substituted for H is a rank for which the third sub-goal can be satisfied. For others, the third sub-goal fails, and Prolog backtracks to try the
next soldier. Alternative answers are produced by searching through all the
soldiers, testing the rank of each against Flume's rank. This is not the most
efficient method: better would be to identify in turn each rank that is higher
than Flume's and then pick out the soldiers holding each of these ranks. To
implement this approach, we would reverse the order of the last two sub-
goals, giving the procedure:

```
subordinate(Lower, Higher) :-
    soldier(name(Lower), rank(L)),
    lower_rank(L, H),
    soldier(name(Higher), rank(H)).
```

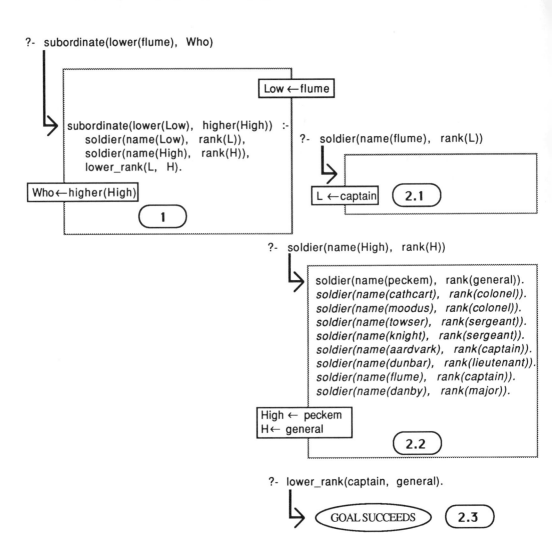

Figure 4.4 Satisfying the goal: ?- subordinate(lower(flume), Who).

However, if subordinate/2 is to be used in a large program, we may not be able to predict the pattern of arguments in every call. Yet, if in the larger program there are many more soldiers and ranks than just those we used for illustration, it will be important to execute a call in an efficient way. The predicate must be treated as a utility and the procedure structured accordingly:

```
subordinate(Lower,  Higher)  :-
    compound(Lower),                % Both names given on input
    compound(Higher),
    soldier(name(Lower),  rank(L)),
    soldier(name(Higher),  rank(H)),
    lower_rank(L,  H).
subordinate(Lower,  Higher)  :-
    compound(Lower),                % Just first name given
    var(Higher),
    soldier(name(Lower),  rank(L)),
    lower_rank(L,  H),
    soldier(name(Higher),  rank(H)).
subordinate(Lower,  Higher)  :-
    var(Lower),                     % Just second name given
    compound(Higher),
    soldier(name(Higher),  rank(H)),
    lower_rank(L,  H),
    soldier(name(Lower),  rank(L)).
subordinate(Lower,  Higher)  :-
    var(Lower),                     % Neither name given on input
    var(Higher),
    soldier(name(Lower),  rank(L)),
    soldier(name(Higher),  rank(H)),
    lower_rank(L,  H).
```

There is now a clause for each of the four argument patterns, and the calls to the type testing predicates ensure mutual exclusivity. The other sub-goals are ordered for efficiency. In general, the fewer variables are in a sub-goal, the less backtracking is involved in satisfying a conjunction of sub-goals and the more efficiently a procedure is executed.

Exercises 4.3

(a)   Extend the procedure for greater_or_equal/2 so that the call:

   ?- greater_or_equal(N, 10).

produces alternative substitutions for N through backtracking.

4.4   Term Constructing Operations

arithmetic_expression/1 is useful, but the procedure for it is rather long because of the need for separate clauses, with identical bodies, for each arithmetic operator.   More convenient would be to list the operators as clauses for arithmetic_operator/1:

```
arithmetic_operator('+').
arithmetic_operator('-').
arithmetic_operator('*').
arithmetic_operator('/').
arithmetic_operator(div).
arithmetic_operator(mod).
```

and write a single clause for arithmetic_expression/1 to handle all the cases where the expression was a structure. The clause would be:

```
arithmetic_expression(E1 Op E2) :-
    arithmetic_operator(Op),
    arithmetic_expression(E1),
    arithmetic_expression(E2).
```

This, however, is syntactically incorrect because Op, the functor of the structure E1 Op E2, is not an atom. The correct method is to use a single variable in the head of the clause and then examine the functor and the components of the structure which is substituted for it by using the built-in predicate =.. (pronounced "univ"). The definition is:

> =../2
> The goal succeeds if the first argument is a structure and the second argument is a list whose head is the functor of the structure and whose tail comprises the components of the structure in order.

The predicate, which is written between its arguments, can be used to decompose a structure into functor and components:

```
?- soldier(name(moodus), rank(colonel)) =.. L.
L = [soldier, name(moodus), rank(colonel)]

?- f =.. L.
L = [f]

?- [a, b, c] =.. [F|A].
F = .
A = [a, [b, c] ]
```

or to construct a structure:

```
?- S =.. [a, b, c].
S = a(b, c)

?- S =.. ['+', a, b].
S = a + b
```

It is the first usage which occurs in the corrected procedure for arithmetic_expression/1:

```
arithmetic_expression(Term)  :-
    Term =.. [Functor, Component1, Component2],
    arithmetic_operator(Functor),
    arithmetic_expression(Component1),
    arithmetic_expression(Component2).
```

With =../2, we can write programs which process arbitrary structures. At the time of writing a program, we do not need to know what structure will be given as argument in a call. An example is ground/1, which succeeds if the argument in a call is a ground term. The procedure is:

```
ground(T) :-                       % Atoms and numbers are
    atomic(T).                     %  ground terms.
ground(T) :-
    compound(T),                   % A structure is ground if . . .
    T =.. [_|Components],
    ground_comps(Components).      %  its components are ground.

ground_comps([ ]).
ground_comps([First|Others])  :-
    ground(First),
    ground_comps(Others).
```

At each recursive call, the procedure for ground_comps/1 reduces the list of arguments by removing the head and passing it as argument to ground/1.

The built-in predicate functor provides another way of building a structure from a functor and components. Its definition is:

> functor/3
> The goal succeeds if the first argument is a structure, the second argument is its functor and the third is its arity.

We can call goals such as:

```
?- functor(T, s, 2).
T = s(_12, _20)

?- functor(a + b, Functor, Arity).
Functor = +
Arity = 2

?- functor(f, Functor, Arity).
Functor = f
Arity = 0
```

With functor/3, one cannot specify the value of components when building a structure. The built-in predicate arg does this. It is defined as follows:

> arg/3
> The goal succeeds if the first argument is an integer N, the second is a structure and the third is the Nth component of the structure. A Prolog error results if the first argument is not an integer or the second argument is not a structure.

So:

```
?- arg(2, soldier(name(moodus), rank(colonel)), R).
R = rank(colonel)
```

```
?- arg(2, [a, b, c, d], [b, c, d]).
yes
```

The effect of the goal:

```
?- T =.. [s, a, b].
```

can be achieved by a conjunction of calls to functor/3 and arg/3:

```
?- functor(T, s, 2), arg(1, T, a), arg(2, T, b).
T = s(a,b)
```

=../2 is simpler to use, but functor/3 and arg/3 are useful when writing programs to process structures of large arity. In general, it is not good programming practice to use such structures, because of the risk of confusing argument positions in procedures which manipulate them. Occasionally, however, such a structure is the most natural representation for a problem. For instance, if we were writing a program to play noughts-and-crosses we might represent the board by a structure with functor board and arity 9, each component representing one square on the board. A procedure to establish the initial state of the board, in which the empty squares are represented by variables, would be:

```
start_game(Board)  :-
      functor(Board, board, 9).
```

To determine whether the square at position P is free:

```
empty_square(P, Board) :-
      arg(P, Board, Square),
      var(Square).
```

To play in a square, assuming it is free:

```
play_in(P, Board, Player) :-
    arg(P, Board, Player).
```

The last term-constructing predicate is name. It is used to construct an atom from a list of integers representing Ascii character codes. It is defined as follows:

> name/2
> The goal succeeds if the first argument is an atom and the second is a list of the Ascii codes for the characters in the atom.

So, we get:

```
?- name(abc, L).
L = [97, 98, 99]

?- name(hat, [H|T]), name(W, [99|T]).
H = 104
T = [97, 116]
W = cat
```

The predicate is used frequently in text processing applications in which words are represented by atoms. A common requirement in such applications is to determine the alphabetical order of two words. This can be done by a program before, which takes two words as arguments and succeeds if the first is alphabetically before the second:

```
before (W1, W2) :-
    name(W1, L1),
    name(W2, L2),
    before_list(L1, L2).

before_list([H|_], [J|_]) :-
    H < J.
before_list([H|M], [H|N]) :-
    before_list(M, N).
before_list([ ], [_|_]).
```

There are three cases in which a call succeeds, and corresponding to each is a clause of the procedure for before_list/2:

- If the first letter of the first word is alphabetically before the first letter of the second, eg. budgie is before canary.

- If the first letter of the two words is the same, but the first word comes before the second when remaining letters of each are compared, eg. budgerigar is before budgie.

- If corresponding letters of the two words are all identical but the first word is shorter than the second, e.g. bud is before budgerigar.

Another use of name/2 is to generate new atoms to represent different objects as they are introduced, e.g. flight1, flight2, etc. The characteristic of these names is that they consist of a root, identifying the type of the object named, and an integer suffix to distinguish each object from others of its type. The program new_name takes a root and generates names from that root. Successive names are generated through backtracking. The procedure for new_name/2 is:

```
new_name(Root, Name) :-
      greater_or_equal(1, N),               % Generate the next suffix.
      convert(N, [ ], N_chars),             % Convert it to Ascii codes.
      name(Root, Root_chars),               % Convert Root to Ascii codes.
      conc(Root_chars, N_chars, Name_chars),    % Join Root and suffix,
      name(Name, Name_chars).               %  and re-convert to an atom.
```

We cannot construct an atom directly from the list of Ascii codes in Root and N, the next integer. The integer must be converted to the list of Ascii codes for the digits in it. The procedure for convert/3 does this:

```
convert(0, L, L).
convert(N, List_so_far, Full_list) :-
      N > 0,
      Last_digit is N mod 10,
      Other_digits is N div 10,
      Ascii is Last_digit + 48,
      convert(Other_digits, [Ascii|List_so_far], Full_list).
```

For a single digit number, the Ascii code for the digit is the number plus 48. For larger integers, we obtain successive Ascii codes, starting with that for the least significant digit, by repeatedly dividing the number by 10 and converting the remainder to a code using the rule for a single digit number. To have the list of codes in the right order, we use ingoing recursion. This is why convert is a three argument predicate and why the extra argument in the call is the empty list. The program behaves as follows:

```
?- new_name(flight, Name).
Name = flight1;

Name = flight2;

Name = flight3;

Name = flight4
```

Exercises 4.4

(a) The plural form of most English nouns is obtained by adding "s" to the singular form. However, if the noun ends in a consonant followed by "y", the plural is formed by replacing the "y" with "ies"; and if the noun ends in a consonant followed by "o", the plural is formed by adding "es". Write clauses for plural_form/2, defining each of these formation rules.

(b) A simple system for encoding messages is to replace each letter of the message by the Nth letter after it in alphabetic order. For example, for N = 2, "a" is replaced by "c", "y" by "a", etc. Given that the letters "a" to "z" have Ascii codes 97 to 122, write a procedure for cifer/3 which takes a word to be encoded and an integer and produces the coded form of the word using this method.

(c) Assuming the representation for the noughts-and-crosses board which we described in this section, write a procedure for select_a_move/2 which takes a board position and returns an integer representing the move selected. The simplest method is to select the first free square.

4.5 Testing for Equality between Terms

There are several built-in predicates which test for equality between terms. You have met is/2 and =:=/2, used in arithmetic. Another test is provided by =, which is defined as follows:

> = / 2
> The goal succeeds if the two arguments match and fails otherwise.

As =/2 exactly replicates the operation of matching terms, you may wonder why it is needed as a built-in predicate. After all, for every clause of the form:

```
proc(X, Y) :-
    sub-goals 1 to k - 1,
    X = Y,                      % Test for match between the
                                % arguments in this sub-goal.
    sub-goals k + 1 to n.
```

there is a formulation:

```
proc(X, X) :-                   % Test for match between the
                                %  arguments in this pattern.
    sub-goals 1 to n, excluding sub-goal k.
```

79

which has the same declarative meaning whatever procedures are called in sub-goals 1 to n. However, as you have seen, the meaning of some built-in predicates can only be expressed in procedural terms, and if these predicates are used, the position of a test for matching may affect the meaning of the program. For instance, if the first sub-goal was: ?- var(X), the two versions of the procedure for proc/2 would behave differently in the call:

   ?- proc(V, atom).

In the first version, the test: ?- var(X) would succeed, and if the other sub-goals succeeded the answer, following the match X = Y, would be:

   V = atom

In the second version, the two arguments would be matched in the head of the clause, the test: ?- var(X) would fail and the answer would be:

   no

   In Chapters 5, 6 and 7, you will learn of problems which do require =/2, but you should always avoid using it unnecessarily. The question in your mind should be: "Do I have to use =/2 here because of the procedural interpretation of my program or is there an identical formulation which simply uses matching?"
   Also provided as a built-in predicate is \=, defined thus:

   \=/2
   The goal succeeds if the two arguments do not match and fails otherwise.

The procedure for different/2, which we used in section 3.4 but did not define, uses \=/2:

   different(A, B) :-
      A \= B.

Note that we cannot use different/2 in a call such as:

   ?- different(george, Other).

to generate values for the variable Other which are different from the atom george. The goal merely fails, as the terms george and Other do match.
   The final built-in predicates in this group are == (pronounced "is identical to") and \== ("is not identical to"). They are defined as:

   ==/2
   The goal succeeds if the arguments have the same functor and arity and corresponding components are identical.

\==/2
The goal succeeds if the two arguments are not identical.

A variable is identical to another variable only if the two variables are sharing. This gives the following behaviour:

```
?- X + 7 == Y + 7.                              X and Y do not share.
no
```

```
?- X = Y,                              Succeeds: X and Y now share.
X + 7 == Y + 7.        Succeeds: X and Y share, so the terms are identical.
X = _71
Y = _71
```

Figure 4.5 illustrates the differences between is, =:=, = and ==.

	Call	Result
First argument:X	X is 7 + 2	Succeeds: substitutes X← 9
	X =:= 7 + 2	Prolog error: X is not an arithmetic expression
Second argument:7 + 2	X = 7 + 2	Succeeds: substitutes X← 7 + 2
	X == 7 + 2	Fails: the terms are not identical
First argument:8 + 1	8 + 1 is 7 + 2	Fails: the terms 8 + 1 and 9 do not match
	8 + 1 =:= 7 + 2	Succeeds: the expressions have the same value
Second argument:7 + 2	8 + 1 = 7 + 2	Fails: the terms 8 + 1 and 7 + 2 do not match
	8 + 1 == 7 + 2	Fails: the terms are not identical

Figure 4.5 Results of calls to is/2, =:=/2, =/2 and ==/2

==/2 is used when it is necessary to distinguish a variable from any other kind of term. For instance, in our noughts-and-crosses example, where a blank square was represented by a variable, we would use ==/2 in a procedure for occupied_by/3 to test whether a square was occupied, and if so whether by player o or player x. The procedure is:

```
occupied_by(P, Board, o) :-
    arg(P, Board, Square),
    Square == o.
```

```
occupied_by(P, Board, x) :-
    arg(P, Board, Square),
    Square == x.
```

A call to the procedure succeeds if the first argument represents a square and the third argument is the player who has played in the square. We must not apply any substitution to Square if it is a variable. Compare this procedure with that for play_in/3 to ensure that you understand the effect of ==/2.

The justification for representing an unoccupied square by a variable rather than by a distinguished atom such as b (for "blank") is that it saves making a new copy of the structure which represents the board each time a move is played. The method is sound because the status of a square does not change once a nought or a cross has been played in it. However, treating a variable as an object in its own right, instead of just as a place-holder waiting to be filled, is a tricky business because of the ever-present danger that a substitution may inadvertently be applied to it. In section 5.2.1, we introduce a programming technique which depends on exactly this trick, but in general you should beware of it. As we develop the noughts-and-crosses program, you will come to appreciate the point more clearly.

4.6 Summary

In this chapter, we have introduced the following ideas:

- Prolog provides arithmetic operators for constructing arithmetic expressions and the built-in predicate is for evaluating them.

- Some built-in predicates require arguments of a particular type. The programmer must observe these type constraints to prevent Prolog errors.

- There are built-in predicates to test the type of a term.

- A utility predicate is used for generating values or testing them and can be called safely with different patterns of arguments.

- =.. functor and arg are built-in predicates for constructing and decomposing structures. name is a built-in predicate for constructing and decomposing atoms.

- Equality between terms is defined in different ways and tested by the four built-in predicates is =:= = and ==.

Chapter 5

Input and Output

So far, input of data to programs has been through the arguments in a goal and output of program results has been through the values substituted for variables. This method is simple and convenient for the programmer when developing a program. For a user, however, it is too restrictive, and in this chapter we describe built-in predicates for input and output and show various ways they can be used to implement a user interface.

5.1   Input and Output of Terms

The built-in predicates read and write input and output terms. They are defined as follows:

> read/1
> The goal reads the next term from the current input stream. It succeeds if the term matches the argument in the call; otherwise it fails. The goal is not re-satisfiable.

> write/1
> The goal writes its argument to the current output stream.

The concept of input and output streams is central to Prolog I/O. By default, the stream for input and output is the file user, identified with the user's terminal. How to change streams is described in section 5.3.

To illustrate read/1 and write/1, we give a program dimensions, whose purpose is to calculate the wall area of a rectangular room:

```
dimensions :-
    write('All measurements for the room must be in feet'),
    nl,
    write('Type in the length of the room: '),
    read(Length),
    write('Type in the width of the room: '),
    read(Width),
```

```
        write('Type in the height of the room: '),
        read(Height),
        Longer_walls is Length * Height,
        write(Longer_walls),
        write(' sq.ft. is the area of each long wall'),
        nl,
        Shorter_walls is Width * Height,
        write(Shorter_walls),
        write(' sq.ft. is the area of each short wall'),
        nl,
        Total is (Longer_walls + Shorter_walls) * 2,
        write(Total),
        write(' sq.ft. is the total wall area'),
        nl.
```

The behaviour of this program is shown below, with the user's input in boldface:

```
?- dimensions.
All measurements for the room must be in feet
Type in the length of the room: 14.
Type in the width of the room: 10.
Type in the height of the room: 8.
112 sq.ft. is the area of each long wall
80 sq.ft. is the area of each short wall
384 sq.ft. is the total wall area
yes
```

There are several points to note here:

- When we wish to output a prompt of several words, we enclose the prompt in single quotes to make it an atom.

- nl is another built-in predicate. Its definition is:

  nl/0
  The goal writes a <newline> character to the current output stream. The goal always succeeds and is not re-satisfiable.

  In the case of the prompts for user input, the call to write/1 is not followed by a call to nl/0, so the user's input is on the same line as the prompt.

- The end of the term input must be marked by a full-stop and a <newline> character.

The predicates carry out actions of reading and writing as *side-effects*.

A side-effect is an action of a predicate that is not undone on backtracking. If Prolog backtracks over a call to read/1 in which the argument was a variable, the substitution of the term read for the variable is undone, but the action of reading the term from the input stream is not. The term cannot be "put back" on the input stream, and its value is lost to the program. Similarly, if a call to read/1 fails because the term read does not match the argument in the call, that term is lost. The following example illustrates the problems of predicates with side-effects. It is a version of the dimensions program, extended to compute how much gloss paint, emulsion paint or wallpaper is required for decorating the room.

The intended behaviour of the program is:

```
?- dimensions_and_quantities.
All measurements for the room must be in feet
Type in the length of the room: 17.
Type in the width of the room: 11.
Type in the height of the room: 8.
136 sq.ft. is the area of each long wall
88 sq.ft. is the area of each short wall
448 sq.ft. is the total wall area
Which material will be used for decorating the room?'
Type "paint(gloss).",   "paint(emulsion)." or "wallpaper.": wallpaper.
5 rolls of wallpaper are required
yes
```

The extended program, then, is to issue a prompt and read one of three possible inputs. First we give a procedure which implements this correctly:

```
dimensions_and_quantities  :-
    . . .
    sub-goals as for dimensions/0, then:
    . . .
    write('Which material will be used for decorating the room?'),
    nl,
    write('Type "paint(gloss).",   "paint(emulsion)." or "wallpaper.": '),
    read(Material),
    compute_quantity(Material,  Total).

compute_quantity(paint(gloss),  Total)  :-          % Gloss paint is used.
    Quantity is Total div 130 + 1,
    write(Quantity),
    write(' litres of gloss paint are required'),
    nl.
compute_quantity(paint(emulsion),  Total)  :-       % Emulsion is used.
    Quantity is Total div 170 + 1,
    write(Quantity),
    write(' litres of emulsion paint are required'),
    nl.
```

```
compute_quantity(wallpaper, Total) :-          % Wallpaper is used.
    Quantity is Total div 180 + 3,
    write(Quantity),
    write(' rolls of wallpaper are required'),
    nl.
```

After reading the user's input, Prolog searches through the clauses for compute_quantity/1 until a clause is found which matches the term which the user had typed in. The design of the program ensures that the call to read/1 does not fail and that Prolog does not backtrack over it. The following alternative procedure would be incorrect:

```
dimensions_and_quantities :-

    . . .
    sub-goals as for dimensions/0
    . . .
    write('Which material will be used for decorating the room?'),
    nl,
    write('Type "paint(gloss).",  "paint(emulsion)." or "wallpaper.": '),
    compute_quantity(Total).

compute_quantity(Total) :-
    read(paint(gloss)),             % Gloss paint is used.
    Quantity is Total div 130 + 1,
    write(Quantity),
    write(' litres of gloss paint are required'),
    nl.
compute_quantity(Total) :-
    read(paint(emulsion)),          % Emulsion is used.
    Quantity is Total div 170 + 1,
    write(Quantity),
    write(' litres of emulsion paint are required'),
    nl.
compute_quantity(Total) :-
    read(wallpaper),                % Wallpaper is used.
    Quantity is Total div 180 + 3,
    write(Quantity),
    write(' rolls of wallpaper are required'),
    nl.
```

The fault is the inclusion of the call to read/1 in the clauses for compute_quantity/1. The call in the first clause would fail if the user's input did not match paint(gloss), and the input would be lost. In the second clause, it would be the next term entered that would be read and tested for a match with paint(emulsion).

To avoid these pitfalls, you should ensure that the argument to read/1 is a variable and that the term read is processed by a separate sub-goal from that containing the call to read/1. The procedure for this sub-goal should have a clause for each anticipated input and perhaps a catch-all clause to trap invalid input.

The built-in predicate tab can be used to format output. It is defined:

tab/1
The argument in the goal must be N, an integer. The goal writes N blank spaces to the current output stream.

We illustrate the use of tab/1 in a program format_term which writes a term in a format that makes clear the structure of the term. The components are written on successive lines, indented to the right of the functor, thus:

```
?- format_term(family(parents(george, lesley), children(bill, ben))).
family(parents(george,
               lesley),
       children(bill,
                ben))
yes

?- format_term(20 - 5 + 2 * 3).
+(-(20,
    5),
  *(2,
    3))
yes
```

The procedure is:

```
format_term(Term) :-
    output_formatted(Term, 0),         % Initially indent is 0 spaces.
    nl.
output_formatted(Term, _) :-
    atomic(Term),
    write(Term).
output_formatted(Term, _) :-
    var(Term),
    write(Term).
output_formatted(Term, Current_indent) :-
    compound(Term),
    Term =.. [Functor|Args],
    write(Functor),
    write('('),
    name(Functor, List),               % Find number of characters
    length(List, L),                   % in functor, to compute
    Next_indent is Current_indent + L + 1,    % indent for
    output_args(Args, Next_indent).    % output of args.
```

```
output_args([Arg], Indent) :-          % Only one argument to output.
    output_formatted(Arg,  Indent),        % Output it as a term,
    write(')').                          %  and close bracket after it.
output_args([First, Second|Others], Indent) :-    % More than one arg.
    output_formatted(First,  Indent),      % Output first as term.
    write(','),                                 % Comma,
    nl,                                      % <newline>
    tab(Indent),                          %  and indent, then
    output_args([Second|Others],  Indent).  % output rest as args.
```

The program uses length/2, described in section 4.1.

Exercises 5.1

(a)   Write a procedure for display_position/1 to print a noughts-and-crosses board position at the current output stream, assuming the representation for the board that we gave in section 4.4.

5.2   More Flexible Input and Output

With read/1 and write/1, the user is constrained by the syntax of Prolog. Input must be as terms, which means putting commas and brackets in the right places and a full-stop at the end. A program which fails if the syntax of the programming language is not respected will be fragile in the hands of an inexperienced user. We introduce two methods for achieving greater flexibility: operator definition and character I/O.

5.2.1   Operator   definition

Some functors of arity 2 can be written between their components, and this makes structures easier to type in correctly and to read when they are output. Examples are the arithmetic operators, which we described in section 4.1, and built-in predicates such as >/2, =../2 and ==/2 which we introduced in later section of Chapter 4. In addition, the programmer can define his own functors as *infix operators*, to be written between the components of a structure, *prefix operators*, written before the single component, or *postfix operators*, written after the single component. We explain the mechanism of operator definition by reference to the pre-defined arithmetic operators and then give examples of the use of programmer-defined operators.

The program format_term showed that an arithmetic expression which the user enters in infix notation as 20 - 5 + 2 * 3 is interpreted as the term +(-(20, 5), *(2, 3)). The expression is interpreted in accordance with the *precedence* and *associativity* of the operators -, + and *. The precedence of an operator defines its order of application in relation to other operators in expressions which are not bracketed. The associativity defines the order of application in unbracketed expressions where two operators have the same precedence. An operator is defined by a call to the built-in predicate op. A typical call to define the arithmetic operators would be:

?- op(31, yfx, ['-', '+']).
yes

?- op(21, yfx, ['*', '/', div]).
yes

?- op(11, xfx, mod).
yes

In each call to op/3, the first argument defines the precedence, the second defines the associativity and the third is the name of the operator, or, where several operators are being defined with the same precedence and associativity, it is a list of names. The precedence is expressed as an integer, a lower number indicating higher precedence. The associativity is denoted by one of the atoms:

xfx   xfy   yfx   fx   fy   xf   xy

These atoms are mnemonics: f represents the operator, x and y represent two types of operand. So, xfx, xfy and yfx are mnemonics for infix operators, fx and fy denote prefix operators and xf and yf denote postfix operators. A type x operand, if unbracketed, may include only operators of higher precedence than the operator f. A type y operand, if unbracketed, may include operators of equal or higher precedence.

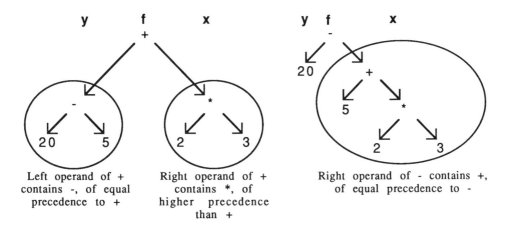

| Left operand of + contains -, of equal precedence to + | Right operand of + contains *, of higher precedence than + | Right operand of - contains +, of equal precedence to - |

Figure 5.1 Correct and incorrect interpretations of the arithmetic expression: 20 - 5 + 3 * 2

Operators of higher precedence are applied first. This excludes interpretations of the expression: 20 - 5 + 2 * 3 in which the multiplication is carried out last. The two other possible interpretations are shown in Figure 5.1. As - requires a right operand of type x and + is not of higher precedence than it, the second interpretation is ruled out.

In effect, the mnemonic yfx denotes an infix operator which associates to the left in expressions where several operators of the same precedence are used, xfy one which associates to the right, and xfx indicates that operands must be fully bracketed in such expressions.

A set of operators is given as Figure 5.2. You can think of these clauses as directives executed when you enter the Prolog system. The set provided varies between implementations of the language, as does the range of integers used, but the order within the precedence hierarchy is fixed.

```
:- op(255, xfx, ':-').
:- op(255, fx, ['?-', ':-']).
:- op(254, xfy, ';').
:- op(253, xfy, ',').
:- op(51, xfy, '.').
:- op(40, xfx, [is, =.., =, \=, ==, \==, =:=, =\=, <, =<, >, >=]).
:- op(31, yfx, ['-', '+']).
:- op(21, yfx, ['*', '/', div]).
:- op(11, xfx, mod).
```

Figure 5.2 Pre-defined operators

To define your own operators, simply include calls to op/3 as directives at the head of a program. If you want these directives to be executed without causing Prolog to respond with yes for each, use the prefix operator :- instead of ?-. If, at the head of the dimensions_and_quantities program, we defined paint as a postfix operator :

:- op(xf, 150, paint).

the user could input:

gloss paint.

or:

emulsion paint.

in response to the prompt:

Which material will be used for decorating the room?

We could also use the operator syntax in the program itself, writing the heads of the first two clauses for compute_quantity/1 as:

compute_quantity(gloss paint) :-

and:

compute_quantity(emulsion paint) :-

Using operator syntax extensively in a program can make the program difficult to read and understand. If clauses include operators with differing precedence and associativity, the reader may have difficulty in discerning the structure of clauses and in recognising which sub-goal calls match which clauses. However, a program user does not need to be aware of the syntactic issues, and for him the advantages of a more natural interface are considerable. We include the *operator definition* technique in our toolkit for this reason.

Operator Definition

The technique is used to make program input easier and output more read-able. The programmer must ensure that:

- Directives defining operators are executed before Prolog reads any clauses which use them.

- The precedence and associativity of operators are carefully considered and fully understood.

- If terms are represented in standard syntax in the program, their structure does match the terms which the user inputs in operator syntax.

The built-in predicate display is useful in connection with the last point. Its definition is:

display/1
The goal takes as argument a term in operator syntax and writes the term to the current output stream in standard syntax in accordance with current operator definitions.

Examples are:

```
?- display(20-5+2*3).
+(-(20,5),*(2,3)
yes
```

```
?- display(gloss  paint).
paint(gloss)
yes
```

As an illustration of the operator definition technique, we give a program to generate a truth table for a Boolean expression constructed using the connectives ~ (not), ^ (and) and v (or). To enable the user to enter the expression in a convenient form, we define the connectives as operators:

```
:- op(90, xfy, v).
:- op(89, xfy, '^').
:- op(88, fy, '~').
```

We also define operators gives and constant, so that we can write a truth table for each connective entirely in operator syntax:

```
:- op(95, xfx, gives).
:- op(94, fx, constant).
```

The truth table is:

```
constant  t.
constant  f.
~t  gives  f.
~f  gives  t.
t ^ t  gives  t.
t ^ f  gives  f.
f ^ t  gives  f.
f ^ f  gives  f.
t v t  gives  t.
t v f  gives  t.
f v t  gives  t.
f v f  gives  f.
```

Before proceeding, we check that the operator definitions do implement the required precedence and associativity:

```
?- display(~a ^ b ^ c).
^(~a, ^(b, c))
yes
```

```
?- display(f v f gives f).
gives(v(f, f), f)
yes
```

The program evaluates an expression by replacing each term with one of the Boolean constants t and f and each sub-expression with a constant value from the truth table. The user obtains successive rows of the truth table by rejecting each answer Prolog gives:

```
truth_table(Variable_expression, Const_expression gives Value) :-
    assign(Variable_expression, Const_expression, Value).

assign(Term, Bool_constant, Bool_constant) :-
    atom(Term),
    constant Bool_constant.
assign(~ E, ~ C, V) :-
    assign(E, C, V1),
    ~ V1 gives V.
assign(E1 ^ E2, C1 ^ C2, V) :-
    assign(E1, C1, V1),
    assign(E2, C2, V2),
    V1 ^ V2 gives V.
assign(E1 v E2, C1 v C2, V) :-
    assign(E1, C1, V1),
    assign(E2, C2, V2),
    V1 v V2 gives V.
```

The procedure for assign/3 has a clause to handle the base case, that of a Boolean expression which is a simple term, and three recursive clauses each handling a compound expression constructed using one connective: ~, ^ or v. In the base case, the term is replaced by a Boolean constant, which evaluates to itself. In the other cases, we recursively assign values to the sub-expressions and then evaluate the whole expression by searching the truth table.
We can call goals such as:

```
?- truth_table(~a ^ b ^ c, Line).
Line = ~t ^ t ^ t gives f;

Line = ~t ^ t ^ f gives f;

Line = ~t ^ f ^ t gives f;

Line = ~t ^ f ^ f gives f;

Line = ~f ^ t ^ t gives t;

Line = ~f ^ t ^ f gives f;

Line = ~f ^ f ^ t gives f;

Line = ~f ^ f ^ f gives f;
no
```

However, if a term occurs more than once in an expression, the program assigns different truth values to different occurrences of it. For an expression such as: a v b ^ a, it produces eight answers, rather than just four:

```
?- truth_table(a v b ^ a, Line).
Line = t v t ^ t gives t;

Line = t v t ^ f gives t;

Line = t v f ^ t gives t;

Line = t v f ^ f gives t
etc.
```

To prevent this, we must check, before replacing a term by a Boolean constant, whether the term has already occurred in the expression and, if so, what value had replaced it. To keep track of terms and the values which replaced them, we could use two lists as extra arguments to the assign procedure. The first list, empty in the initial call, would accumulate new terms and values by ingoing recursion. The second would be returned as an output argument each time the base case was reached. As each term was met, we would check whether it was in the list, and if it was not we would add it, recording in a structure with functor value and arity 2 the term and the value which had replaced it.

However, we can represent the growing list in a single argument by using a *hollow term*. A hollow term, in contrast to a ground term, is a structure that does contain variables. In the present problem, the hollow term is a list whose end is marked by a variable instead of by the empty list. In the initial call to evaluate a Boolean expression, the list is just a variable. As each new term is evaluated, we substitute for this variable a list whose head is a structure recording the term and the value which replaced it and whose tail is another variable. Because the list remains a hollow term, we can always apply further substitutions to it.

We use put_in_list/2 to insert an item in a list represented as a hollow term:

```
put_in_list(Item, [Item|_]).
put_in_list(Item, [Element|Es]) :-
    Item \== Element,
    put_in_list(Item, Es).
```

The first clause succeeds in two ways:

- By matching a new item and an element in the list: this prevents duplication.

- By applying a substitution to the variable at the end of the list: this adds a new item to it.

The procedure behaves as follows:

    ?- put_in_list(a,L), put_in_list(b,L), put_in_list(b,L).
    L = [a, b|_72]

The substitutions applied to L are illustrated in Figure 5.3.

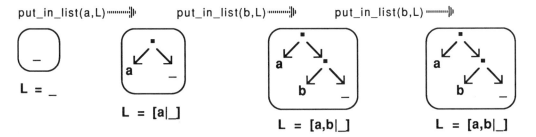

Figure 5.3 Substitutions applied to the list L

This behaviour is exactly what we require for the truth table program: if a term is already in the list, we wish to retrieve the value associated with it, and if it is not, we add the term and a value to the list. In the modified program, assign is a four argument predicate:

    truth_table(Variable_expression, Const_expression gives Value) :-
        assign(Variable_expression, Hollow, Const_expression, Value).

In the base case, we put another item in the list which the extra argument represents, and in the recursive cases we pass it on:

    assign(Operand, L, Bool_constant, Bool_constant) :-
        atom(Operand),
        put_in_list(value(Operand, Bool_constant), L),
        constant(Bool_constant).
    assign(~ E, L, ~ C, V) :-
        assign(E, L, C, V1),
        ~ V1 gives V.
    assign(E1 ^ E2, L, C1 ^ C2, V) :-
        assign(E1, L, C1, V1),
        assign(E2, L, C2, V2),
        V1 ^ V2 gives V.
    assign(E1 v E2, L, C1 v C2, V) :-
        assign(E1, L, C1, V1),
        assign(E2, L, C2, V2),
        V1 v V2 gives V.

The program gives the correct result in the call which previously produced an error:

```
?- truth_table(a v b ^ a, Line).
Line = t v t ^ t gives t;

Line = t v f ^ t gives t;

Line = f v t ^ f gives f;

Line = f v f ^ f gives f;
no
```

As we explained in section 4.5, there are risks in treating a variable as an object. The use of one to represent the end of a list makes it more difficult to determine whether an item really is in such a list. We could not use member/2, as given in section 3.4, because the item being searched for would always match the variable at the end of the list. We must check that the item at the head of the list is not a variable. A procedure for found_in_list/2 is:

```
found_in_list(Item, [Element|_]) :-
    nonvar(Element),
    Item = Element.
found_in_list(Item, [E|Es]) :-
    nonvar(E),
    found_in_list(Item, Es).
```

This gives the required behaviour:

```
?- found_in_list(cat, [can, cat, car|_]).
yes

?- found_in_list(cab, [can, cat, car|_]).
no

?- found_in_list(X, [matthew, mark, luke, john|_]).
X = matthew;

X = mark;

X = luke;

X = john;
no
```

In the truth table example, where we do not have to distinguish whether an item really is in a list, the use of a hollow term is appropriate. Indeed, the technique is valid in many situations where we wish to avoid encumbering numerous procedures with two extra arguments, and it belongs in our toolkit.

Hollow Terms

The technique is an alternative to ingoing recursion when a program needs access to results accumulated so far. It comprises the following steps:

- One extra argument is needed to all procedures which examine results so far or add to them.

- In the initial call, the argument is a variable.

- Progressive substitution is applied to the argument, but the structure substituted always contains at least one variable.

- A single procedure both tests for the existence of a value in the hollow term and adds a new value to it.

- The programmer must take great care when writing procedures in which it is necessary to distinguish between an item in the hollow term and a variable.

Exercises 5.2.1

(a) Write operator definitions for the verb stands, prepositions by, on and under and articles the and a, so that the layout of a room can be described in a program by facts such as:

    a table stands by the window.
    the television stands on the table.
    a box stands under the table.

and the user can ask questions such as:

    ?- What stands by the window.
    ?- What stands under Something.
    ?- the television stands Where.

(b) The connective -> ("implies") is of lower precedence than ~, ^ and v. The truth table for it is:

    a   b   a -> b
    t   t   t
    t   f   f
    f   t   t
    f   f   t

Extend the truth table program to deal with expressions which include this connective.

5.2.2   Input and output of characters

Operator definitions make term output more readable and input easier, but a program still fails if the syntax of current operator definitions is not respected.   As we have suggested, this fragility is unacceptable in many environments.   For robustness, the programmer must be able to control the program's response when a user enters invalid data.   This means reading input character by character and defining in the program classes of character and responses for each.   Two built-in predicates provide character input: get0 and get.   They are defined as follows:

> get0/1
> The goal reads the next character from the current input stream. It succeeds if the Ascii code for the character matches the argument in the goal; otherwise it fails.   The goal is not re-satisfiable.

> get/1
> The goal reads characters from the current input stream until a printing character is read.   It succeeds if the Ascii code for the printing character matches the argument in the goal; otherwise it fails.   The goal is not re-satisfiable.

We use get0/1 in conjunction with name/2 in a program to read characters from the current input stream and return as output argument a list of words read.   The top level of the program is a procedure for read_words/1:

```
read_words(List_of_words)  :-
    get0(C),
    form_words(C,  List_of_words).
```

The character read is processed in the procedure for form_words/2.   The procedure has three clauses, each defining one character class and the processing required for a character in the class:

```
form_words(C, [ ]) :-          % Return empty list if . . .
    end_of_input(C).           %  C marks end of input.
form_words(C, Words) :-
    separates_words(C),        % C separates words.
    get0(C1),                  % Read next character
    form_words(C1, Words).     %  and pass it to recursive call.
form_words(C, [W|Ws]) :-
    occurs_in_word(C),         % C is a character of a word
    form_a_list(C, List, C1),  % Form a list of characters,
    name(W, List),             %  convert it to an atom
    form_words(C1, Ws).        % Recursive call to form tail of list
```

The three classes of character are defined by three guard predicates. The procedures for them are:

```
end_of_input(46).                    % "."

separates_words(32).                 % <space>
separates_words(10).                 % <carriage-return>
separates_words(13).                 % <line-feed>
separates_words(9).                  % <tab>

occurs_in_word(C) :-
      C > 64,                        % "A" to "Z"
      C < 91.
occurs_in_word(C) :-
      C > 96,                        % "a" to "z"
      C < 123.
occurs_in_word(40).                  % "("
occurs_in_word(41).                  % ")"
occurs_in_word(44).                  % ","
occurs_in_word(58).                  % ":"
occurs_in_word(59).                  % ";"
```

If the user enters a character which falls into none of these classes, the call fails.

form_a_list/3 takes as input the first character of a word and returns a list of all the characters in the word and the first character after the end of the word. The procedure is:

```
form_a_list(C, [ ], C) :-
      end_of_input(C).
form_a_list(C, [ ], C) :-
      separates_words(C).
form_a_list(C, [C|Cs], C2) :-
      occurs_in_word(C),
      get0(C1),
      form_a_list(C1, Cs, C2).
```

The program behaves as follows, with the user's input in boldface:

```
?- read_words(S).
```
A sentence can continue over several lines;
punctuation marks are treated (like characters in a word).
```
S = [A, sentence, can, continue, over, several, lines;, punctuation, marks,
are, treated, (like, characters, in, a, word)]
```

You should study carefully how successive characters are read and processed in this program. The program exemplifies the method described in section 5.1. In particular, there is no backtracking over sub-goals. Each character read is "passed forward" to another sub-goal to be processed.

read_words/1 is useful in many text processing applications, though for most it would have to be extended to handle other classes of character. We suggest one extension in the exercises.

Output of characters is achieved by the built-in predicate put. It is defined thus:

> put/1
> The argument should be an integer which is an Ascii character code. The goal succeeds by writing the corresponding character to the current output stream.

Output to the terminal is more conveniently achieved by write/1 than by put/1, not least because the programmer does not have to have a table of Ascii character codes to use write/1. put/1 is frequently used in conjunction with get0/1 in processing text files. File handling is the subject of the next section.

Exercises 5.2.2

(a) Modify the procedure for read_words/1 so that punctuation marks are included as separate words in the list.

5.3 File Handling

To read input from and write output to external files, the current input and output streams must be altered. For input, the predicates are see, seeing and seen. The analogous set for output is tell, telling and told. These are defined as follows:

> see/1
> The argument should an atom representing a file name, and a file with this name should exist. The predicate succeeds and, as a side-effect, makes the named file the current input stream. If the file was not already open for input, it is opened, and reading starts at the beginning of it. If the file was open for input, reading continues from the point in the file already reached.

> seeing/1
> The goal succeeds if its argument matches the name of the file which is the current input stream and fails otherwise.

> seen/0
> The goal succeeds and, as a side-effect, the file which is the current input stream is closed. The file user becomes the current input stream.

tell/1
The argument should be an atom representing a file name. The goal succeeds and, as a side-effect, makes the named file the current output stream. If the file did not exist, it is created and opened for output. If it did exist, but was not open for output, it is opened and its previous contents are lost. If the file was already open for output, further output is appended to it.

telling/1
The goal succeeds if its argument matches the name of the file which is the current output stream and fails otherwise.

told/0
The goal succeeds and, as a side-effect, the file which is the current output stream is closed. The file user becomes the current output stream.

A program can open several files, but at any point in the program just one is the current stream for input and one for output. Only the special file user can be open for input and for output.

The programs write_file_of_terms and read_file_of_terms show how to use these predicates to write and read files of terms. The programs do not define how the terms to be written are obtained or how the terms read are to be processed, but they exemplify a program structure which you can use in any problem which involves file handling. The argument to each is the name of a file. First, the procedure for write_file_of_terms/1:

```
write_file_of_terms(To)  :-
    telling(Currently),          % Identify current output stream.
    tell(To),                    % Re-direct output.
    write_each_term,
    tell(Currently).             % Revert to previous output stream.

write_each_term  :-
    next(Term),                  % Obtain next term to be written.
    write(Term),                 % Mark end of term with "."
    write('.'),  nl,             % and <newline>
    fail.                        % This goal always fails.
write_each_term  :-
    told.                        % Close output file.
```

The predicate fail is built-in. It always fails when called as a goal, like a predicate without a procedure. We give examples of programs using fail in section 6.2. Its purpose here is to force Prolog to backtrack to the sub-goal: ?- next(Term) which, we assume, generates terms to be output through backtracking. When there are no more, the sub-goal fails, and the second clause for write_each_term/1 closes the output file.

Now, the procedure for read_file_of_terms/1:

```
read_file_of_terms(From)  :-
    seeing(Currently),             % Identify current input stream.
    see(From),                     % Take input from named file.
    read(Term),                    % Read next term
    process_term(Term).
    see(Currently).                % Revert to previous input stream.

process_term(Term)  :-
    end_of_file_marker(Term),      % End of input file reached?
    seen.                          % Close input file.
process_term(Term)  :-
    end_of_file_marker(T),
    Term \== T,
    actions_on(Term),              % Process term read,
    read(Next),                    %   read next term
    process_term(Next).            %   recursive call to process it.
```

The recursion in the procedure for process_term/1 stops when the term read is the end of file marker. Implementations differ in the term used for this purpose. In some systems, it is the atom end_of_file, in others it is the structure :- end.

Many text processing applications require characters to be read from an input file and written, in a modified form, to an output file. Our program convert_char_files exemplifies the structure of a program for such an application. The arguments are the input and output file names:

```
convert_char_files(Chars_in, Chars_out)  :-
    seeing(Input),
    telling(Output),
    see(Chars_in),
    tell(Chars_out),
    get0(C),
    change_char(C),
    see(Input),
    tell(Output).
change_char(C)  :-
    end_of_file_char(C),
    seen,
    told.
change_char(C)  :-
    end_of_file_char(Eof),
    C \= Eof,
    change(C, C1),
    put(C1),
    get0(C2),
    change_char(C2).
```

We assume that the procedure for change/2 defines the processing required on the characters of the input file. Recursion in the procedure for change_char/1 stops when the end of file character is read. Usually, this is the character with Ascii code 26, but again this is implementation-dependent.

Exercises 5.3

(a) Write a version of the program convert_char_files which converts upper-case letters in the input file to lower-case in the output.

(b) Write a version of the program convert_char_files which replaces multiple adjacent <space> characters in the input file with a single <space> character in the output file.

5.4   Summary

In this chapter, we have introduced the following ideas:

- Prolog input and output is stream-oriented. There are built-in predicates to associate files with streams.

- I/O may be term-based or character-based.

- The built-in predicates which read and write terms or characters do so by side-effects. The programmer must take care to ensure that input is not lost because of backtracking.

- The operator definition technique makes term input easier and term output more readable.

- A hollow term is a term which is not ground. It is sometimes more convenient to use a hollow term than ingoing recursion to accumulate results.

- A standard structure for programs which read and process files of terms can be adapted for any application which has this requirement. An equivalent structure forms the basis for any program which generates terms for storage in an external file.

Chapter 6

Controlling Program Execution

In this chapter, we introduce built-in predicates which enable the programmer to exercise a measure of control over Prolog's search strategy. All
are procedural devices and tend to obscure the declarative interpretation of
programs. An important consideration throughout the chapter is how good
programming practice can mitigate this tendency.

6.1   Reducing Search: the "cut"

The built-in predicate ! (pronounced "cut") increases the efficiency of program execution by reducing search. It eliminates alternatives which Prolog
would otherwise investigate on backtracking. The cut always succeeds
when called as a goal and is not re-satisfiable on backtracking. It has two
side-effects in a clause for a procedure:

- It cuts out backtracking to preceding sub-goals in the clause.

- It prevents any subsequent clauses for the procedure from being used
  to satisfy a goal.

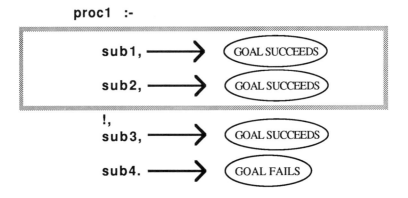

Figure 6.1 The cut prevents backtracking to earlier sub-goals in a clause

Figure 6.1 illustrates the first of these side-effects. The failure of sub-goal sub4 causes Prolog to seek to re-satisfy sub3. If sub3 cannot be re-satisfied, Prolog backtracks to the cut. Now, the call to proc1 immediately fails because the cut has cut out backtracking to sub2 or sub1.

The second side-effect is shown in Figure 6.2.

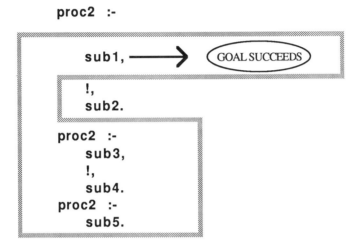

Figure 6.2 The cut cuts out subsequent clauses for a procedure

The cut in the first clause for proc2 cuts out the second and third clauses. If the sub-goal sub2 fails, the call to proc2 fails. It is important to distinguish this situation from that shown in Figure 6.3 where the call to sub1 has failed.

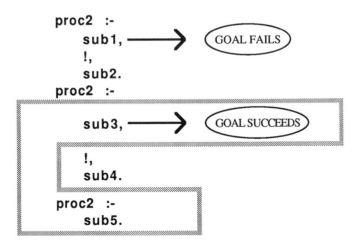

Figure 6.3 The cut in a clause is not reached, so the second can be used

As the cut in the first clause is not reached, the second clause for proc2 is used after the failure of sub1. The call to proc2 now succeeds if the sub-goal sub4 succeeds and fails otherwise. If sub3 had failed, the cut in the second clause would not have been reached, and Prolog would have used the third clause in trying to satisfy the goal.

There are two reasons for using the cut:

- To prevent fruitless searches for ways of re-satisfying a goal on back-tracking, when the programmer knows that the goal is not re-satisfiable.

- To ensure that just one clause is used to satisfy a goal, when case analysis has shown that clauses represent mutually exclusive cases.

We illustrate these usages in the next two sections.

6.1.1 Preventing fruitless searches

In a program to manipulate sets, we might choose to represent a set by a list. If so, we would use member/2, for which we gave a procedure in section 3.4, to test for set membership. Consider the situation in which the test occurs as a sub-goal in another procedure:

```
proc(Arg1, . . . , Argn) :-
    generate_item(Item),        % Generate an item.
    generate_set(Set),          % Generate a set.
    member(Item, Set),          % If Item is a member of Set . . .
    test(Arg1, Item),           %  apply further tests, and . . .
    action(Item, Set, Argn).    %  take the required action.
```

If Item is a member of Set but the call to test/2 fails, Prolog backtracks to the set membership test and searches the remainder of the list for another occurrence of Item. As a set does not contain duplicates, we know that this search is fruitless. With the cut, we can eliminate all search on back-tracking. The procedure is:

```
member(H, [H|_]) :- !.
member(H, [_|T]) :-
    member(H, T).
```

Now, the sub-goal: ?- member(Item, Set) fails immediately on back-tracking because when, on first satisfying the goal, the base case was reached, the cut in the clause representing that case prevented the recursive clause from being used to try to re-satisfy the goal. Prolog backtracks directly to try to generate another set, in the sub-goal: ?- generate_set(Set).

Used in this way, the cut does not alter the results produced by a program. It is purely a device to reduce search. For most implementations of Prolog, the cut also reduces the memory requirement of a running program. The saving comes about through the reduction in the number of points to which Prolog might have to backtrack, each of which it has to record. For large programs, the reduction can be considerable.

Despite these benefits, the utmost care is required for safe use of the cut. Though it may not alter the behaviour of a whole program, its inclusion in a procedure always alters the behaviour of that procedure. You must be aware of the alteration, and you must satisfy yourself that it does not compromise the operation of the whole program. In our example, the cut prevents the procedure for member/2 from being used to generate members of a list. So:

```
?- member(Item, [red, orange, yellow, green, blue]).
Item = red;
no
```

Alternative substitutions cannot be generated because the cut in the clause for the base case cuts out the backtracking which would otherwise produce alternatives by the recursive case. This restriction is not pertinent if we are sure that member/2 will only be used for testing for list membership.

The effect of the cut is to transform a procedure which may generate alternative substitutions for variables in a goal (sometimes referred to as a *non-deterministic* procedure) into one which can produce just a single answer (a *deterministic* procedure). It is this action which makes the predicate valuable for enforcing mutual exclusion, and in the next section we examine this usage.

6.1.2   Enforcing mutual exclusion

We illustrate this technique by re-considering the procedure for hidden_flatten/3 which we gave in section 3.4. There, we first wrote a procedure which was faulty through failing to enforce mutual exclusion. We then removed the fault, giving:

```
hidden_flatten([ ], L, L).
hidden_flatten([ [H|T] | L], S, F) :-
        hidden_flatten(L, S, Lf),
        hidden_flatten([H|T], Lf, F).
hidden_flatten([H|T], S, [H|L]) :-
        different(H, [_|_]),
        hidden_flatten(T, S, L).
```

The sub-goal: ?- different(H, [_|_]) is the guard which enforces mutual exclusion between the second and third clauses. We can make the procedure deterministic by using the cut, instead of a guard, in the second clause:

107

```
hidden_flatten([ ], L, L).
hidden_flatten([ [H|T] | L], S, F) :- !,
    hidden_flatten(L, S, Lf),
    hidden_flatten([H|T], Lf, F).
hidden_flatten([H|T], S, [H|L]) :-
    hidden_flatten(T, S, L).
```

If, at any level of recursion, the input list matches the pattern in the head of the second clause: [[H|T] | L], the cut stops the third clause being used at that level to re-satisfy the goal on backtracking.

The important decision is where to place the cut to make a procedure deterministic. The guiding principle is that in each clause where it is needed, the cut should appear immediately after the test which recognises the case that the clause handles. The cut is not required in clauses which are already exclusive with respect to all subsequent ones. That is why we did not use the cut in the first clause for hidden_flatten/3: the case of the empty list excludes the other cases.

To see how this principle is applied, consider the problem of writing a program to produce the Soundex code representation of a name. The code provides a way of reducing similar-sounding names to a common code. Names are abbreviated according to the following rules:

- The first letter of the name remains.

- All subsequent vowels, "h", "w" and "y" are omitted.

- Double letters are replaced by single.

- The maximum length of the coded name is four letters.

A procedure for soundex/2 should behave as follows:

```
?- soundex(barrington, Code).
Code = brng
```

```
?- soundex(llewellyn, Code).
Code = lln
```

```
?- soundex(smith, Code), soundex(smythe, Code).
Code = smt
```

We can formulate the rules for the treatment of characters after the first as a series of cases:

- If four letters have been output, terminate the output.

- If there are no more characters in the input, terminate the output.

- If the current letter of the input is a vowel, "h", "w" or "y", discard it and generate the output from the remaining letters of the input.

- If the current letter of the input is the same as the preceding one, discard it and generate the output from the remaining letters of the input.

- Otherwise, define the current letter of the input to be the next letter of the output, and generate the remainder of the output from the remaining letters of the input.

Besides completing the first stage in the application of the case analysis technique, the identification of cases, this formulation encompasses part of the second and third stages. It describes how each case is recognised, though this description remains to be translated into a definition of Prolog terms, and it describes in loose English the processing required in each case. The first two are base cases; the third and fourth are recursive; and the last, also recursive, is a catch-all. We note also that the cases are mutually exclusive: for a given name there is just one correct encoding. We can express the cases as clauses for reduce/4:

```
% reduce(Input_list, Count_of_output, Previous_letter, Output_list)

reduce(_, 4, _, [ ]) :- !.              % Output is empty list . . .
reduce([ ], _, _, [ ]) :- !.            % in both base cases.
reduce([Current|Others], Count, _, Code) :-
    vowel_h_w_y(Current), !,
    reduce(Others, Count, Current, Code).
reduce([Letter|Others], Count, Letter, Code) :- !,
    reduce(Others, Count, Letter, Code).
reduce([Current|Others], Count, _, [Current|Code]) :-
    N is Count + 1,
    reduce(Others, N, Current, Code).
```

```
vowel_h_w_y(97)         % "a"
vowel_h_w_y(101),       % "e"
vowel_h_w_y(105).       % "i"
vowel_h_w_y(111).       % "o"
vowel_h_w_y(117).       % "u"
vowel_h_w_y(104).       % "h"
vowel_h_w_y(119).       % "w"
vowel_h_w_y(121).       % "y"
```

The formulation of the clauses for reduce/4 follows very naturally from the case analysis of the problem. The programmer's skill is in recognising from the case analysis what arguments are needed in the procedure and choosing suitable representations for them. The first case suggests that one argument must be a count of letters output so far, and we represent it by an integer. Other arguments are the letters input and output; these we represent by lists of Ascii codes. The fourth case requires a comparison between a letter of the input and the one which preceded it. Evidently, we need another argument to denote the previous letter. An integer representing an Ascii code serves the purpose.

You should also study how the processing requirements are expressed in clauses for each case. Look especially at how, in those for the recursive cases, the arguments to recursive calls are formed from the arguments given in the heads of clauses, and satisfy yourself that each call does approach a base case.

The procedure for soundex/2, the top level of the program, converts between the representation of names as atoms and as lists of Ascii codes and initiates the call to recursively reduce a name to its code:

```
soundex(Name, Code) :-
    name(Name, [First|Others]),
    reduce(Others, 1, First, Reduced),
    name(Code, [First|Reduced]).
```

Note that, as the First letter of the output is generated before calling the recursive procedure, the count of letters output is 1 in the call to reduce/4.

The main lesson of this example concerns the positioning of the cut in clauses for reduce/4. In the first and fourth clauses, the cut is the first subgoal in the body of the clause because the case is identified by a pattern in the clause head. It is also identified in this way in the second clause, but as the case of the empty list excludes the three following cases, the cut is not strictly required. Its use here simply enhances efficiency. When the case is identified by a sub-goal, as in the third clause, the cut is placed immediately after that sub-goal. Backtracking alternatives are not eliminated as Prolog tests for each case, but as soon as a case is recognised, other cases are excluded.

The value of this usage of the cut is the gain in efficiency and ease of programming which derives from not having to formulate for each guard in a clause its inverse in subsequent clauses. If you do exercise 6.1.2(c), you will appreciate the benefits of this. However, there is a drawback. The correct behaviour of a program from which explicit guards are omitted depends on the presence of the cut and on the order of clauses. Removing cuts which enforce mutual exclusion would alter the results which a program gave: the program would admit incorrect alternatives on backtracking. Changing the order of clauses would cause an incorrect result to be given when a goal was first satisfied.

The cut compromises the declarative interpretation of a procedure. Each clause now has an implicit extra sub-goal which is the inverse of the guards in each preceding clause. For instance, the last clause in the procedure for reduce/4 defines how to obtain the next character of the output, but the declarative reading must be qualified by the procedural interpretation. Under that interpretation, the final clause is stating a relationship between input and output arguments which only holds if the condition expressed in each preceding clause has been tested and does not hold.

On occasions, it is hard to see whether the cut is an adequate replacement for explicit guards. Consider the procedure for max/3 which we gave in section 4.2:

```
max(N1, N2, N2) :-
    N2 >= N1.
max(N1, N2, N1) :-
    N2 < N1.
```

The test: ?- N2 < N1 is the the inverse of: ?- N2 >= N1, and enforces mutual exclusion between the two clauses. If we preferred to enforce it by the cut, we might write:

```
max(N1, N2, N2) :-
    N2 >= N1, !.
max(N1, N2, N1).
```

However, though this procedure behaves correctly when the third argument is a variable in the call, it may not when that argument is a number:

```
?- max(3, 7, 3).
yes
```

The cut in the first clause is not reached because the call does not match the pattern in the head; but the call succeeds because it does match the second clause.

One solution is to alter the first clause, postponing the test for a match between the second and third arguments until after the cut:

```
max(N1, N2, N3) :-
    N2 >= N1, !,
    N3 = N2.
max(N1, N2, N1).
```

This program illustrates the point we made in section 4.5 that the procedural interpretation of a program sometimes obliges us to use =/2 instead of matching. In this instance, however, a better solution is to stick to the first formulation and avoid the cut altogether!

Prolog provides a built-in predicate fail_if for expressing the inverse of a condition, and, in view of the drawbacks of the cut, it is sometimes preferable to use it rather than the cut for enforcing mutual exclusion. The predicate is defined as follows:

fail_if/1[1]
The argument must be a structure. The structure is called as a goal. fail_if fails if the goal succeeds and succeeds otherwise. It is not re-satisfiable on backtracking.

In the following versions of a procedure for union/3, to determine the union of two sets represented as lists, the first version uses fail_if while the second includes the cut. The set C is the union of sets A and B if it comprises just those elements that occur in A or in B:

```
% union(A, B, C) - Version with fail_if

union([ ], S, S).
union([H|T], S1, S2) :-
    member(H, S1),
    union(T, S1, S2).
union([H|T], S1, [H|S2]) :-
    fail_if(member(H,  S1)),
    union(T, S1, S2).
```

```
% Version with cut

union([ ], S, S).
union([H|T], S1, S2) :-
    member(H, S1), !,
    union(T, S1, S2).
union([H|T], S1, [H|S2]) :-
    union(T, S1, S2).
```

In each version, the three clauses express three mutually exclusive cases:

- The first list represents an empty set.

- The head of the first list is a set element which occurs in the second set.

- The head of the first list is a set element which does not occur in the second set.

The advantage of the first version is that the clauses can be placed in any order and each can be understood without reference to the others. In the second version, fail_if(member(H, S1)) is an implicit condition in the third clause. However, by avoiding repetition of the test for set membership, the second version has the merit of being more efficient.

_____

[1] In most implementations, this predicate is called not. fail_if is the name to be used in the Prolog standard.

Exercises 6.1.2

(a) Representing a set by a list, write procedures for the following set-processing predicates:

intersection/3   The set C is the intersection of sets A and B if it comprises just those elements that occur in both A and B.

subset/2   The set B is a subset of the set A if every element of B occurs in A.

difference/3   Set C is the difference of sets A and B if it comprises just those elements that occur in A but not in B.

equal_sets/2   Sets A and B are equal if they contain the same elements.

disjoint/2   Sets A and B are disjoint if there is no element in either that occurs in the other.

Remember that a set is unordered, unlike a list.

(b) Using the representation for the noughts-and-crosses board given in section 4.4, write a procedure for game_over/2. A call succeeds if the first argument represents a completed game and the second argument gives the result of the game as the structure winner_is(Player), where Player is the winner, or as the atom 'The game is drawn'. A game is completed if one player has a winning line or all squares of the board are occupied.

(c) Re-write the procedure you wrote for exercise 4.3(a) using the cut instead of guards.

6.2 Forcing Backtracking and Repetition: fail and repeat

The built-in predicate fail, which always fails when called as a goal, is used to force Prolog to backtrack. In section 5.3, we used it to force a non-deterministic procedure for next/1 to generate all alternatives. We might have used it in the program to print a truth table, which we gave in section 5.2.1. The top-level procedure in that program was:

```
truth_table(Variable_expression, Const_expression gives Value) :-
    assign(Variable_expression, Hollow, Const_expression, Value).
```

The procedure for assign/4 is non-deterministic, generating at each call another row of the table, and the user forces it to generate all rows by rejecting each answer. We might prefer to build the backtracking into the program, using fail:

```
truth_table(Variable_expression)  :-
    assign(Variable_expression, Hollow, Const_expression, Value),
    write(Const_expression gives Value),
    nl,
    fail.
```

giving:

```
?- truth_table(~a ^ b ^ c).
~t ^ t ^ t gives f
~t ^ t ^ f gives f
~t ^ f ^ t gives f
~t ^ f·^ f gives f
~f ^ t ^ t gives t
~f ^ t ^ f gives f
~f ^ f ^ t gives f
~f ^ f ^ f gives f
no
```

As the substitutions made in the non-deterministic procedure are undone when Prolog backtracks to it, we use the side-effect of write/1 to display the value substituted. Unless we include a sub-goal with a side-effect somewhere between the non-deterministic procedure which generates values and the fail goal which rejects each, we simply lose all these values.

If a program is to obtain a series of values by using one of the built-in predicates which read input, instead of by a non-deterministic procedure, the program structure with fail is not adequate. The following example shows why not:

```
process_values  :-
    read(Value),            % Get an input value.
    process(Value, Result), % Process it.
    write(Result),          % Display the result and  . . .
    nl,
    fail.                   %  backtrack to get the next input value.
```

The problem here is that the built-in predicate read reads a new value only when first called as a goal and not on backtracking. As a result, the call to process_values/0 fails after processing the first input value. To overcome this problem, we use repeat/0, a built-in predicate which succeeds when called as a goal and is always re-satisfiable on backtracking:

```
process_values :-
    repeat,
    read(Value),            % Get next input value.
    process(Value, Result), % Process it.
    write(Result),          % Display the result and . . .
    nl,                     % backtrack to get the next input value.
    fail.
```

Now, Prolog backtracks to the sub-goal: ?- repeat, and each time it is re-satisfied, read/1 is called anew and does deliver a new value. Unfortunately, there is a different problem, which is that this program never terminates! If the programmer does intend the program to terminate, there must be some value which the user enters to indicate the end of the input. Assuming that value is the atom end, the correct program structure is:

```
process_values :-
    repeat,
    read(Value),            % Get next input value . . .
    act_on(Value), !.       %  and act on it.

act_on(end) :- !.           % Terminate processing, or . . .
act_on(Value) :-
    process(Value, Result), % Process the value.
    write(Result),          % Display the result and . . .
    nl,
    fail.                   % backtrack to get the next value.
```

The cut at the end of the procedure for process_values/0 ensures that when the procedure is called as a sub-goal of a larger program, failure of a later sub-goal does not cause Prolog to backtrack to repeat but to whatever sub-goal preceded the call to process_values/0. Without the cut here, Prolog would never be able to backtrack to before the sub-goal: ?- repeat.

The structure which we have shown is a very commonly-used one in programs which interact with a user in a dialogue style. We call this structuring technique *forced backtracking*, and we include it in the programmer's toolkit.

Forced Backtracking

The technique provides a structure for programs which interact with a user through a repeated series of prompts and responses. It comprises the following steps:

- Identify the condition which terminates the interaction. Usually, this is a special data value.

- Identify whether the procedure which generates data values does so
  on backtracking or only when first called as a goal. In the latter case,
  it must be preceded by a call to repeat.

- The procedure which processes input has two clauses: the first
  recognises the terminating value, and the second processes input
  values. The last sub-goal in the second clause is fail. In the second
  clause, the result of processing an input must be recorded by a side-
  effect.

We could obtain the same sequencing as through forced backtracking by
using recursion:

```
process_values :-
     read(Value),              % Get an input value . . .
     act_on(Value).            %  and act on it.

act_on(end) :- !.             % Terminate processing, or . . .
act_on(Value) :-
     process(Value, Result),   % Process the value.
     write(Result),            % Display the result . . .
     nl,
     process_values.           %  and process the next value.
```

When deciding between forced backtracking and recursion, you should
bear three points in mind:

- Forced backtracking is only suitable if the procedures being repeated
  achieve their action through side-effects.

- With a recursive formulation, results can be accumulated by ingoing
  recursion in the arguments to the top-level goal. The programmer is
  not wholly dependent on side-effects for results.

- In general, recursion uses more memory as the program runs, though
  some implementations have mechanisms which avoid the memory
  overhead in some types of recursive procedure. This consideration
  may be significant if, for instance, you are deciding on the design for
  the top level of an interactive command-driven program and you
  anticipate a long sequence of commands in a single run of the
  program.

To illustrate how the various options for controlling execution provide the
means of structuring a larger program, we give the remaining procedures of
the noughts-and-crosses program:

```
play(First_player, Result) :-
    start_game(Board),                            % See section 4.4
    play_game(First_player, Board, Result).

play_game(_, Board, Result) :-
    game_over(Board, Result), !,    % See answer to exercise 6.1.2(b)
    display_position(Board),        % See answer to exercise 5.1(a)
    write('The game is over'),
    nl.
play_game(Player_to_move, Board, Result) :-
    get_move(Player_to_move, Board, Move),
    play_in(Move, Board, Player_to_move),         % See section 4.4
    next_player_is(Player_to_move, Next_player),
    play_game(Next_player, Board, Result).

get_move(o, Board, Move) :-                       % User to move
    display_position(Board),
    get_users_move(Board, Move).
get_move(x, Board, Move) :-                       % Computer to move
    select_a_move(Board, Move),     % See answer to exercise 4.4(c)
    write('My move' is Move),
    nl.
next_player_is(o, x).
next_player_is(x, o).

get_users_move(Board, Move) :-
    repeat,
    write('Type in a number between 1 and 9'),
    nl,
    write(' for the square you want to occupy: '),
    read(Move),
    verify_move(Board, Move), !.

verify_move(Board, Move) :-                       % Move is valid if . . .
    integer(Move),                  %  it is an integer which . . .
    Move >= 1,                      %  represents a square . . .
    Move =< 9,
    empty_square(Move, Board),      %  that is empty.  See section 4.4
    !
verify_move(_, Invalid) :-
    write(Invalid is impossible),
    nl,
    fail.
```

The program makes the user play the noughts but allows him to choose whether to play first. In the call to play/2, the first argument, given as input, indicates which player is to start the game, and the second, returned as output, reports the result.

We use a recursive structure in the procedure for play_game/3 because we wish to build up the structure representing the board in the second argument and return the result of the game as output in the third. We use forced backtracking in the procedure for get_users_move/2 to control a dialogue which is repeated until the user enters a valid move.

In the following example, the user's input is shown in boldface.

```
?- play(x, Result).
```

My move is 1
Position is:

x _ _

_ _ _

_ _ _

Type in a number between 1 and 9
 for the square you want to occupy: **5.**
My move is 2
Position is:

x x _
_ o _

_ _ _

Type in a number between 1 and 9
 for the square you want to occupy: **7.**
My move is 3
Position is:

x x x
_ o _
o _ _

The game is over

Result = winner_is(x)

It is interesting to see how we can extend the program to allow the user who loses to re-select moves made during the game. We have to build the possibility of backtracking into the part of the program where the user selects a move. That selection is made within the procedure for get_users_move/2. To allow alternative selections, we introduce a higher-level procedure, of which the existing procedure forms the first clause:

```
user_tries_a_move(Board, Move) :-
    get_users_move(Board, Move).
```

This gets one move, as at present. A second clause enables the goal to be re-satisfied if the user does want to select an alternative for the move:

```
user_tries_a_move(Board, Move) :-
    display_position(Board),
    write('Do you want to try a different move'),
    write(' in this position (y/n)? '),
    get(121),                            % Succeeds if user enters "y"
    user_tries_a_move(Board, Move).
```

By making the procedure for user_tries_a_move/2 recursive, we ensure that it is re-satisfiable for so long as the user enters y in response to the prompt. He can have as many tries as he likes at selecting a winning move! Finally, we alter the procedure for get_move/3 to call the new procedure when the user has the move:

```
get_move(o, Board, Move) :-             % User to move
    display_position(Board),
    user_tries_a_move(Board, Move).
```

With the new version, the previous interaction can continue if the user rejects the first answer:

Result = winner_is(x);

Position is:
x x _
_ o _
_ _ _

Do you want to try a different move in this position (y/n)? **n**
Position is:
x _ _
_ _ _
_ _ _

Do you want to try a different move in this position (y/n)? **y**

The user thinks this is where he went wrong!

Type in a number between 1 and 9
 for the square you want to occupy: **3.**
My reply is 2
Position is:
x x o

_ _ _

_ _ _

Type in a number between 1 and 9
 for the square you want to occupy: **5.**

My reply is 4

Position is:

```
x  x  o
x  o  _

_  _  _
```

Type in a number between 1 and 9
 for the square you want to occupy: **7.**
Position is:

```
x  x  o
x  o  _
o  _  _
```

The game is over

Result = winner_is(o)

We are able to encapsulate a considerable extension to the program's power in a very small extension to the code because Prolog's backtracking search strategy reflects a natural human approach to problem-solving. The approach is to make a series of decisions, and if something goes wrong, to re-consider the decisions, starting with the most recent. Of course, human problem-solving is vastly more sophisticated than this. For instance, experience gives us the capacity often to recognise at once which of our decisions is at fault and correct our plan from that point, rather than laboriously working back from the most recent decision. An important topic in Chapter 11 is how to enhance Prolog's mechanical approach to capture more expertise. At this stage, our purpose is to illustrate how the Prolog programmer can solve a programming problem in a concise way by making the language work for him. A simple control structure in a large program is a sign of success in this endeavour.

Exercises 6.2

(a) Modify the procedure for truth_table/1 so that a call succeeds after printing the truth table.

(b) Re-write the procedure for get_users_move/2 using recursion instead of forced backtracking.

6.3 Other Options for Control

As in all programming languages, there are in Prolog different ways of obtaining a particular program behaviour. In section 6.3.1, we mention other built-in predicates which can be used instead of the methods we have taught for expressing alternatives. They do not bring any more power to the language when used for this purpose, and we try to persuade you of the superior merits of the methods we recommend! In section 6.3.2, we show how the cut and fail can be used in combination to achieve a control effect which is difficult to realise by the methods we have described so far.

6.3.1   Expressing   alternatives

The best way of expressing alternatives in a procedure is to describe each in a separate clause. It is possible, however, to express them in a single clause. For example, instead of:

```
occurs_in_word(C)  :-
        C > 64,                        % "A" to "Z"
        C < 91.
occurs_in_word(C)  :-
        C > 96,                        % "a" to "z"
        C < 123.
```

which we gave in section 5.2.2 as the first clauses of the procedure for a predicate which defined whether a given character could occur as part of a word, we might write:

```
occurs_in_word(C)  :-
        C > 64,                        % "A" to "Z"
        C < 91;
        C > 96,                        % "a" to "z"
        C < 123.
```

Here, ; expresses disjunction: the goal is satisfied if either the first two sub-goals are satisfied or the last two are.

One drawback of ; is the difficulty of understanding a clause which includes both ; and ,. For a clause:

```
proc1  :-
        sub1, sub2; sub3.
```

is the meaning of the body: (sub1 and sub2) or sub3 or is it: sub1 and (sub2 or sub3)? The answer is that the first interpretation is correct. Rule bodies which include both symbols are interpreted as a disjunction of conjuncts, not as a conjunction of disjuncts.

The programmer can use brackets to make the meaning clearer:

```
proc2  :-
        (sub1, sub2); sub3.
```

or to alter the normal interpretation:

```
proc3 :-
    sub1, (sub2; sub3).
```

Even if he does so, the structure of the procedure is obscure. It is not clear what cases are recognised, nor which sub-goal handles each. A procedure using ; can always be re-written using , only, as you will see if you do exercise 6.3.1(b).

Prolog provides a built-in predicate true, defined as:

> true/0
> The goal always succeeds and does nothing. It is not re-satisfiable on backtracking.

This predicate can be used in dubious ways in conjunction with ;. If you did exercise 6.2(a), you probably wrote:

```
truth_table(Variable_expression) :-
    assign(Variable_expression, Hollow, Const_expression, Value),
    write(Const_expression gives Value),
    nl,
    fail.
truth_table(_).
```

After the failure of the first clause, the second ensures that the goal is satisfied. The same effect is achieved by:

```
truth_table(Variable_expression) :-
    assign(Variable_expression, Hollow, Const_expression, Value),
    write(Const_expression gives Value),
    nl,
    fail;
    true.
```

Of course, the second version is much less readable. If this clause was in a large program, it would be all too easy for a reader to overlook the trick at the end of it.

You may wonder why these nefarious predicates are part of the language. In fact, there are some very special situations in which their use is necessary. These we mention in section 7.2.1. Unfortunately, lazy programmers use them in reprehensible ways just because they exist.

Exercises 6.3.1

(a) Under what combinations of success and failure of sub-goals sub1, sub2 and sub3 would a call to proc2 succeed where a call to proc3 would fail? Use the program truth_table to check your intuition.

(b)   Re-write the procedures for proc2 and proc3 using only conjunction. Do you think the answer to the question in the previous exercise is more obvious now?

6.3.2   The cut and fail combination

Consider the problem of writing a procedure for after_month/2. A call is to succeed if the arguments are the names of two months of the year and the second comes after the first in a year. In many respects, the problem is analogous to that of determining the order of two military ranks which we examined in section 3.1.   We represent the calendar by facts for next_month/2:

```
next_month(jan, feb).
next_month(feb, mar).
next_month(mar, apr).
next_month(apr, may).
next_month(may, jun).
next_month(jun, jul).
next_month(jul, aug).
next_month(aug, sep).
next_month(sep, oct).
next_month(oct, nov).
next_month(nov, dec).
next_month(dec, jan).            % The calendar is cyclic.
```

At first sight, there appear to be two cases, as in the procedure for lower_rank/2, handled by clauses:

```
after_month(M1, M2) :-
    next_month(M1, M2).
after_month(M1, M2) :-
    next_month(M1, M3),
    after_month(M3, M2).
```

But this is not adequate:

```
?- after_month(feb, jul).
yes

?- after_month(dec, mar).
yes

?- after_month(jul, feb).
yes
```

In fact, every month is recognised as coming after any other! The fault is our failure to recognise December as a special case. As the month after it does not come in the same year, a call should fail when the first argument is dec. The case is handled by a new clause:

```
after_month(dec, _) :- !,
        fail.                           % No month comes after dec.
```

The clause must be placed first because the other clauses handle cases which only hold if the given month is not December. The cut ensures mutual exclusion between this clause and the other two: there is only one correct way of processing December. The action when the case is recognised is to cause the call to fail. Now, we have:

```
?- after_month(feb, jul).
yes

?- after_month(dec, mar).
no

?- after_month(jul, feb).
no
```

Backtracking alternatives are only eliminated when the cut is reached. So, the procedure can be used non-deterministically:

```
?- after_month(oct, M).          What months come after oct?
M = nov;

M = dec;
no
```

to some extent:

```
?- after_month(M, mar).          What months come before mar?
no
```

In general, it is good programming practice, having identified a case, to express the processing required in that case in terms of the conditions which, if satisfied, make the call succeed. You should only use the cut and fail combination if a predicate defines when a relationship does not hold, rather than when it does. For instance, a case analysis of the list member-ship relationship includes the case of the empty list, of which no item is a member. However, we do not translate this analysis into:

```
member(_, [ ]) :- !,
        fail.
```

We ensure failure in this case by not providing a clause to handle it. Beware of writing redundant clauses.

Exercises 6.3.2

(a) Why does a call to after_month/2 fail when the first argument is a variable? Write a procedure for the predicate so that a call such as:

> ?- after_month(M, mar).

succeeds and generates alternatives.

6.4 Summary

In this chapter, we have introduced the following ideas:

- The cut is a procedural device which eliminates backtracking alternatives but obscures the declarative interpretation of a procedure.

- By making a procedure deterministic, the cut can prevent fruitless searches or enforce mutual exclusion between clauses.

- Careful placing of the cut and ordering of clauses in which it is used are essential for correct use of the predicate.

- fail_if can be used as an alternative to the cut for enforcing mutual exclusion between clauses of a procedure, but the procedure may be less efficient.

- Used together, repeat and fail are an alternative to recursion as a means of structuring a program. Forced backtracking depends on side-effects to deliver results because substitutions applied to variables are undone by the backtracking.

- true and ; used for controlling program execution detract from the clarity of the program.

- The cut and fail combination forces a goal to fail. Its use should be confined to occasions when the definition of a predicate is partly in terms of when a call fails.

Chapter 7

Programs as Data

At the beginning of this book, we stated that every object in a Prolog program is a term of one type or another. In this chapter, we explore the implications of this for the kinds of program we can write.

What type of term are the clauses of a program? With facts, it is straightforward. The fact:

    union([ ], S, S).

is a structure with functor union and arity 3. In the next clause for this procedure, it is not apparent what the structure is:

    union([H|T], S1, S2) :-
        member(H, S1), !,
        union(T, S1, S2).

The answer is that the rule is the structure shown as a tree diagram in Figure 7.1.

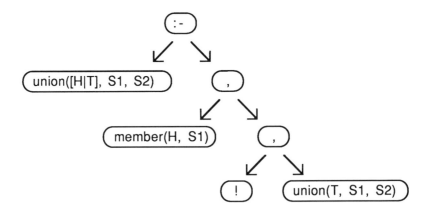

Figure 7.1 Structure of a rule

The functor is :-, the structure has arity 2 and the components are the head and body of the rule. :- was defined as an operator in Figure 5.2, as were all the other symbols we have used with special meanings in our programs:

?-   for introducing a goal;

:-   for introducing a directive (a prefix operator);

,   for denoting a conjunction of goals;

;   for denoting a disjunction of goals.

The operators , and ; are built-in predicates, defined as follows:

,/2
The two arguments should be structures. A call succeeds if the two arguments are satisfied when called in succession as goals. It is re-satisfiable if the second goal is re-satisfiable or if the first can be re-satisfied and the second can be satisfied anew after it.

;/2
The two arguments should be structures. A call succeeds if either the first or the second argument is satisfied when called as a goal. It is re-satisfiable if the second goal can be satisfied after the first or if either is re-satisfiable.

When a rule whose body comprises conjoined sub-goals is used to try to satisfy a goal, it is ,/2 that is called. Obviously, by appealing to the definition of ,/2 to explain the meaning of the body of a rule with conjoined sub-goals, we arrive at exactly the same statement of when a call using that rule succeeds as by saying that it has a series of sub-goals which must be satisfied in turn. However, to understand and write programs which process rules as items of data, you must recognise the structure of a rule body with more than one sub-goal and know the meaning of the predicate which is its functor.

7.1 Modifying the Clauses of a Program

The built-in predicates asserta and assert enable the programmer to add new clauses to the Prolog database. They are defined as follows:

asserta/1
The argument in the goal should be a structure. The goal is always satisfiable and is not re-satisfiable on backtracking. As a

side-effect, the structure is added to the Prolog database as a clause, before any existing clauses for the same procedure.

assert/1
The definition is the same as that of asserta/1, except that the new clause is added after existing clauses for the procedure.

As these predicates add the new clause by a side-effect, the clause remains even if Prolog backtracks over the goal. The built-in predicates retract and retractall are for removing clauses from the Prolog database.

retract/1
The argument in the goal should be a structure. The Prolog database is searched for the first clause which matches the structure. If a match is found, the goal is satisfied and as a side-effect the clause is removed from the Prolog database; otherwise it fails. On backtracking, the goal is re-satisfiable by removing subsequent matching clauses.

retractall/1
The argument in the goal should be a structure. The goal is always satisfiable, and, as a side-effect, all clauses (zero or more) whose heads match the structure are removed from the Prolog database. The goal is not re-satisfiable on backtracking.

If retractall/1 were not built-in, we could write a procedure for it:

```
retractall(Head) :-
    retract(Head),                % Remove all facts.
    fail.
retractall(Head) :-
    retract((Head :- Body)),      % Remove all rules.
    fail.
retractall(_).                    % Then succeed.
```

The syntax of Prolog requires a structure of the form: Term1 :- Term2 to be enclosed in brackets when it occurs as a component of another structure.
We illustrate three usages of these predicates in the following sections.

7.1.1   Managing a database

In many programming applications, programs process a body of stored data, allowing the user to update this database and using it to provide information and reports to the user. The typical structure of a database application in Prolog is illustrated in Figure 7.2.

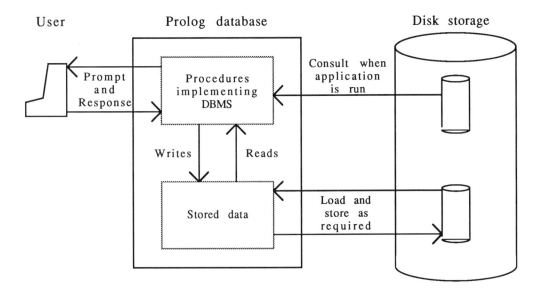

Figure 7.2 Structure of a database application in Prolog

The figure illustrates the important distinction between the database management system (DBMS) and the database. The database cannot be represented in arguments to procedures because it exists independently of the programs which manipulate it. It must be represented by clauses in the Prolog database and be manipulated by calls to assert and retract.

For illustration, we use the example of a database which records information about the members of a social club: their surname and age, how much their subscription is and whether they have paid it. In the database, we record the details of each member as a fact of the form: member(Name, Age, Subscription_status). We do not record the amount of the subscription separately for each member, as this is determined according to the member's age by the rule:

```
subscription_is(Age, pounds(10)) :-
    Age < 18.
subscription_is(Age, pounds(20)) :-
    Age >= 18.
```

Some operations on the database are:

- Adding details of a new member:

  ```
  add_member(M) :-
      assert(M).
  ```

- Displaying membership details:

```
        print_details(member(Name, Age, Status)) :-
            member(Name, Age, Status),
            subscription_is(Age, Subs),
            write(member(Name, Age, Subs, Status)),
            nl,
            fail.
        print_details(_).
```

- Removing details of members:

```
        remove_members(M) :-
            retract(M),
            fail.
        remove_members(_).
```

- Recording that a member has paid the subscription:

```
        record_payment(member(Name, Age)) :-
            retract(member(Name, Age, unpaid)),
            assert(member(Name, Age, paid)).
```

The following interaction illustrates these predicates. First, we enrol some members:

```
?- add_member(member(holmes, 33, unpaid)).
yes

?- add_member(member(sutcliffe, 44, paid)).
yes

?- add_member(member(sutcliffe, 42, paid)).
yes

?- add_member(member(sutcliffe, 17, unpaid)).
yes

?- add_member(member(hobbs, 27, unpaid)).
yes
```

Display the list of members:

```
?- print_details(_).
member(holmes, 33, pounds(20), unpaid)
member(sutcliffe, 44, pounds(20), paid)
member(sutcliffe, 42, pounds(20), paid)
member(sutcliffe, 17, pounds(10), unpaid)
member(hobbs, 27, pounds(20), unpaid)
yes
```

As we used assert and not asserta in the procedure for add_member/1, the members are in the order in which they were enrolled.

Record that Holmes has now paid:

```
?- record_payment(member(holmes,  33)).
yes
```

Check who has not paid:

```
?- print_details(member(_, _, unpaid)).
member(sutcliffe, 17, pounds(10), unpaid)
member(hobbs, 27, pounds(20), unpaid)
yes
```

Eject all members who have not paid:

```
?- remove_members(member(_, _, unpaid)).
yes
```

Establish who is left:

```
?- print_details(_).
member(sutcliffe, 44, pounds(20), paid)
member(sutcliffe, 42, pounds(20), paid)
member(holmes, 33, pounds(20), paid)
yes
```

Holmes is now at the end of the list because a replacement record was added for him when we recorded his payment.

If the club treasurer frequently had to remove defaulters, we could provide a separate operation to do this, as a procedure for remove_unpaid/0:

```
remove_unpaid :-
      retractall(member(_, _, unpaid)).
```

If the club agreed to a reduced subscription for the under-fifteens, the change could be entered as:

```
?- asserta((subscription_is(Age, pounds(5)) :- Age < 15, !)).
```

Of course, we would not wish the treasurer to call asserta/1 directly because it would be too easy to alter the programs of the DBMS inadvertently.

The risk that a program may be altered is the main reason why you must be very cautious in using assert and retract. Once the clauses of a program are altered, that program is liable to produce errors whose cause is very hard to pin down. The rogue alteration could be anywhere in the program.

In the database application, this risk was minimised by the clear logical separation of programs and data. We only changed the stored data.

Exercises 7.1.1

(a) Write procedures for load/1 and store/1, to read a database from a named file and write it to a file. If you use the structure given in section 5.3, you have only to write procedures for action_on/1 and next/1.

7.1.2 Accumulating results with forced backtracking

We use forced backtracking to make Prolog satisfy and re-satisfy a goal exhaustively. By the side-effects of assert and retract, we can accumulate results, which the backtracking would otherwise preclude, within a procedure which is structured using this technique.

To count how many members the club has, we have to make Prolog exhaustively satisfy the goal: ?- member(Name, Age, Status). Forced backtracking does this. To record the number of times the goal is satisfied, we use a counter stored as a clause in the Prolog database. In a call to count_members/2, the first argument is a structure indicating which members are to be counted, the second an integer which is the answer. The procedure is:

```
count_members(member(Name, Age, Status), _) :-
    initialise_counter(no_of_members, 0),
    member(Name, Age, Status),
    increment_counter(no_of_members, 1),
    fail.
count_members(_, Count) :-
    finalise_counter(no_of_members, Count).
```

In the first clause, we initialise the no_of_members counter to 0 and increment it by 1 each time the second sub-goal is satisfied. This clause eventually fails, leaving the counter at its final value. In the second clause, we retrieve that value.

The procedures for the predicates which manipulate the counter are:

```
initialise_counter(Name, Initial_value) :-
    retractall(counter(Name, _)),
    assert(counter(Name, Initial_value)).

increment_counter(Name, Inc) :-
    retract(counter(Name, Old_value)),
    New_value is Old_value + Inc,
    assert(counter(Name, New_value)), !.
```

```
finalise_counter(Name, Final_value) :-
    retract(counter(Name, Final_value)).
```

The purpose of requiring the counter to be named is to enable several to be used in a single program, if necessary. The sub-goal: ?- retractall(counter(Name, _)) prevents duplication when we initialise a counter. The cut at the end of the procedure for increment_counter/2 ensures that a call is not re-satisfiable. Without it, the sub-goal: ?- retract(counter(Name, Old_value)) would be re-satisfiable, removing from the Prolog database the new value which the third sub-goal had added.

The structure of the procedure for count_members/2 is typical of programs which accumulate results in this way. There is a phase where results are added to the Prolog database, followed by a phase in which they are collected. It is essential that all clauses added are indeed collected in the second phase. Otherwise a program would modify itself, and though it might give correct results when first used, it would deliver incorrect results forever thereafter!

There are two built-in predicates which force a goal to be satisfied and re-satisfied exhaustively while preserving a result each time the goal is satisfied. They are:

bag/3[1]
The goal is always satisfiable and is not re-satisfiable. The form of a call is: ?- bag(Term, Goal, List). Term is a term representing the result which is to be preserved each time Goal is satisfied. Goal should be a structure. It is called as a goal and re-satisfied exhaustively through backtracking. List is the list of all Terms in the order in which they are generated.

set/3
The definition is the same as that of bag/3, except that the list is in sorted order[2] and duplicates are removed.

In view of the difficulties of using assert and retract safely, these predicates offer a useful alternative. To count the number of members in the club, we could write:

```
?- bag(_, member(_, _, _), L), length(L, Count).
L = [_12, _13, _14, _15, _16]
Count = 5
```

assuming the existence of the procedure for length/1 from section 4.1.

---

[1]bag and set are the names to be used in the Prolog standard. In many implementations, these predicates are called bagof and setof, respectively.

[2]The Prolog standard defines an order of all terms. See Appendix 3.

Here, we only wanted to know how many times the goal: ?- member(_, _, _) could be satisfied. More commonly, we wish to know the substitutions made for variables in a goal each time it is satisfied. To do this, we include the variables in the term which is the first argument, as in the following examples of the club with its five initial members.

Display a list of members who have not paid:

```
?- bag(defaulter(Name, Age), member(Name, Age, unpaid), L).
Name = _12
Age = _13
L = [defaulter(sutcliffe, 17),
     defaulter(hobbs, 22)]
```

Display full details of all members:

```
?- bag(member(Name, Age, Subs, Status), (member(Name, Age, Status),
    subscription_is(Age, Subs)), L).
```

```
Name = _12
Age = _13
Status = _14
Subs = _15
L = [member(sutcliffe, 44, pounds(20), paid),
     member(sutcliffe, 42, pounds(20), paid),
     member(sutcliffe, 17, pounds(10), unpaid),
     member(holmes, 33, pounds(20), unpaid),
     member(hobbs, 27, pounds(20), unpaid)]
```

In this example, the second argument is a conjunction of goals. The notation:

```
(member(Name, Age, Status), subscription_is(Age, Subs))
```

is an abbreviation for the term:

```
','(member(Name, Age, Status), subscription_is(Age, Subs))
```

The syntax of Prolog provides a list-like notation for structures with functor , and arity 2. So, the term:

```
','(a, ','(b, c))
```

can be written:

```
(a, b, c).
```

This notation aggravates the confusion which arises from the function of the comma character as both functor and separator of components. For instance, the structures f(a, b, c) and f((a, b, c)) look as though they have the same arity, but they do not, as Figure 7.3 makes clear.

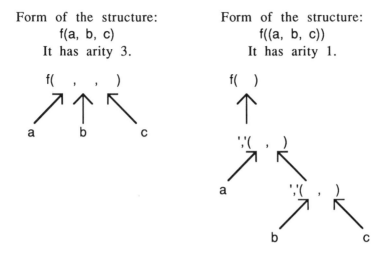

Figure 7.3 Form of similar-looking structures

Sometimes, we need to inspect results as they are being accumulated. In these situations, bag and set are unsuitable. Our next example illustrates this.

The problem involves graph traversal. Given a description of a directed graph, we want to know what nodes can be reached from a given node.

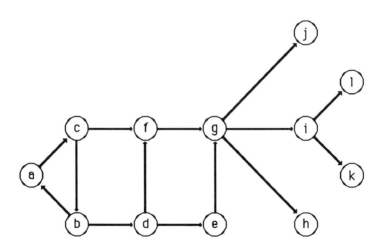

Figure 7.4 A directed graph

Figure 7.4 shows a directed graph. We represent it by a series of facts for arc/2:

```
arc(a, c).                    arc(b, a).
arc(b, d).                    arc(c, b).
arc(c, f).                    arc(d, e).
arc(d, f).                    arc(e, g).
arc(f, g).                    arc(g, h).
arc(g, i).                    arc(g, j).
arc(i, k).                    arc(i, l).
```

Our interpretation of a fact of the form arc(A, B) is:

"There is an arc from node A to node B."

In the procedure for reachable/2, the first argument is the starting node and the second is the list of reachable nodes. The procedure exhibits clearly the two-phase structure:

```
reachable(From, _) :-
    traverse_graph(From).
reachable(_, Nodes_reached) :-
    collect_nodes(Nodes_reached).

traverse_graph(Node) :-
    reached(Node), !, fail.
traverse_graph(From) :-
    assert(reached(From)),
    arc(From, To),
    traverse_graph(To).
collect_nodes([Node|Others]) :-
    retract(reached(Node)), !,
    collect_nodes(Others).
collect_nodes([ ]).
```

The adding phase is the first clause, in which a fact: reached(Node) is added to the Prolog database for each reachable Node. The collecting phase is the second clause, in which these facts are retracted and collected in a list. The two clauses for traverse_graph/1 handle the two cases for a node which is reached:

- The node has already been reached by a different route. To establish this, we inspect the results accumulated so far by a call to reached/1. If the node has been reached, we force Prolog to backtrack to follow other routes.

- The node has not previously been reached. We record the node, find an outgoing arc from it and continue the traversal along that arc. As the traverse_graph sub-goal eventually fails, backtracking forces all outgoing arcs to be explored.

The behaviour of the program is:

?- reachable(f, Nodes).   No duplicate routes from f.
Nodes = [f, g, h, i, k, l, j]

?- reachable(d, Nodes)   Some duplicate routes from d.
Nodes = [d, e, g, h, i, k, l, j, f]

?- reachable(a, Nodes)   Some cycles in routes from a.
Nodes = [a, c, b, d, e, g, h, i, k, l, j, f]

Exercises 7.1.2

(a)   What would be the order of the nodes in the answers to the three
      calls to reachable/2 if the nodes reached were recorded in the
      Prolog database by the sub-goal: ?- asserta(reached(From))?

7.1.3   Global variables

The two-phase structure does not guarantee that a program which uses
assert and retract will not be left in an altered state after it is run. We
must ensure that in the calling sequence of sub-goals there is no failure
which would prevent the collecting phase being reached, once the adding
phase has been passed. In general, this can be assured if the predicates are
used only within low-level procedures and the results accumulated are then
returned to higher-level procedures in an argument to a call. If we use
them at the top level of a large program, there may well, in the dynamic
calling sequence, be an extensive series of deeply-nested sub-goals between
the two phases. Any failure in the series disrupts the co-ordination
between the two phases.
    Despite these problems, we are sometimes justified in using assert and
retract to return a result to the top level of a program from a low-level
procedure if the normal methods of indicating a result, by the success or
failure of the call or by a substitution applied to a variable, are unsuitable.
We may wish to ensure that subsequent sub-goals are reached; if so, the call
must not fail. If we return results in an argument, the whole series of
nested sub-goals has to carry this extra argument. Instead, we may decide
that a procedure is to indicate a result by a side-effect on the Prolog
database. In this, we are treating the Prolog database as a global variable.
It can be very convenient to do so. Any procedure can record a result there,
and that result is visible to any other, whatever the distance between the
two in the dynamic calling sequence of goals. Of course, we abandon the
principles of the two-phase structure, but we can guard against the consequences by using a predicate whose side-effects on the Prolog database are
undone on backtracking. The procedure is:

```
undoable_assert(Clause) :-
    assert(Clause).
undoable_assert(Clause) :-
    retract(Clause), !,
    fail.
```

We would use undoable_assert/1 if we anticipated the results accumulated in the Prolog database being removed in the collecting phase, but wished to ensure that, if failure of an intermediate sub-goal prevented that phase being reached, the Prolog database would remain unaltered. The second clause removes an asserted clause on backtracking, and the cut and fail combination at the end of it ensures that backtracking is not interrupted. In terms of its effect on control within a program, undoable_assert/1 behaves exactly as assert/1.

Another problem of global variables is their effect on program structure. In a program which uses global variables, there are sub-goals in one part of the program which have no procedures and are comprehensible only in terms of the clauses added as side-effects by procedures elsewhere. The result is a program whose text is hard to understand and whose operation is hard to test and debug. In section 7.2.1, we introduce a structuring technique to control the effects of using the Prolog database as a global variable and, in particular, to make clear the association between one procedure which adds a clause to the Prolog database and another whose operation depends on the presence of that clause. With our method, we can reliably use the Prolog database as a global variable, and for this reason we include this strategy as one of those which our next toolkit technique supports.

Database Modification

The technique is used:

- To manage a database.

- To prevent results of a procedure execution being lost on backtracking.

- To facilitate communication between parts of a program through global variables.

The technique is based on the use of the Prolog database for recording the progress of a computation. It comprises the following elements:

- The built-in predicates asserta and assert are used to add results to the Prolog database. In managing a database, the order of clauses added may be significant, and the choice between asserta and assert must be carefully considered. In the second and third uses, the two predicates may be used indifferently.

- The built-in predicates retract and retractall are used to remove results from the Prolog database. In the second and third uses, the Prolog database must not be permanently altered. This is achieved by structuring a program as an adding phase followed by a collecting phase. It is essential to ensure that once the adding phase is passed, the collecting phase is always reached.

- In the second use, the database modification should be confined to low levels of a program, and the adding and collecting phases should be close together. In this way, the effects of database modification are localised.

7.2 Meta-Programming

If we wished to have a message encoded, we might use a predicate which took the words of the message as input and returned the code words as output. Representing messages input and output as lists of atoms, a procedure would be:

```
encode([ ], [ ]).
encode([Word|Ws], [Code|Cs]) :-
    cifer(Word, Code),
    encode(Ws, Cs).
```

The procedure for cifer/2 would embody the encryption algorithm. If, for the sake of security, we wished to vary it periodically, we might express each algorithm as a procedure for a different predicate and change the procedure for encode/2 to call whichever we wished to use. A better method, however, uses the built-in predicate call and avoids having to change the encoding procedure. The definition is:

```
call/1
The argument should be a structure. It is called as a goal. The
call to call/1 succeeds, is re-satisfiable or fails exactly as the
goal which is its argument.
```

In the revised procedure, the name of the encryption algorithm is the second argument:

```
encode([ ], _, [ ]).
encode([Word|Ws], Algorithm_name, [Code|Cs]) :-
    Goal =.. [Algorithm_name, Word, Code],
    call(Goal),
    encode(Ws, Algorithm_name, Cs).
```

At each level of recursion, we construct a goal term from the name of the algorithm as functor and the next plain text word and code word as components and call that goal.

Independently of particular encryption algorithms, the procedure describes how to encode a message. It states that the encryption algorithm is to be applied to successive plain text words, yielding each time one word of cifer text.

A program which defines how other programs are to be used is called a *meta-program*. The procedure for encode/3 is a meta-program, and the procedures for encryption are the *object program*. Meta-programming is easy in Prolog, thanks to the identity of programs and data. In the next two sections, we investigate two applications of it.

7.2.1 Meta-programming and program structure

On a very modest scale, our revised encoding procedure provided a higher-level structure for the procedures that implemented encryption algorithms. It defined how all were applied. We now extend the idea of a meta-program as a device for program structuring to the problem of controlling the use of the Prolog database as a global variable.

We illustrate the problem by considering the design of the input validation component of an interactive system. The role of this component is to determine whether the user's input represents a meaningful command, by applying a sequence of checks. To provide helpful error messages, the program must carry out all the checks appropriate to the command, even if an early one reveals a user error. If an error is detected during a complex check, information may have to be communicated from a low level to higher levels of the program. From our discussion in section 7.1.3, you should recognise this as a situation in which it is appropriate to use the Prolog database as a global variable.

Notice that this analysis of the design problem applies to all the commands to the system. A meta-program for this problem both controls the database modification and defines a structure for validation of all commands. The object program comprises procedures to implement each validation check and each command.

The first part of the meta-program defines the actions taken in a validation check:

```
validate(Check, _) :-
    call(Check), !.
validate(_, Error_message) :-
    assert(error(Error_message)).
```

If there is an error, the sub-goal: ?- call(Check) fails, and the error message associated with the check is added to the Prolog database as a clause for error/1. In the object program, the first part of a procedure to process a command is a series of calls to validate/2. In each, the first argument is the goal term which applies the check and the second is a term representing the error message to be output if the check reveals an error.

The second part of the meta-program defines the manner in which a command is executed:

```
execute(_) :-
    retract(error(Message)), !,
    report_error(Message).
execute(Action) :-
    call(Action).

report_error(Message) :-
    report_to_user(Message),
    retract(error(Next_message)), !,
    report_error(Next_message).
report_error(_).
```

The goal term which carries out the action of the command is the argument in the call from the object program to execute/1. The procedure specifies that if validation revealed errors in the command, a query is executed by reporting these to the user; otherwise it is executed by carrying out the action defined in the goal term.

This part of the meta-program is the collecting phase for clauses for error/1 added to the Prolog database by the procedure for validate/2. The structure of the procedure for report_error/1 ensures that all the clauses are collected. We do not give a procedure for report_to_user/1, as the details of it depend on the form of the terms representing error messages.

In our club membership example, we validate a command to add a new member by checking:

- That the person to be added is not already a member, assuming that a member is uniquely identified by their name and age.

- That the age given is reasonable.

- That the fees status given is either paid or unpaid.

A revised procedure for add_member/1 which uses the meta-program to carry out these checks is:

```
add_member(member(Name, Age, Status)) :-
    validate(fail_if(member(Name, Age, _)),
        'This person is already a member'),
    validate((Age >= 5, Age =< 85),
        'Age must be between 5 and 85'),
    validate((Status = paid ; Status = unpaid),
        'Fees status must be "paid" or "unpaid"'),
    execute(assert(member(Name, Age, Status))).
```

Conformity to a common structure in procedures which process commands has not constrained the form in which validation checks and actions may be defined in the object program. In validating the member's age, the check comprises a conjunction of goals, and in validating the fees status it is a disjunction. We could even define the action: ?- execute(true) if no action was required, as might be the case if the query were an operating system command prefaced by an escape character.

By this meta-program, we gain several benefits in writing the object program. Firstly, procedures which process commands have a common structure, emphasising their common role. Secondly, we are relieved of the risks associated with global variables. We can include calls to validate/2 at any level of a validation routine. The discipline is provided by the meta-program.

A validation check is most naturally specified as a structure which succeeds when called as a goal if its components are valid and fails otherwise. The final benefit of the meta-program is that it enables us to adopt this design for each check in the object program without the worry that later checks may not be reached and that Prolog will attempt to re-satisfy goals in which earlier ones were applied. We use an extended version of this meta-program in the implementation of an electronic diary in Chapter 12.

7.2.2 A Prolog interpreter in Prolog

An *interpreter* for a programming language is a meta-program which executes programs written in that language. To write an interpreter for Prolog, we need the built-in predicate clause:

> clause/2
> In a call, the first argument should be a structure. Prolog searches its database for a clause whose head matches this structure. The call succeeds if such a clause is found and the body of it matches the second argument; otherwise it fails. A fact is treated as though its body was the atom true. On backtracking, the goal is re-satisfiable by matching with subsequent clause heads.

The following interpreter defines how Prolog tries to satisfy a goal:

```
satisfy(true).
satisfy((Goal, Goals)) :-
    satisfy(Goal),
    satisfy(Goals).
satisfy(Goal ; Goals) :-
    satisfy(Goal)   ;   satisfy(Goals).
```

```
satisfy(Goal)  :-
    bip(Goal),
    call(Goal).
satisfy(Goal)  :-
    clause(Goal, Sub_goals),
    satisfy(Sub_goals).
```

In a call to satisfy/1, the argument is the goal which we wish Prolog to try to satisfy. The first clause is the base case, the case of the goal: ?- true. It is reached after the goal to be satisfied in the object program has matched a fact. In the second clause, we state that a conjunction of goals is satisfied by satisfying each in turn, and in the third that a disjunction of goals is satisfied if either is satisfied. The fourth clause handles the case where the call in the object program is to a built-in predicate. It assumes that the interpreter includes facts for bip/1, identifying each:

```
bip(arg(_, _, _)).
bip(assert(_)).
    . . .
    down to
    . . .
bip(write(_)).
```

A built-in predicate is satisfied by calling it as a goal, without reference to the object program. The list would not include clauses for ,/2 or ;/2, whose behaviour is defined in the interpreter.

Unfortunately, executing a cut in the object program as: ?- call(!) does not handle the cut correctly because when it occurs in the argument of a call to call/1, the cut behaves as though the argument is a procedure body, and it only cuts out backtracking alternatives among any preceding goals in that argument. Instead of cutting out alternatives in the object program, the call in the interpreter has no effect at all! However, as the meaning of the cut is hard to capture in any interpreter written in Prolog, we shall disregard this limitation of our very simple one.

The final clause states that a goal is satisfied if there is a clause in the object program whose head matches the goal and whose body can be satisfied.

Subject to the limitation we have mentioned, the answers the interpreter gives are exactly those we would get if we had called the object program goal directly. For an object program consisting of the procedure for permute/2 which we gave in the answer to exercise 3.4(a), we have:

```
?- satisfy(permute([a, e, i, o, u], [a, u, i, e, o]).
yes

?- satisfy(permute([1,2,3],  P)).
P = [1, 2, 3];

P = [1, 3, 2];
```

P = [2, 1, 3];

P = [2, 3, 1];

P = [3, 1, 2];

P = [3, 2, 1];
no

The significance of the interpreter, which is otherwise a singularly useless artifact, is that it shows an object program being executed under the control of a program we have written, instead of under the control of the Prolog system. With suitable enhancements, the interpreter can offer a more helpful programming environment than the basic Prolog system.

We illustrate the possibilities with an interpreter that reports how a goal in an object program was satisfied. It has a second argument and returns in this argument a structure recording the sub-goals satisfied in the course of satisfying a goal in the object program. The procedure is:

```
satisfy(true, 'match with a fact').
satisfy((Goal, Goals), and(Proof, Proofs)) :-
    satisfy(Goal, Proof),
    satisfy(Goals, Proofs).
satisfy(';'(Goal, Goal), Proof) :-
    satisfy(Goal, Proof)  ;  satisfy(Goals, Proof).
satisfy(Goal, by(Goal, 'built-in predicate')) :-
    bip(Goal),
    call(Goal).
satisfy(Goal, by(Goal, Proof)) :-
    clause(Goal, Sub_goals),
    satisfy(Sub_goals, Proof).
```

There are two special cases of satisfying a goal, handled by clauses one and four: when it is satisfied by a match with a fact and when it is satisfied as a built-in predicate. In these cases, the proof of how the goal is satisfied is represented by the atoms 'match with a fact' and 'built-in predicate' respectively. When the goal is satisfied following a match with a clause in the object program, the proof is represented by a structure with functor b y and arity 2, the two components being the goal satisfied and a term representing how its sub-goals are satisfied.

As the second argument is liable to be a large structure, we output it formatted instead of as a substitution for a variable:

```
satisfy_and_display(Goal)  :-
    satisfy(Goal, Proof),
    display_proof(Proof, 2).
```

```
display_proof(and(P, Ps), Indent) :-
    display_proof(P, Indent),
    display_proof(Ps, Indent).
display_proof(by(Goal, Proof), Indent) :-
    tab(Indent),
    write(Goal),
    write(' by '),
    display_proof_of_goal(Proof, Indent).

display_proof_of_goal(Proof, _) :-
    special_case(Proof), !,
    write(Proof),
    nl.
display_proof_of_goal(Proof, Indent) :-
    nl,
    N is Indent + 4,
    display_proof(Proof, N).

special_case('match with a fact').
special_case('built-in predicate').
```

The information provided by the interpreter is useful if calls to our object program succeed but yield the wrong substitutions. If, in the procedure for permute/2, we had defined the clause for the base case incorrectly as:

```
permute([ ], _).
```

the error in the first answer to the question:

```
?- permute([1, 2, 3], P).
P = [1, 2, 3, |_46]
```

could be traced to this fault. The significant line of the proof is in boldface:

```
?- satisfy_and_display(permute([1, 2, 3], P)).
```

```
              permute([1,2,3],[1,2,3|_133]) by
                 remove(1,[1,2,3],[2,3]) by match with a fact
              permute([2,3],[2,3|_133]) by
                 remove(2,[2,3],[3]) by match with a fact
              permute([3],[3|_133]) by
                 remove(3,[3],[ ]) by match with a fact
              permute([ ],_133) by match with a fact
```

```
P = [1,2,3|_133]
```

The display reveals where the variable _133 has crept into the answer.

In section 9.3, we investigate further the concept of an interpreter as an aid to finding faults in an object program.

7.3   Summary

In this chapter, we have introduced the following ideas:

- Rules, as well as facts, are terms which can be treated as items of data. A rule has functor :- and arity 2.

- assert and asserta are built-in predicates which add clauses to the Prolog database. retract and retractall remove clauses from it. They are all potentially harmful because their actions are achieved as side-effects which may leave a program in an altered state after it is run.

- The technique of database modification is the basis for safely using assert, asserta, retract and retractall. It is a technique for managing a database, for accumulating results which would be lost on back-tracking or for safely using the Prolog database as a global variable.

- A meta-program is a program which defines how another program, called the object program, is to be used. A meta-program can be a means of structuring an object program.

- An interpreter for a programming language is a meta-program which executes programs written in that language. A Prolog interpreter in Prolog can extend the facilities offered by the Prolog system.

Chapter 8

Grammar Rules

In this chapter, we discuss the topic of parsing and investigate the application of Prolog to the problem of writing parsers. An appreciation of how Prolog is applied to this problem is valuable for two reasons. Firstly, a very important class of grammar for describing natural language, called a *phrase-structure grammar*, can be represented easily and naturally as a Prolog program, and this has stimulated a great deal of investigation of the structure of natural language to use Prolog as a tool (Pereira & Shieber, 1987). Indeed, this use was the aim of the designers of Prolog. Secondly, as the notation for a phrase-structure grammar in Prolog is different from the syntax of facts and rules, mastery of the language must include an understanding of the relationship between this notation and the standard syntax.

8.1 Phrase-Structure Grammar

The parsing problem is to determine whether a sequence of words is a sentence of a language and to produce a representation of the structure of the sentence if it is. The representation is called the *parse tree* for the sentence. The starting point is a *grammar* for the language in question. A grammar is a set of rules which defines how sentences of the language are constructed. A phrase-structure grammar expresses the rules in terms of components of the language and how they may be concatenated. A phrase-structure grammar for a very small subset of English is given in Figure 8.1. The rules are numbered for easy reference.

A rule such as:

VerbPhrase → Verb NounPhrase

is to be interpreted as stating that the component called *VerbPhrase* is a sentence element composed of the component *Verb* immediately followed by the component *NounPhrase*. The components whose names begin with an upper-case letter are the *non-terminal symbols* of the grammar. These are the grammatical categories of the language. The *terminal symbols*, written with an initial lower-case letter, are the words of the language.

1	Sentence	→	NounPhrase VerbPhrase
2	NounPhrase	→	Determiner Noun
3	VerbPhrase	→	Verb NounPhrase
4	VerbPhrase	→	Verb
5	Determiner	→	the
6	Determiner	→	a
7	Noun	→	woman
8	Noun	→	girl
9	Verb	→	sees
10	Verb	→	calls

Figure 8.1 A phrase-structure grammar

In the grammar, there is one distinguished non-terminal, called the *starting symbol*, which describes the components of a complete sentence of the language. A grammar must have at least one rule with the starting symbol on the left of the arrow. In the grammar of Figure 8.1, *Sentence* is the starting symbol.

One way of approaching the parsing problem for this very simple grammar is to begin with the starting symbol on the left side of rule 1 and repeatedly re-write the left side by replacing it with the components on the right side. When the component on the right is a terminal symbol, we check whether the next word in the sequence matches the symbol. The sequence is a sentence if the starting symbol can be fully re-written, with all the words checked.

To see how this parsing strategy works and how a parse tree is built, consider the problem of parsing the sequence: "The woman calls". The effect of re-writing the starting symbol is to build the parse tree of Figure 8.2.

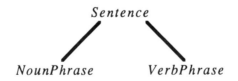

Figure 8.2 Parse tree built by re-writing rule 1

Next, we take the first of these components and, finding it on the left side of rule 2, re-write it as *Determiner Noun*. The parse tree expands to that of Figure 8.3.

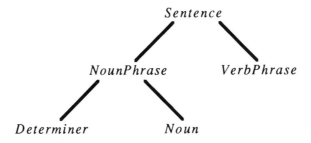

Figure 8.3 Parse tree after re-writing using rule 2

The first rule for *Determiner* re-writes it as a terminal symbol, and as the first word in the sequence does match the symbol, parsing can proceed. The rule for *Noun* is re-written in the same way after checking the next word, and this completes the re-write of the symbol *NounPhrase*. The parse tree is in Figure 8.4.

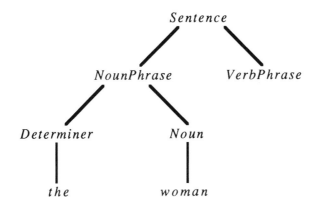

Figure 8.4 The parse tree after fully re-writing *NounPhrase*

The non-terminal *VerbPhrase* is re-written, using rule 3, as *Verb NounPhrase*. To re-write *Verb*, we try rule 9. This fails because the word in the sequence does not match the terminal *sees*. It does, however, match the right side of rule 10, and after also re-writing *NounPhrase* as *Determiner Noun*, we get the parse tree of Figure 8.5.

At this point, parsing breaks down. Though we have checked all the words in the sequence, we have not fully re-written the starting symbol. We must backtrack to seek other ways of re-writing previous symbols, dismantling the parse tree and working back through the sequence as we go.

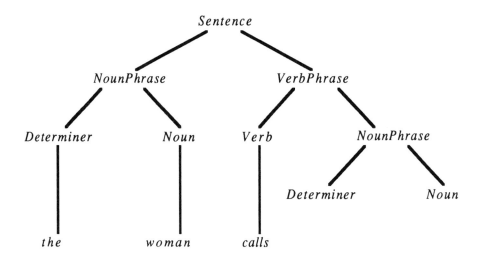

Figure 8.5 The parse tree after applying rules 3, 10 and 2
in re-writing *VerbPhrase*

There is no other way to re-write *Verb*, so "calls", the last word of the
sequence, remains to be checked. By using rule 4 instead of rule 3, we can
re-write *VerbPhrase* as *Verb*. After applying rule 10 again and re-
checking the word "calls", we complete the re-write of the starting symbol,
leaving the parse tree of Figure 8.6.

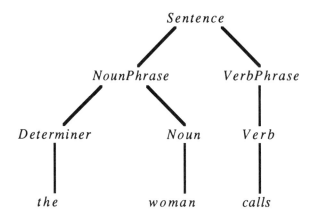

Figure 8.6 The parse tree after fully re-writing the starting symbol

At this point, having checked every word of the sequence, we confirm it as a
sentence of the language which the grammar describes.

8.2   Definite Clause Grammar

You probably realised that our parsing strategy for the phrase-structure
grammar was exactly Prolog's search strategy in trying to satisfy a goal.   To
automate the laborious process which we described in the previous section,
we have only to represent the rules of the grammar as clauses of a Prolog
program and construct a goal which provides the sequence of words as input
and yields the parse tree as output.   In Prolog's grammar rules notation, the
phrase-structure grammar of Figure 8.1 is:

```
sentence -->
    noun_phrase,
    verb_phrase.

noun_phrase -->
    determiner,
    noun.

verb_phrase -->
    verb,
    noun_phrase.
verb_phrase -->
    verb.

determiner --> [the].
determiner --> [a].

noun --> [woman].
noun --> [girl].

verb --> [sees].
verb --> [calls].
```

Each grammar rule is a structure with functor --> and arity 2.   The components are the left and right sides of the rule.   Non-terminal symbols must
conform to the syntax of Prolog atoms.   Terminals may be atoms or variables and are enclosed in square brackets.

When a program is loaded into the Prolog system, clauses with functor
--> are transformed into clauses of standard Prolog.   A grammar rule which
re-writes a symbol as non-terminals is transformed into a Prolog rule whose
head is the left side of the grammar rule and whose body comprises the
symbols on the right side as conjoined sub-goals.   The rule is augmented by
two arguments.   In the head of the rule, the first argument represents the
sequence to be parsed.   It is given as the first argument to the first sub-goal.
For each sub-goal, the first argument represents the sequence remaining to
be parsed and the second represents the sequence left after a component
has been parsed.   The second argument in the head of the rule is the

sequence left after the last sub-goal has been satisfied. For instance, the grammar rule:

```
noun_phrase -->
    determiner,
    noun.
```

is transformed into the rule:

```
noun_phrase(L0, L2) :-
    determiner(L0, L1),
    noun(L1, L2).
```

The sequence of words to be parsed and the sequence remaining after parsing are represented as lists. The whole rule is to be interpreted as stating:

"The list L0 begins with a noun phrase and L2 is the list which remains after it has been removed if:

- The list L0 begins with a determiner and L1 is the list which remains after it has been removed, and

- The list L1 begins with a noun and L2 is the list which remains after it has been removed."

A grammar rule which re-writes a symbol as a terminal is transformed into a Prolog rule whose body is a call to the built-in predicate 'C', defined as:

'C'/3[1]
The goal succeeds if the first argument is a list, the second is its head and the third is its tail."

The rule:

```
noun --> [woman].
```

is transformed into:

```
noun(L0, L1) :-
    'C'(L0, woman, L1).
```

The rule is to be interpreted as stating:

---

[1]The name of this predicate varies between implementations of the language.

"The list L0 begins with the noun "woman" and L1 is the list which remains after it has been removed if L0 has the atom woman as its head and the list L1 as its tail."

A Prolog grammar rule can have any sequence of terminals and non-terminals on its right side. Adjacent terminals can be put in a single list; in the rule shown in Figure 8.7, we write [r, s] instead of [r], [s]. Figure 8.7 illustrates the mechanism for translating a grammar rule into a Prolog rule.

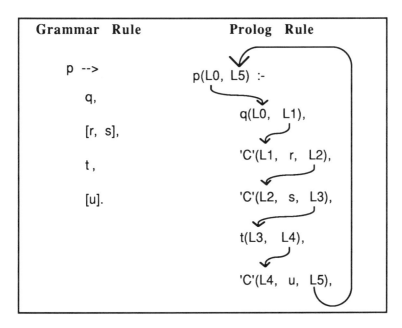

Figure 8.7 Translation of a grammar rule into a Prolog rule

In section 8.2.2, we give an example of a rule from a grammar of English that has a terminal and a non-terminal on the right side.

To determine whether our example sequence is a sentence, we call the goal:

```
?- sentence([the, woman, calls], [ ]).
yes
```

The second argument is the empty list because in parsing we wish to check all the words of the sequence.

This Prolog grammar is only a partial solution to the parsing problem. It discriminates between sentences of the language and sequences which are not sentences, but it does not produce a parse tree for a sentence. To do this, we add an argument to each grammar rule and build the parse tree up by progressive substitution, exactly as we did in the procedure for sentence/1 in section 2.5. The revised grammar, including some more terminal symbols, is:

```
sentence(s(Np, Vp)) -->
    noun_phrase(Np),
    verb_phrase(Vp).

noun_phrase(np(D, N)) -->
    determiner(D),
    noun(N).

verb_phrase(vp(V, Np)) -->
    verb(V),
    noun_phrase(Np).
verb_phrase(vp(V)) -->
    verb(V).

determiner(d(the)) --> [the].
determiner(d(a)) --> [a].

noun(n(woman)) --> [woman].
noun(n(women)) --> [women].
noun(n(girl)) --> [girl].
noun(n(girls)) --> [girls].

verb(v(see)) --> [sees].
verb(v(see)) --> [see].
verb(v(call)) --> [calls].
verb(v(call)) --> [call].
```

When a grammar rule with arguments is transformed into a clause of standard Prolog, the two extra arguments are added as the last two. So, the grammar rule:

```
sentence(s(Np, Vp)) -->
    noun_phrase(Np),
    verb_phrase(Vp).
```

becomes the rule:

```
sentence(s(Np, Vp), L0, L2) :-
    noun_phrase(Np, L0, L1),
    verb_phrase(Vp, L1, L2).
```

and the grammar rule:

```
noun(n(woman)) --> [woman].
```

becomes the rule:

```
noun(n(woman), L0, L1) :-
    'C'(L0, woman, L1).
```

The call to parse the example sentence is now:

```
?- sentence(S, [the, woman, calls], [ ]).
S = s(np(d(the), n(woman)), vp(v(call)))
```

On the parse tree, we choose to represent the verb by its *infinitive* form, rather than by the form with suffix "s" that occurs in the input. In replacing the inflected forms of verbs that occur in sentences, we aim to simplify the processing in the phase that would follow parsing. We do not consider that phase in this chapter, but it is evident that the actions in it would be more easily programmed if its procedures deal with just a single form of each verb.

A grammar in Prolog which builds a parse tree is called a *definite clause grammar*. A definite clause grammar is a much more powerful mechanism for describing natural language than a phrase-structure grammar. We investigate two features of natural language which can be readily captured.

8.2.1 Person and number agreement

Consider the following pairs of sequences:

[1] A woman calls
[2] *A woman call

and:

[3] The women call
[4] *A women call

In each pair, the two sequences have an identical phrase structure: they are constructed from the same components in the same order, but only the first is a sentence of English. We indicate that a sequence is not a sentence by the asterisk.

Sequence [2] is not acceptable because it does not conform to the rule of English which prescribes that the verb in the verb phrase must agree in person and number with the noun phrase which is the subject of the sentence. This is a *context-sensitive* rule. The question of whether the verb in a verb phrase is valid depends on the context in which it occurs, namely the person and number of the subject noun phrase which precedes it. The rule is illustrated in Figure 8.8 by the example of the parse tree for the sentence: "A woman calls". The figure illustrates a second context-sensitive rule of English: that a determiner and a noun which are components of a noun phrase must agree in number. It is this rule which leads us to reject sequence [4].

155

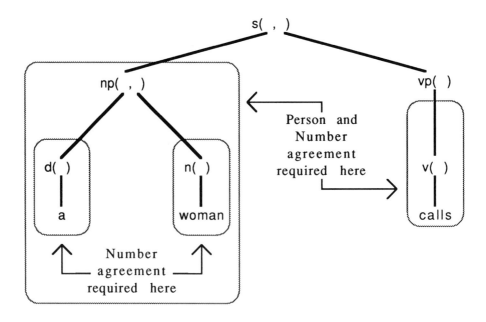

Figure 8.8 Context-sensitive rules apply between components of a sentence

To capture these rules, we introduce an argument to carry the contextual information:

```
sentence(s(Np, Vp)) -->
    noun_phrase(Np, F),
    verb_phrase(Vp, F).
```

This rule states that a verb phrase and a following noun phrase are only valid components of a sentence if each is of form F. A revised rule describing a noun phrase expresses the second context-sensitive rule:

```
noun_phrase(np(D, N), form(third, Number)) -->
    determiner(D, Number),
    noun(N, Number).
```

The form of the noun phrase is represented by a structure with functor form and arity 2, the two components denoting person and number. Every noun phrase composed of a determiner and a noun is in the third person.

In the rules which describe the terminal symbols, we substitute the value singular or plural for the variable Number:

```
determiner(d(the), _) --> [the].
determiner(d(a), singular) --> [a].
```

```
noun(n(woman), singular) --> [woman].
noun(n(women), plural) --> [women].
noun(n(girl), singular) --> [girl].
noun(n(girls), plural) --> [girls].
```

When the determiner is "the", no substitution is made because this word occurs in both singular and plural noun phrases: "the woman" and "the women".

The rules for a verb phrase are:

```
verb_phrase(vp(V, Np), F) -->
    verb(V, F),
    noun_phrase(Np, _).
verb_phrase(vp(V), F) -->
    verb(V, F).
```

A noun phrase following the verb is not subject to rules of agreement with any other component, so in the first clause, we use the anonymous variable in the call to noun_phrase/4. The clauses for verb/4 specify the forms of each verb that the grammar recognises:

```
verb(v(see), form(first, singular)) --> [see].
verb(v(see), form(second, singular)) --> [see].
verb(v(see), form(third, singular)) --> [sees].
verb(v(see), form(_, plural)) --> [see].
verb(v(call), form(first, singular)) --> [call].
verb(v(call), form(second, singular)) --> [call].
verb(v(call), form(third, singular)) --> [calls].
verb(v(call), form(_, plural)) --> [call].
```

The extended grammar enforces both context-sensitive rules, as the following examples show:

```
?- sentence(_, [a, woman, calls], [ ]).
yes

?- sentence(_, [a, woman, call], [ ]).
no

?- sentence(_, [the, women, call], [ ]).
yes

?- sentence(_, [a, women, call], [ ]).
no
```

Exercises 8.2.1

(a) Write clauses for noun_phrase/4 to recognise the personal pronouns: "I", "we", "me", "us", "you", "he", "she", "it", "they", "him", "her" and "them", as used in sentences such as: "She sees me" and "They call you".

8.2.2   Surface structure and deep structure

We recognise that a pair of sentences such as:

[5] The woman sees the girl
[6] The girl is seen by the woman

are similar despite their different phrase structures.   Sentence [5] is in the *active voice*. You can think of a sentence in the active voice as being one in which the subject noun phrase describes the agent that is carrying out the action.   Sentence [6] describes the same action, but is in the *passive voice*. The subject noun phrase is not the agent but is the participant to whom the action is applied.   Linguists account for the relationship between sentences such as [5] and [6] by postulating that the two have an identical *deep structure* and that the *surface structure* of [6] is derived from the deep structure by the application of a *transformational rule*, specifically the *passivization* rule.   Besides defining a re-ordering of noun phrases, this rule specifies a change in the form of the verb and the introduction of the preposition "by".   It is illustrated in Figure 8.9.

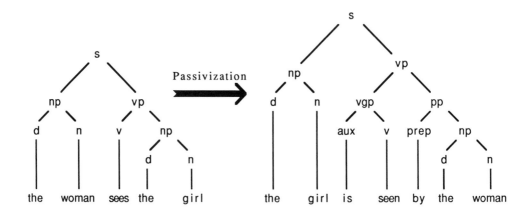

Figure 8.9 The relationship between active and passive sentences is explained by a transformational rule

We would like our grammar to carry out the transformation in reverse, producing a parse tree to represent the deep structure whether the sentence given is active or passive. The problem in producing this representation is that when we parse the subject noun phrase, we do not know where on the parse tree it belongs. If the sentence is passive in voice, which we identify only when we parse the verb, the subject noun phrase has to be moved to a position within the verb phrase. In the extended grammar, the initial noun phrase, which is recognised in a call to noun_phrase/4, is simply passed as argument in a call to verb_phrase/6. The parse tree is returned from this call:

```
sentence(Parse_tree, Voice) -->
    noun_phrase(Np, F),
    verb_phrase(Np, F, Parse_tree, Voice).
```

The second argument in the call to sentence/4 is an indicator of the surface structure of the sentence: active or passive in voice.

The procedure for verb_phrase/6 is:

```
verb_phrase(SNp, F, s(SNp, vp(V, Np)), active) -->
    verb(V, F),
    noun_phrase(Np, _).
verb_phrase(SNp, F, s(SNp, vp(V)), active) -->
    verb(V, F).
verb_phrase(SNp, F, s(Np, vp(V, SNp)), passive) -->
    verb_group(V, F),
    agent_phrase(Np).
```

The first two clauses specify that SNp, the variable denoting the subject noun phrase which was given as input, is the first branch of the parse tree whose root is the node s. In these clauses, the voice is active and there is no transformation of the surface structure in obtaining the deep structure. The third clause specifies that in the passive voice SNp is identified as the second branch of the vp node of the tree and the noun phrase which in the deep structure occupies the position of the subject is Np, obtained from parsing an agent phrase after the verb group. The rules for verb group and agent phrase are:

```
verb_group(V, F) -->
    auxiliary_verb(F),
    verb(V, form(past_participle)).

agent_phrase(Np) -->
    [by],
    noun_phrase(Np, _).
```

The rules which introduce new terminal symbols are:

```
auxiliary_verb(form(first,singular)) --> [am].
auxiliary_verb(form(second, singular)) --> [are].
auxiliary_verb(form(third, singular)) --> [is].
auxiliary_verb(form(_, plural)) --> [are].

verb(v(see), form(past_participle)) --> [seen].
verb(v(call), form(past_participle)) --> [called].
```

In the passive voice, person and number agreement are to be enforced between the subject noun phrase and the auxiliary verb.

With these extensions, the grammar produces identical deep structures for corresponding active and passive sentences:

```
?- sentence(S, V1, [the, woman, sees, the, girl], [ ]),
    sentence(S, V2, [the, girl, is, seen, by, the, woman], [ ]).
S = s(np(d(the), n(woman)), vp(v(see), np(d(the), n(girl))))
V1 = active
V2 = passive
```

A feature of the passive voice which the grammar does not recognise is the possibility that the agent phrase may be omitted, as in: "The girl is seen". To handle this, we add a second clause to the procedure for agent_phrase/3:

```
agent_phrase(someone) --> [ ].
```

In this rule, the symbol [ ] is a special terminal symbol denoting the empty sequence. The rule is transformed into the fact:

```
agent_phrase(someone, L, L).
```

The fact states:

> "An agent phrase is recognised without removing any element from the list L. Such an agent phrase is represented by the atom: someone."

With this refinement, we get:

```
?- sentence(S, V, [the, girl, is, seen], [ ]).
S = s(np(someone), vp(v(see), np(d(the), n(girl))))
V = passive
```

Exercises 8.2.2

(a) Some noun phrases do not have a determiner: "The women sing songs". Write a clause for noun_phrase/4 to describe this feature of English.

8.3   Adding a Dictionary

Extending our grammar to recognise more English verbs would lead to a
rapid escalation in its size because we would have to add a rule for each
form of each verb.   We can prevent this by using the facility to include calls
to ordinary Prolog procedures on the right side of grammar rules.   The idea
is to describe the general form of a verb in a single grammar rule and
include all the particular verbs and their forms as clauses of standard Prolog
in a separate dictionary.   The grammar rule is:

```
verb(v(Inf), F) -->
    [V],
    {is_verb(V, Inf, F)}.
```

The call to is_verb/3 is a call to a Prolog procedure.   By enclosing it in curly
brackets, we ensure that it is not augmented by the two extra arguments
when the grammar rule is transformed into standard Prolog:

```
verb(v(Inf), F, L0, L1) :-
    'C'(L0, V, L1),
    is_verb(V, Inf, F).
```

The rule is to be intepreted as stating:

> "The list L0 has a verb at its head and L1 is the list which re-
> mains after it has been removed if V is the head of L0, L1 is the
> tail of L0 and V is a verb of form F whose infinitive form is Inf."

The procedure for is_verb/3 is:

```
is_verb(Inf, Inf, form(first, singular)) :-
    verb_entry(Inf, _, _).
is_verb(Inf, Inf, form(second, singular)) :-
    verb_entry(Inf, _, _).
is_verb(V, Inf, form(third, singular)) :-
    verb_entry(Inf, V, _).
is_verb(Inf, Inf, form(_, plural)) :-
    verb_entry(Inf, _, _).
is_verb(V, Inf, form(past_participle)) :-
    verb_entry(Inf, _, V).
```

Each clause for verb_entry/3 constitutes the dictionary entry for a single
verb; the first component is the infinitive form, the second is the third
person singular form and the third is the past participle:

```
verb_entry(see, sees, seen).
verb_entry(call, calls, called).
```

The dictionary entries might also include information about the meaning of words. For instance, if the entry for the verb "see" included the information that the word referred to an action carried out by an animate being and the entries for nouns indicated whether the word denoted an animate being or an inanimate object, we would be able to reject a sequence such as: "The brick sees the girl" even though its phrase structure is valid and it respects context-sensitive rules. How much semantic information to use in parsing depends on the application for which a grammar is to be used. The point is that the grammar rules notation lets us include semantic or other tests of arbitrary complexity within a grammar simply by embedding Prolog sub-goals in curly brackets in the right sides of grammar rules.

Exercises 8.3

(a) Write a grammar rule for nouns and dictionary entries for them in the style of those for verbs.

(b) Extend the entries for verbs and nouns to include the semantic information described in this section and modify the grammar to enforce the semantic check referred to.

8.4 Pragmatic Issues in Parser Design

There are many issues to be considered in the design of a grammar and many different phrase-structure grammars for even the simplest language. In this section, we examine some of the main issues which you must bear in mind, and we point out some of the pitfalls to be avoided.

The question of efficiency is often an important consideration. A parser which does not backtrack over the input sequence is likely to be an efficient one. Consider the rules of our grammar which describe the structure of a verb phrase in the active voice:

```
verb_phrase(SNp, F, s(SNp, vp(V, Np)), active) -->
    verb(V, F),
    noun_phrase(Np, _).
verb_phrase(SNp, F, s(SNp, vp(V)), active) -->
    verb(V, F).
```

In processing the sentence: "The woman calls", Prolog backtracks over the word "calls", examining it when trying to use the first clause for verb_phrase/6 and again when using the second. The inefficiency is trivial, but would not be so if there were complex dictionary look-up or semantic analysis routines associated with processing the word "calls". The backtracking occurs because the constituent verb is the first element of both rules. It can be eliminated by factoring out the common element into a single rule:

```
verb_phrase(SNp, F, s(SNp, vp(V, Np)), active) -->
    verb(V, F),
    object_np(Np).

object_np(Np) -->
    noun_phrase(Np, _).
object_np([ ]) -->  [ ].
```

By moving the choice point down to the rules for an object noun phrase, we eliminate the source of the inefficiency. However, this grammar of a verb phrase is only *weakly equivalent* to our first version: it recognises the same verb phrases, but it does not ascribe the same parse trees to them. You can see the differences by comparing Figure 8.6 with Figure 8.10.

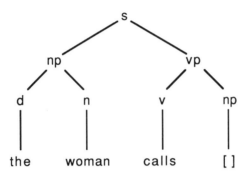

Figure 8.10 Parse tree for the sentence : "The woman calls" produced by the second grammar of verb phrases

For an efficient grammar of verb phrases which is *strongly equivalent*, we must construct the parse tree for the verb phrase after parsing the object noun phrase:

```
verb_phrase(SNp, F, s(SNp, Vp), active) -->
    verb(V, F),
    object_np(V, Vp).

object_np(V, vp(V, Np)) -->
    noun_phrase(Np, _).
object_np(V, vp(V)) -->  [ ].
```

A grammar which never backtracks over input is called a *deterministic* grammar. A non-deterministic grammar, though less efficient, has the merit that the structure of the parse tree it builds does mirror in a direct and natural way the hierarchy of its rules. Sometimes, the most natural way of describing a language is by phrase-structure rules that are left-recursive, and a direct translation into rules of a definite clause grammar is impossible.

An example is the phrase-structure grammar for a language of arithmetic expressions shown in Figure 8.11.

1	*Expression*	→	*Term*
2	*Expression*	→	*Expression AddOp Term*
3	*Term*	→	*Factor*
4	*Term*	→	*Term MultOp Factor*
5	*Factor*	→	*Integer*
6	*AddOp*	→	+
7	*AddOp*	→	-
8	*MultOp*	→	*
9	*MultOp*	→	/

Figure 8.11 A phrase-structure grammar for a language of arithmetic expressions

Assuming that we have a definition for *Integer*, the grammar ascribes to the expression: "4 - 3 + 5 * 6" a parse tree, shown in Figure 8.12, which represents both the precedence and the associativity of arithmetic operators.

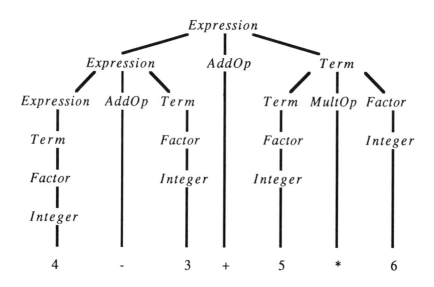

Figure 8.12 Parse tree for the expression: "4 - 3 + 5 * 6"

A naive translation of this grammar into a definite clause grammar yields the following clauses for expression/2:

```
expression -->
    term.
expression -->
    expression,
    add_op,
    term.
```

Though declaratively sound, the second clause is fatally flawed in its procedural interpretation:

> "An expression is found if an expression is found, followed by an adding operator and a term."

With this clause, Prolog would generate endless recursive sub-goals to find an expression. To prevent this, we replace the two rules defining *Expression* with one rule which recognises the first symbol of an expression and a second which recognises the symbols which optionally follow. In this way, we ensure that Prolog does progress through the input sequence. The rules are:

```
expression -->
    term,
    more_terms.

more_terms -->
    add_op,
    term,
    more_terms.
more_terms -->   [ ].
```

The remaining clauses of the grammar, including a similar treatment of the left recursion in the rules for *Term*, are:

```
term -->
    factor,
    more_factors.

more_factors -->
    mult_op,
    factor,
    more_factors.
more_factors -->   [ ].

factor -->
    [N],
    {integer(N)}.
```

```
add_op --> ['+'].
add_op --> ['-'].

mult_op --> ['*'].
mult_op --> ['/'].
```

Though the grammar now has a sound procedural interpretation, it is not obvious how we are to construct a satisfactory parse tree. Reflecting directly the rules used in parsing an expression, we arrive at that of Figure 8.13.

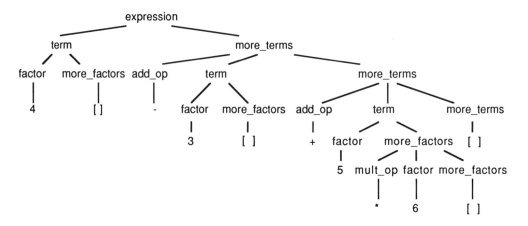

Figure 8.13 A possible parse tree for the expression: " 4 - 3 + 5 * 6"

This is unlikely to be a satisfactory representation of an arithmetic expression, whatever processing is to be applied to it after syntactic analysis, because it obscures the structure of the expression. A more useful parse tree for the same expression is shown in Figure 8.14.

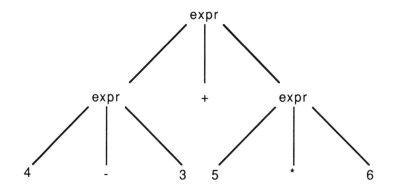

Figure 8.14 A clearer parse tree for the expression: "4 - 3 + 5 * 6"

As the example in section 8.2.2 showed, the form of a parse tree is not constrained by the order of rule applications, and we can construct the parse tree of Figure 8.14 by manipulation of the arguments in the grammar rules. The resulting program is:

```
expression(E) -->
    term(T),
    more_terms(T, E).

more_terms(Part, Complete) -->
    add_op(Op),
    term(T),
    more_terms(expr(Part, Op, T), Complete).
more_terms(T, T) -->  [ ].

term(T) -->
    factor(F),
    more_factors(F, T).

more_factors(Part, Complete) -->
    mult_op(Op),
    factor(F),
    more_factors(expr(Part, Op, F), Complete).
more_factors(F, F) -->  [ ].

factor(N) -->
    [N],
    {integer(N)}.

add_op('+') -->  ['+'].
add_op('-') -->  ['-'].

mult_op('*') -->  ['*'].
mult_op('/') -->  ['/'].
```

We get:

```
?- expression(E, [4, -, 3, +, 5, *, 6], [ ]).
E = expr(expr(4, -, 3), +, expr(5, *, 6))

?- expression(E, [4, +, 3, *, 6, +, 5, +, 6], [ ]).
E = expr(expr(expr(4, +, expr(3, *, 6)), +, 5), +, 6)
```

The precedence of a mult_op over an add_op is enforced by the hierarchy of rules. We obtain the correct associativity for adjacent operators of equal precedence by the manner in which we combine sub-expressions in the arguments to the procedures for more_terms/4 and more_factors/4. In the first clause of each, the Part expression which is given as input argument is combined with the operator Op and the next term T (or factor F) into a structure that represents a sub-expression and is the first argument in a call to more_terms/4 (or more_factors/4). Thus, each sub-expression which has on its left a sub-expression with an operator of equal precedence is combined with that sub-expression before being joined to any on its right. How to enforce right-associativity within an identically-structured grammar, we leave to you as exercise 8.4(b).

Failure to specify the associativity of operators or connectives is a common source of *ambiguity* in a grammar. A grammar is ambiguous if it ascribes two or more different parse trees to a sentence or if a single parse tree can be ascribed by different sequences of rule applications. The following definite clause grammar for English sentences with conjunctions is ambiguous:

```
sentence_sequence(S) -->
    sentence(S).
sentence_sequence(conj(S1, C, S2)) -->
    sentence_sequence(S1),
    conjunction(C),
    sentence_sequence(S2).

conjunction(but) --> [but].
coinjunction(and) --> [and].
```

If "s1", "s2" and "s3" are valid sentences, the grammar ascribes two parse trees to the sentence: "s1 and s2 but s3", as shown in Figure 8.15.

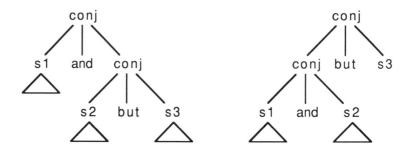

Figure 8.15 Two parse trees for the sentence: "s1 and s2 but s3"

The triangles represent portions of the parse tree not fully expanded.

It can be very hard to detect ambiguities in a complex grammar. In this, Prolog is a very valuable tool, for its search strategy is a means of checking all possible ways of deriving a parse tree for a sentence. We simply have to reject the answer which a call to parse a sentence first produces:

```
?- sentence_sequence(S, [s1, and, s2, but, s3], [ ]).
S = conj(s1, and, conj(s2, but, s3));

S = conj(conj(s1, and, s2), but, s3);
no
```

We could prevent Prolog finding the second parse on backtracking simply by placing a cut at the end of the second clause for sentence_sequence/3, but this would not resolve the ambiguity inherent in the grammar. It would merely ensure that, under the procedural interpretation of Prolog rules with the cut, just a single parse was produced. As the definition of ambiguity makes no mention of a procedure for applying rules, a definite clause grammar must be declaratively sound in order to meet the criterion for being unambiguous. This precludes use of the cut. To eliminate the ambiguity, we should re-write the rules, making clear the associativity of the conjunctions "and" and "or".

If we are designing a grammar for a query language or a programming language, it is essential that the grammar is unambiguous. However, all natural languages are rich in ambiguity, and grammars for them are necessarily ambiguous. For example, two parse trees may be ascribed to the sentence: "A good chemist dispenses with accuracy", as Figure 8.16 shows.

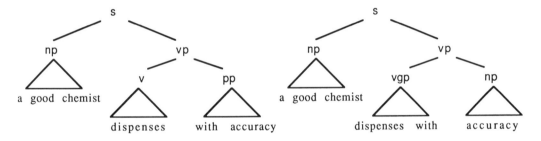

Figure 8-16 Two parse trees for the ambiguous sentence:
"A good chemist dispenses with accuracy"

Presumably, the first represents the intended meaning, but we cannot expect a grammar to discern this. The best we can hope for is that the grammar generates all possible interpretations of an ambiguous sentence and that the succeeding semantic analysis phase is able to to make the right choice among them.

Exercises 8.4

(a) An arithmetic expression may include brackets to override the normal precedence of operators. Extend the grammar to recognise brackets. The brackets should not appear on the parse tree, but it must reflect their effect on the meaning of the expression.

(b) Write a grammar of Boolean expressions, to include the operators "and" and "or". Assume that "and" is of greater precedence, that both are right-associative and that the terms of expressions are relational expressions. For example, the parse tree for the expression:

"8 = 3 + 5 or 7 > 9 * 2 or 3 = 5 * 10 and 5 = 7"

is as shown in Figure 8.17.

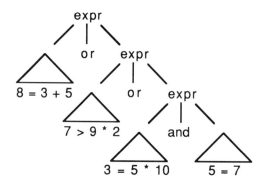

Figure 8.17 Parse tree showing precedence and associativity of Boolean operators

(c) Supplement the grammar you wrote for exercise 8.4(b) with a semantic analysis phase to evaluate the expression and return the atom true or false. Evaluation of sub-expressions should stop as soon as the value of the whole is known. The value of the expression in Figure 8.17 is known as soon as the leftmost sub-expression has been evaluated.

8.5   Summary

In this chapter, we have introduced the following ideas:

* A grammar is a set of rules for forming sentences of a language.

* A phrase-structure grammar expresses the rules in terms of components of the language and how they may be concatenated.

* The parsing problem is to determine whether a sequence of words is a sentence of a language and to produce a representation of the structure of the sentence if it is.

* The grammar rules notation enables a phrase-structure grammar to be

represented as a Prolog program, called a definite clause grammar. The parsing problem is solved by calling a procedure of the program as a goal.

- A definite clause grammar can capture features of natural language which are described by context-sensitive rules or by transformational rules.
- A definite clause grammar can have calls to Prolog procedures in the right side of its rules.

- Pragmatic issues you must consider when writing a definite clause grammar include its efficiency and the problems of left-recursive rules and of ambiguity.

- The cut should not be used in a definite clause grammar because it has only a procedural interpretation and does not resolve ambiguity.

Chapter 9

Testing, Debugging and Documentation

How to test a Prolog program, how to find faults in it when it gives erroneous results and how to describe its behaviour are questions which have pervaded the whole of Part 1 of this book. However, our emphasis has been on teaching good design, based on the programmers' toolkit. Illustrating the methods by which we may check the soundness of our programming efforts has been incidental to our main purpose. In this chapter, we bring together the lessons about testing, debugging and documentation which have been implicit in what has gone before. As the toolkit equips you to solve problems, so we now offer a set of prescriptions which you will be able to follow to check the validity of the solutions you devise.

9.1 Testing

The first consideration in designing test data for a procedure is to ensure that every clause is exercised by at least one of the tests. If the procedure was developed by case analysis, this is easy: we identify an item of test data to exemplify each case, and we use the outcome of the third stage of case analysis, in which we identified the processing required for each case, to predict the result of each test. In all testing, it is essential that you identify the correct outcome before running the test. Otherwise, it is too easy, given the natural reluctance of every programmer to admit that his creation may be faulty, to persuade yourself that the observed result is the correct one.

As an example, we consider how to test the procedure for reduce/4 which we gave in section 6.1.2 as part of the solution to the Soundex coding problem. We identified three recursive cases. Figure 9.1 shows test data for each. The actual result is as expected in each test:

```
?- reduce([97, 98], 1, _, Res).
Res = [98];
no
```

Case	Test data in a call		
	Arguments input		Expected result
Current letter is a vowel, "h", "w" or "y"	[97, 98] 1 _		[98]
Current letter is the same as the preceding one	[98, 99] 1 98		[99]
Catch-all	[98, 99] 1 100		[98, 99]

Ascii codes: 97 = "a", 98 = "b", 99 = "c", 100 = "d"

Figure 9.1 Test data for recursive clauses of the procedure for reduce/4

```
?- reduce([98, 99], 1, 98, Res).
Res = [99];
no
```

```
?- reduce([98, 99], 1, 10, Res).
Res = [98, 99];
no
```

In these tests, we test the second base case indirectly, as the recursive cases reduce the input argument to the empty list.   We could exercise the clause for the first base case directly by a test such as:

```
?- reduce([99], 4, _, Res).
```

for which the expected result is:

```
Res = [ ];
no
```

Better, however, is to test it indirectly by calling the procedure with an input list for which we expect a list of the maximum length to be produced without exhausting the input.   In this way, we thoroughly check the arithmetic in the clause for the catch-all case:

```
?- reduce([98, 99, 100, 102, 103], 1, 99, Res).

Res= [98, 99, 100];
no
```

To check that a procedure which you intend to be deterministic is indeed so, you must always reject the first answer Prolog produces. If the procedure is deterministic, there will be no alternatives.

You must test a non-deterministic procedure very carefully to ensure that it can indeed be called with all the patterns of argument you envisage and that it produces exactly the intended alternative answers. In section 3.5, we gave two procedures for sub_list/2, and the answer to exercise 3.5(b) gives a third. The three behave identically when used to determine whether one list is a sublist of another, but their behaviours differ in quite subtle ways when they are used non-deterministically. The version developed by case analysis and the first of the two developed by analysis of logical relationships can safely be used to generate sublists of a given list, though the latter generates duplicate sublists among its alternative answers. The third is unsound in this usage because it starts an endless series of recursive calls after producing its alternatives.

Testing a non-deterministic procedure includes checking what it does after it has exhausted the alternative answers, so test data, though it must be complex enough to exercise the procedure fully, must not be so elaborate that it is impractical for all the answers to be enumerated. This is particularly important in the case of procedures for utility predicates, which we expect to be used to generate values. In section 4.3, we tested the procedure for in_range_integer/3 by a call:

```
?- in_range_integer(1, N, 10).
```

rather than:

```
?- in_range_integer(1, N, 500).
```

Sometimes, we have to modify a procedure to constrain the set of values to a size which enables it to be readily enumerated. In section 12.4.1, we give a utility procedure which computes the day of the week on which a given date falls or generates dates which do fall on a given day. Because there are so many alternatives in the second usage, we modify the procedure to constrain a lower-level procedure which generates successive months to generate just two for testing purposes.

The discipline of testing every procedure exhaustively is a very worthwhile one for the Prolog programmer. Save for the actions of the built-in predicates which modify the Prolog database, one procedure cannot have a side-effect on another. We can be absolutely confident that when we have tested a procedure as an independent component, its interaction with other components as part of a large program will not produce errors. The importance of this approach to testing becomes clear in Part 2, where we embark on much larger-scale Prolog programming and encounter a new set of difficulties, which can only be resolved if we are not also worrying about the correctness of low-level procedures. Nonetheless, our discipline of *incremental testing* is a severe one. You may not find the meticulous bottom-up approach to testing very appealing as you become experienced in Prolog programming and discover that you can often write correct programs without testing the numerous procedures individually. It is natural to want to short-circuit a laborious testing strategy; indeed, we did so ourselves by not testing the procedure for vowel_h_w_y/1 before using it in that for reduce/4! Inevitably, you will be faced with having to find faults in large programs whose procedures you have not tested separately. There is a comforting term for this process, which we use to try to shift the blame for faults from ourselves to the computer: *debugging*. Debugging, the process of finding and correcting our mistakes, is the subject of the next section.

Exercises 9.1

(a) Thoroughly test the procedure for permute/2 which you wrote using remove/3 in answer to exercise 3.4(a). What limitations do you find? Can you write a different procedure for the predicate which overcomes the limitations?

9.2 Debugging

A characteristic of programming is the mis-match between cause and effect: a small fault can make a large program produce wildly inaccurate results. This is strikingly true of Prolog, where typing mistakes are liable to alter the meaning of a program, instead of giving rise to faulty syntax. The first stage in debugging is to proof-read your program very carefully. The most obvious mistake is to mis-spell the functor of a structure or the name of a variable. Equally common, but less easy to spot, are the following:

- Typing "." instead of "," before the last of a series of conjoined sub-goals. The last sub-goal drops out of the procedure body to be treated by Prolog as a fact.

- Omitting "," between arguments. When this mistake occurs in the head of a clause, Prolog interprets the clause as belonging to a procedure of a different arity; in a sub-goal, it results in a procedure call of the wrong arity.

- Typing a variable with an initial lower-case letter. The supposed variable becomes an atom and does not match as intended.

If a careful reading of the program text does not reveal any typing mistakes, the second stage of debugging is to examine the program as it runs. All Prolog systems have a debugging mode of operation, in which information about the behaviour of the user's program is displayed to him, but they differ widely in the views of program execution that they present. None is as sophisticated as the graphical illustrations we used in Chapters 2 and 3. We describe the most common, called the *procedure box* view of program execution. This view of the procedure for subordinate/2 is illustrated in Figure 9.2.

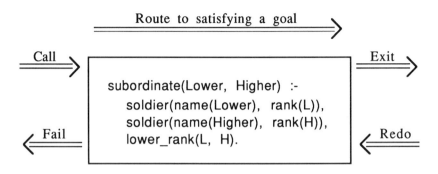

Figure 9.2 Procedure box view of the procedure for subordinate/2

When the procedure is called as a goal, the procedure box is entered by the *call port*. A series of sub-goals is generated, which are wholly contained within the box, and if these are satisfied the route out of the box is via the *exit* port. If the user rejects the answer produced, the box is re-entered at the *redo* port. The route out is via the exit port again if the goal is re-satisfiable or via the *fail* port if it is not. This view is repeated for all sub-goals. In debugging mode, Prolog displays a message as it passes through a port, showing the form of the procedure call at that port.

For illustration, we assume that the user has omitted the clause:

```
next_rank(captain, major).
```

from the procedure for next_rank/2. As a result, some calls to subordinate/2 produce errors:

```
?- subordinate(cathcart, peckem).
yes

?- subordinate(towser, aardvark).
yes

?- subordinate(towser, peckem).
no

?- debug.
Debug mode switched on.
yes

?- trace.
yes
```

```
?- subordinate(towser,  peckem).
   (1)  1   Call: subordinate(towser,peckem)
   (2)  2   Call: soldier(name(towser),rank(_6))
   (2)  2   Exit: soldier(name(towser),rank(sergeant))
   (3)  2   Call: soldier(name(peckem),rank(_7))
   (3)  2   Exit: soldier(name(peckem),rank(general))
   (4)  2   Call: lower_rank(sergeant,general)
   (5)  3   Call: next_rank(sergeant,general)
   (5)  3   Fail: next_rank(sergeant,general)
   (6)  3   Call: next_rank(sergeant,_61)
   (6)  3   Exit: next_rank(sergeant,lieutenant)
   (7)  3   Call: lower_rank(lieutenant,general)
   (8)  4   Call: next_rank(lieutenant,general)
   (8)  4   Fail: next_rank(lieutenant,general)
   (9)  4   Call: next_rank(lieutenant,_80)
   (9)  4   Exit: next_rank(lieutenant,captain)
  (10)  4   Call: lower_rank(captain,general)
  (11)  5   Call: next_rank(captain,general)
  (11)  5   Fail: next_rank(captain,general)
  (12)  5   Call: next_rank(captain,_99)
  (12)  5   Fail: next_rank(captain,_99)
  (10)  4   Redo: lower_rank(captain,general)
  (10)  4   Fail: lower_rank(captain,general)
   (9)  4   Redo: next_rank(lieutenant,_80)
   (9)  4   Fail: next_rank(lieutenant,_80)
   (7)  3   Redo: lower_rank(lieutenant,general)
   (7)  3   Fail: lower_rank(lieutenant,general)
   (6)  3   Redo: next_rank(sergeant,_61)
   (6)  3   Fail: next_rank(sergeant,_61)
   (4)  2   Redo: lower_rank(sergeant,general)
   (4)  2   Fail: lower_rank(sergeant,general)
   (3)  2   Redo: soldier(name(peckem),rank(_7))
   (3)  2   Fail: soldier(name(peckem),rank(_7))
   (2)  2   Redo: soldier(name(towser),rank(_6))
   (2)  2   Fail: soldier(name(towser),rank(_6))
   (1)  1   Redo: subordinate(towser,peckem)
   (1)  1   Fail: subordinate(towser,peckem)
no
```

The built-in predicates used in this sequence are:

debug/0
The debug mode of operation is switched on.

trace/0
Debug mode is switched on if it is not already on. In a traced execution, a message is displayed at each port of every goal and sub-goal of a program's execution.

In the traced execution, each message gives the *invocation number* in brackets, the *depth count*, the name of the port and the goal which Prolog is trying to satisfy. Each of a series of conjoined sub-goals, for example the goals: ?- soldier(name(towser), rank(_6)), ?- soldier(name(peckem), rank(_7)) and ?- lower_rank(sergeant,general), which are sub-goals of the top-level goal, has the same depth count. It denotes the number of goals which have been called but whose execution has not ended. Every procedure call has a unique invocation number, including, for example, the recursive calls to lower_rank/2 at invocations 4, 7 and 10. The procedure box view has a parallel in the system of boxes and numbers which we used in Chapters 2 and 3 to describe the procedural behaviour of Prolog. In Figure 2.1, there are three goal invocations, each shown in a separate box. The depth of the goal in box **1** is 1, and that of the sub-goals in boxes **2.1** and **2.2** is 2.

Knowing the fault in the program, you probably spotted in the trace of its execution that the error was the failure of invocation 12. However, an exhaustive trace produces too much information too rapidly for a user to have a realistic chance of finding a fault. If you have no clue about where the faults lie, for there will certainly be several, debugging a large program in this way is a hopeless proposition. You should never get into the situation of needing to try. If you follow our guidelines on testing even partially, you will have confined the faults to just those procedures which you have not tested bottom-up. This is much more promising: we have a chance of finding faults when we know where to look. Also, the Prolog debugging system allows the programmer to focus on the suspect parts of a program by *leashing* the execution of it and by setting *spy-points*, and in this way the amount of information produced can be reduced to manageable proportions.

When the debugging system is leashed, the display halts at some or all of the ports of a procedure invocation to allow the user to examine the progress of the computation and to specify how it should proceed. The behaviour of the built-in predicate leash varies somewhat between implementations, but a typical definition is:

leash/1
The leashing mode of the display is set according to the form of the argument in the call, as follows:

off   The display does not stop.
loose The display stops at call ports.
half   The display stops at call and redo ports.
tight The display stops at call, redo and fail ports.
full   The display stops at all ports.

When the display stops, the user inputs a single character to indicate the manner in which debugging should proceed. Once again, the options vary, but the most useful are:

c Creep through program execution. The display stops at the next leashed port. Use this option when you think you are in the region of a fault.

s Skip tracing this goal. This option is available only at call and redo ports. If our procedure for soldier/2 had sub-goals but we believed them to be fault-free, we would use this option to go on quickly to the call to lower_rank/2.

q Quasi-skip tracing this goal. This option is available only at call and redo ports. Tracing is skipped, except of sub-goals on which spy-points have been set. This option is particularly useful when you wish to see the form of successive recursive calls to a procedure whose execution you are spying.

f Fail the call. Use this at the call port of a procedure when you can see from the form of the goal that it will fail, for instance, when a procedure has a number of clauses handling different cases and the call in question is handled by a later clause. You are spared watching Prolog test the call against the wrong cases. Notice that you could not use this option if the goal, though failing, had a side-effect on the Prolog database on which a procedure elsewhere in the program depended. This illustrates the point we made in section 7.1.3 about the difficulty of testing programs which use global variables.

r Re-try the current goal by transferring to its call port. This is very useful when you suspect you have overlooked a fault. If r is followed by an integer n, the goal re-tried is the procedure with invocation number n. This option enables you to revert to any stage of program execution. However, modifications to the Prolog database are not undone, nor are other side-effects of program execution.

a Abort execution. This is the right action once you have spotted a fault. In the example, we could have aborted execution after the failure of invocation 12. Once we have identified the fault, we gain nothing by watching Prolog continue.

Spy points are set by calls to the built-in predicate spy:

spy/1
The argument in the call is either a structure of the form: P/A or an atom. In the first case, a spy point is set on the procedure for the predicate P with arity A. In the second, one is set on each procedure for the named predicate, whatever its arity.

They are removed by calling nospy/1, whose argument has the same form as that in a call to spy/1. Spy points are removed from the procedures for the named predicates. Alternatively, a call to nodebug/0 removes all spy points and switches off the debug mode.

When a spy point has been set on a procedure, program execution proceeds normally until the spied procedure is called. The message for the call port is then displayed, and unless leashing is off, Prolog halts for the user to select an option for continued execution. When Prolog leaves the exit or the fail port of the spied procedure, normal execution resumes and halts only when a spied procedure is called again. This is an alternative to exhaustive tracing by trace as a means of observing program behaviour. By careful leashing and use of spy-points, the debugging example could be shortened to:

```
?- subordinate(towser, peckem).
no

?- debug.
Debug mode switched on.
yes

?- spy(lower_rank/2).
Spy-points set on:
    lower_rank/2
yes

?- leash(half).
Leashing set to half (call, redo)
yes

?- subordinate(towser, peckem).
   (4)  2  Call: lower_rank(sergeant,general) c
   (5)  3  Call: next_rank(sergeant,general) s
   (5)  3  Fail: next_rank(sergeant,general)
   (6)  3  Call: next_rank(sergeant,_61) s
   (6)  3  Exit: next_rank(sergeant,lieutenant)
   (7)  3  Call: lower_rank(lieutenant,general) c
   (8)  4  Call: next_rank(lieutenant,general)  s
   (8)  4  Fail: next_rank(lieutenant,general)
   (9)  4  Call: next_rank(lieutenant,_80) s
   (9)  4  Exit: next_rank(lieutenant,captain)
  (10)  4  Call: lower_rank(captain,general) c
  (11)  5  Call: next_rank(captain,general) s
  (11)  5  Fail: next_rank(captain,general)
  (12)  5  Call: next_rank(captain,_99) s
  (12)  5  Fail: next_rank(captain,_99) a

execution aborted
no
```

Though spy-points reduce the verbiage that the debugging mode of operation generates, they depend for effect on you having assessed correctly where a program's faults are likely to be. Of course, you should always make this assessment before starting your debugging attempts. Otherwise, you will be confused by the output from Prolog in debugging mode, to the point where you may overlook even a fault which is staring you in the face.

9.3   An Enhanced Interpreter for Debugging

When we have difficulty in expressing in Prolog the logic of a complex predicate, our first attempts are likely to contain many faults. A large program which includes such procedures untested suffers from having faults occurring not singly but in clusters, and is particularly tiresome to debug. We risk repeating several times a cycle in which we watch a traced execution of the program, find and correct the first fault that we notice, but discover that the program fails again scarcely further on in its execution. If the debugging system allowed us to correct the sub-goal which had erroneously failed, program execution could resume until the next fault manifested itself, and we would break the cycle. In this section, we extend the interpreter of section 7.2.2 to support this facility.

A failure of a sub-goal in the object program causes a call to satisfy/2 in the interpreter also to fail. Our method is to add another clause for satisfy/2 to detect a failing goal in the object program and then, by an interaction with the user, to determine whether the goal should have succeeded. The procedure is:

```
satisfy(true, 'match with a fact') :- !.
satisfy((Goal, Goals), and(Proof, Proofs)) :- !,
    satisfy(Goal,  Proof),
    satisfy(Goals,  Proofs).
satisfy(';'(Goal, Goal), Proof) :- !,
    satisfy(Goal, Proof)   ;   satisfy(Goals, Proof).
satisfy(Goal, by(Goal, 'built-in predicate')) :-
    bip(Goal), !,
    call(Goal).
satisfy(Goal, by(Goal, Proof)) :-
    clause(Goal, Sub_goals),
    satisfy(Sub_goals, Proof).
satisfy(Goal, by(Goal, 'by user intervention')) :-
    satisfied(Goal).
```

We now use the cut because we do not wish the user to be asked about the failure of a goal if that goal had initially been handled by one of the first four clauses.

The procedure for satisfied/1 is:

```
satisfied(Goal)  :-
    write('Should  goal:  ?-  '),
    write(Goal),
    write(' fail  (y/n)  ?  '),
    get(110).                    % succeeds if next character input is "n"
```

If the user's answer is that Goal should not fail, the interpreter considers Goal to be satisfied by user intervention, and the execution of the object program continues. The proof of a goal which is satisfied in this way is a new special case:

```
special_case('by  user  intervention').
```

We illustrate the behaviour of the extended interpreter by reference to an object program which describes the family tree shown in Figure 9.3.

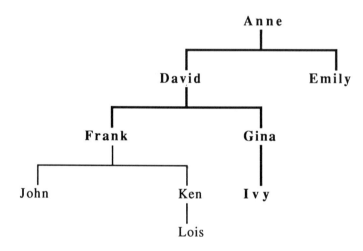

Figure 9.3 A family tree

```
mother(anne,david).
mother(anne,emily).
mother(gina,ivy).

father(david,frank).
father(david,gina).
```

Notice that the program omits some family relationships. It also includes a procedure for descendant/2, defining when one person is recognised as having another as a descendant:

```
descendant(Ancestor,Descendant)  :-
        parent(Ancestor,Descendant).
```

```
descendant(Ancestor,Descendant) :-
        parent(Ancestor,Child),
        descendant(Child,Descendant).

parent(Parent, Child) :-
        father(Parent,Child).
parent(Parent, Child) :-
        mother(Parent,Child).
```

Because of the omissions, calls fail unexpectedly:

```
?- descendant(anne, john).
no
```

We can identify the fault with the interpreter:

```
?- satisfy_and_display(descendant(anne,john)).
Should goal: ?- father(anne,john) fail (y/n) ? y
Should goal: ?- mother(anne,john) fail (y/n) ? y
Should goal: ?- parent(anne,john) fail (y/n) ? y
Should goal: ?- father(anne,_17) fail (y/n) ? y
Should goal: ?- father(david,john) fail (y/n) ? y
Should goal: ?- mother(david,john) fail (y/n) ? y
Should goal: ?- parent(david,john) fail (y/n) ? y
Should goal: ?- father(frank,john) fail (y/n) ? n

descendant(anne,john) by
  parent(anne,david) by
    mother(anne,david) by match with a fact
  descendant(david,john) by
    parent(david,frank) by
      father(david,frank) by match with a fact
    descendant(frank,john) by
      parent(frank,john) by
          father(frank,john) by user intervention

yes
```

However, if the failing goal is:

```
?- descendant(anne, lois).
no
```

our interpreter proves inadequate:

```
?- satisfy_and_display(descendant(anne,lois)).
Should goal: ?- father(anne,lois) fail (y/n) ? y
```

Should goal: ?- mother(anne,lois) fail (y/n) ? **y**
Should goal: ?- parent(anne,lois) fail (y/n) ? **y**
Should goal: ?- father(anne,_17) fail (y/n) ? **y**
Should goal: ?- father(david,lois) fail (y/n) ? **y**
Should goal: ?- mother(david,lois) fail (y/n) ? **y**
Should goal: ?- parent(david,lois) fail (y/n) ? **y**
Should goal: ?- father(frank,lois) fail (y/n) ? **y**
Should goal: ?- mother(frank,lois) fail (y/n) ? **y**
Should goal: ?- parent(frank,lois) fail (y/n) ? **y**
Should goal: ?- father(frank,_151) fail (y/n) ? **n**
Should goal: ?- father(_151,lois) fail (y/n) ? **n**

```
descendant(anne,lois) by
  parent(anne,david) by
    mother(anne,david) by match with a fact
  descendant(david,lois) by
    parent(david,frank) by
      father(david,frank) by match with a fact
    descendant(frank,lois) by
      parent(frank,_151) by
        father(frank,_151) by user intervention
      descendant(_151,lois) by
        parent(_151,lois) by
          father(_151,lois) by user intervention
```

yes

The problem is that when the user indicates that the goal: ?- father(frank, _151) should not fail, he means that there is a substitution for _151 for which the goal should succeed, not that it should succeed for all substitutions. We must modify the procedure for satisfied/1 so that when the incorrectly-failing goal includes variables, the user is asked to supply substitutions for which the goal should succeed. The modified procedure is:

```
satisfied(Goal) :-
    write('should goal: ?- '),
    write(Goal),
    write(' fail (y/n) ? '),
    get(110),              % succeeds if next printing character is "n"
    fill_vars(Goal, Goal).
```

In the procedure for fill_vars/2, we look for variables in the second argument. For each, we ask the user to supply a value. The purpose of passing the goal term also as the first argument is to enhance the display of the term, as values are substituted for variables in it:

```
fill_vars(_, Term) :-
    atomic(Term).
```

```
fill_vars(Goal, Term) :-
    compound(Term),
    Term =.. [Functor|Arguments],
    fill_vars_in_args(Goal, Arguments).
fill_vars(Goal, Term) :-
    var(Term),
    write('enter a value for: '),
    write(Term),
    nl,
    write(' for which: ?- '),
    write(Goal),
    nl,
    write(' should succeed: '),
    read(Value),
    fill(Goal, Value, Term).

fill_vars_in_args(_, [ ]).
fill_vars_in_args(Goal, [Arg|Args]) :-
    fill_vars(Goal, Arg),
    fill_vars_in_args(Goal, Args).
```

The user may be aware of numerous values which could be substituted for a variable to make a goal succeed. On backtracking, therefore, the procedure for fill_vars/2 must prompt the user to enter a different value and be re-satisfiable for so long as he does so. The user enters the atom: no_more to indicate that there are no more possible substitutions. We support the required behaviour through the call to fill/3. The procedure is:

```
fill(_, no_more, _) :- !,
    fail.
fill(_, Term, Term).
fill(Goal, _, Term) :-
    write('enter another value for: '),
    write(Term),
    nl,
    write(' for which: ?- '),
    write(Goal),
    nl,
    write(' should succeed (or "no_more"): '),
    read(Value),
    fill(Goal, Value, Term).
```

The series of questions and answers is as before until the user is asked about the goal: ?- father(frank,_151). We show the user first entering a value for the variable different from that which leads to the call succeeding. Frank has two sons, but it is Ken, not John, who is Lois' father.

```
?- satisfy_and_display(descendant(anne,lois)).
   . . .
```

Questions as before until:

```
   . . .
Should goal: ?- father(frank,_151) fail (y/n) ? n
Enter a value for: _151
  for which: ?- father(frank,_151)
  should succeed: john.
Should goal: ?- father(john,lois) fail (y/n) ? y
Should goal: ?- mother(john,lois) fail (y/n) ? y
Should goal: ?- parent(john,lois) fail (y/n) ? y
Should goal: ?- father(john,_225) fail (y/n) ? y
Should goal: ?- mother(john,_225) fail (y/n) ? y
Should goal: ?- parent(john,_225) fail (y/n) ? y
Should goal: ?- descendant(john,lois) fail (y/n) ? y
Enter another value for: _151
  for which: ?- father(frank,_151)
  should succeed (or "no_more"): ken.
Should goal: ?- father(ken,lois) fail (y/n) ? n
```

```
descendant(anne,lois) by
  parent(anne,david) by
    mother(anne,david) by match with a fact
  descendant(david,lois) by
    parent(david,frank) by
      father(david,frank) by match with a fact
    descendant(frank,lois) by
      parent(frank,ken) by
        father(frank,ken) by user intervention
      descendant(ken,lois) by
        parent(ken,lois) by
          father(ken,lois) by user intervention
```

yes

To find and correct the failing goals, the interpreter asked the user nineteen questions. If the user had entered the correct name when first asked about Frank's children, the total would have been twelve. This is rather tiresome for the user, and we would like to make fewer demands upon him. However, it is characteristic of Prolog that programs have a complex procedural behaviour even if they express simple logical relationships and their declarative interpretation can readily be grasped. Consider the following procedure for sort_integers/2:

```
sort_integers(List, Sorted) :-
    permute(List, Sorted),
    ordered(Sorted).
```

```
ordered([_]).                          % A one element list is ordered.
ordered([First, Second|Others]) :-
    First =< Second,
    ordered([Second|Others]).
```

The declarative interpretation is clear: Sorted is a sorted version of List if it is a permutation of List and elements of it are in order. Procedurally, the program's behaviour is complex, with extensive backtracking in the search for the correct permutation. If there was a fault in the program, finding it with our interpreter would necessitate a long series of questions because the interpreter intervenes to ask whether a goal should have failed every time Prolog backtracks in the object program. For example, if the fault is the omission of the clause for permute/2 which handles the base case and the failing goal is:

```
?-  sort_integers([3,1],S).
```

the user has to answer twelve questions before the interpreter produces the proof:

```
sort_integers([3,1],[1,3])  by
   permute([3,1],[1,3])  by
      remove(1,[3,1],[3])  by
         remove(1,[1],[ ]) by match with a fact
      permute([3],[3])  by
         remove(3,[3],[ ]) by match with a fact
         permute([ ],[ ]) by user intervention
   ordered([1,3])  by
      1=<3 by built-in predicate
      ordered([3]) by match with a fact
```

Included in the twelve is the question:

```
Should goal: ?- remove(_162,[ ],_165) fail (y/n) ?
```

which is asked four times, and the questions:

```
Should goal: ?- permute([ ],_110) fail (y/n) ?
```

and:

```
Should goal: ?- ordered([3,1]) fail (y/n) ?
```

each asked three times. To prevent repetition, we must record the user's answers in the interpreter and check them before asking each question. We record goals which should have succeeded as clauses for succeeded/1 and those which correctly failed as clauses for failed/1. In determining whether a goal may be satisfied by user intervention, we first check the answers already obtained. The revised procedure for satisfied/1 is:

```
satisfied(Goal)  :-
    succeeded(Goal).
satisfied(Goal)  :-
    failed(Previous),
    is_instance(Goal, Previous), !,
    fail.
satisfied(Goal)  :-
    write('Should goal: '),
    write(Goal),
    write(' fail (y/n) ? '),
    nl,
    get(110),
    fill_vars(Goal, Goal),
    assert(succeeded(Goal)).
satisfied(Goal)  :-
    assert(failed(Goal)),
    fail.
```

In this instance, we use database modification to accumulate results and prevent them being lost on backtracking. The first clause checks whether the current goal matches one which has already been satisfied. The second determines if there is a previously-failed goal of which the current goal is an instance. If this case holds, the cut and fail combination makes the call to satisfy/1 fail immediately.

The third and fourth clauses record the user's answers in the Prolog database. The third adds a clause for succeeded/1, recording an instance of the goal, each time the call to fill_vars/2 succeeds. The fourth clause is reached if the goal should correctly fail or if the user has enumerated all instances for which it should succeed, and it adds a clause for failed/1.

A term T1 is an instance of a term T2 if there is a set of substitutions which, applied to the variables in T2, make the two terms identical. Our implementation of is_instance/2 actually applies these substitutions:

```
?- is_instance(member(a, [a, b, c]), member(X, [X|Y])).
X = a
Y = [b,c]

?- is_instance(member(X, [X|Y]), member(a, [a, b, c])).
no
```

The procedure is:

```
is_instance(Term, Variable)  :-
    var(Variable),
    Variable = Term.
```

```
is_instance(Term1, Term2) :-
    atomic(Term2),
    Term1 == Term2.
is_instance(Term1, Term2) :-
    compound(Term1),
    compound(Term2),
    Term1 =.. [Func|T1args],
    Term2 =.. [Func|T2args],
    args_is_instance(T1args, T2args).

args_is_instance([ ], [ ]).
args_is_instance([T1|T1s], [T2|T2s]) :-
    is_instance(T1, T2),
    args_is_instance(T1s, T2s).
```

With these enhancements, the interpreter asks just five questions before displaying the proof:

```
?- satisfy_and_display(sort_integers([3,1],M)).

Should goal: ?- remove(_162,[ ],_165) fail (y/n) ? y
Should goal: ?- permute([ ],_110) fail (y/n) ? n
Enter a value for: _110
 for which: ?- permute([ ],_110)
 succeed: [ ].
Should goal: ?- ordered([3,1]) fail (y/n) ? y
Enter another value for: _110
 for which: ?- permute([ ],_110)
 should succeed (or "no_more"): no_more.
Should goal: ?- remove(_109,[1],_112) fail (y/n) ? n
Enter a value for: _109
 for which: ?- remove(_109,[1],_112)
 should succeed: 1.
Enter a value for: _112
 for which: ?- remove(1,[1],_112)
 should succeed: [ ].
Enter another value for: _112
 for which: ?- remove(1,[1],_112)
 should succeed (or "no_more"): no_more.
Enter another value for: _109
 for which: ?- remove(_109,[1],_112)
 should succeed (or "no_more"): no_more.
Should goal: ?- permute([1],_55) fail (y/n) ? n
Enter a value for: _55
 for which: ?- permute([1],_55)
 should succeed: [1].
Enter another value for: _55
```

for which: ?- permute([1],_55)
should succeed (or "no_more"): **no_more.**

sort_integers([3,1],[1,3]) by
    . . .
Proof as before.
    . . .

The study of Prolog programming environments is an area of active
research, and very sophisticated debugging tools are being developed for
these environments.   A useful summary of recent work is given in Brna et
al, 1987.   It is important not to forget, however, that no computer-based aid
to debugging can reveal the cause of program failure; it can only provide
better information about the symptoms of failure.   In simple cases, this
information may directly illuminate the fault, but as we show in Chapter 11,
this is not so for a complex problem.

Exercises 9.3

(a)   As it stands, the interpreter has an adding phase for the clauses for
succeeded/1 and failed/1 but not a collecting phase.   Write the
collecting phase.

(b)   Spy-points can be used in conjunction with the interpreter to reduce
further the number of questions the user has to answer.   Given the
following procedure for set_spy_point/1:

```
set_spy_point(Predicate/Arity)   :-
    assert(suspect(Predicate/Arity)).
```

modify the interpreter so that it only asks about calls to procedures
recorded as suspect.

9.4   Documentation

In this section, we focus on aspects of documentation which are particular to
Prolog.   We are concerned with documentation for the reader of a program,
not with end-user documentation, the principles of which apply whatever
the language of implementation.
    Program   documentation   should   explain   both   a   predicate   and   the
procedure that implements it.   Documentation for the predicate gives the
declarative view, in terms of the form of the arguments and the relationship
between them.   To document flatten/2, we would record that the two
arguments are lists and the second contains the same elements in the same
order as the first, but with nested sublists removed.   It is helpful to give
some examples which do satisfy the predicate.   So:

?- flatten([[a, or, b], and, [not, c]], [a, or, b, and, not, c]).

and:

?- flatten([[ ], [ ]], [[ ], [ ]]).

are both true. The second example makes clear that the predicate admits the empty list as an element which can occur in a list.

Side-effects of execution also form part of the description of a predicate. This applies both to one such as add_member/1, which uses database modification to manage a body of stored data and whose side-effect we view as long-term, and to traverse_graph/1, which is simply the adding phase of a program which uses the Prolog database to accumulate results.

Documentation for a procedure begins by stating the patterns of arguments which are permitted in calls. This is a statement of restrictions on the declarative view, and, of course, it depends for accuracy on the thoroughness of the testing. There may be restrictions even if the declarative interpretation is very simple, as we demonstrated through the procedures for max/3 in section 6.1.2. We had to specify whether a procedure could be called to test if integer n was the minimum of l and m or only to generate n such that the predicate is satisfied for l, m, n.

If a procedure can be used non-deterministically, we document the order of the answers it produces. If there are any oddities in the order, such as the inclusion of duplicates, these should be mentioned, though if the procedure's behaviour is idiosyncratic when it is used non-deterministically, you may consider it safer to record that this usage is prohibited.

The best way to explain how a procedure works is by reference to the toolkit techniques used to develop it. If a procedure was developed through case analysis, explain the clauses as handlers for cases; if it uses forced backtracking, highlight the sub-goal that generates values, the one that has the side-effect by which values are reported and the one that initiates backtracking. Record also the terminating value which ends the backtracking. It is not necessary to document well-written procedures in more detail than this. They are clear enough for a reader who knows the declarative interpretation of a predicate and understands the techniques in the procedure to see how the means achieve the end. However, if a procedure includes unexpected devices or tricks, you should explain them. For instance, we thought the design of the procedure for fill_vars/2 in section 9.3 was tricky enough to merit special comment. It is probably not obvious to a reader who sees the call:

?- fill_vars(Goal, Goal).

as a sub-goal within the procedure for satisfied/1 why a two argument predicate is used. Our comment was not a full explanation of how the device enhanced the display of a term, but we surmised that a reader would be able to follow our method, once acquainted with our purpose.

In Part 1 of this book, we have studied the design of well-structured and correct procedures, but we have not examined how to design and implement large Prolog programs. The documentation for a large program is not just an amalgam of comments on its components. It must also record how the components are realised as goals and sub-goals and describe the controlling logic under which they interact. How this is done, we consider in our two case studies in Part 2.

Exercises 9.4

    (a)   Document the graph-traversal program of section 7.1.2. Make sure that you distinguish clearly between documentation of the predicate and of the procedure for it.

9.5 Summary

In this chapter, we have introduced the following ideas:

- The expected results of a test must be identified before the test is run.

- A Prolog program should be tested incrementally, as its component procedures are written.

- Debugging is the process of finding and correcting mistakes.

- Many program errors are caused by minor typing mistakes. The first stage of debugging is to proof-read the program.

- The procedure box model is a view of how a Prolog program is executed.

- The procedural behaviour of a Prolog program is very complex, and in debugging mode a great deal of information is displayed. To avoid being overwhelmed with information, you must first narrow the potential sources of a program error and then make careful use of leashed execution and of spy-points when running the debugging system.

- An enhanced interpreter for debugging can make fault-finding easier, but is liable to ask too many questions of the programmer.

- Documentation of a predicate describes the declarative view; documentation of a procedure states restrictions on the declarative view and describes the techniques used in writing a program.

Part 2

Case Studies in Prolog Programming

Chapter 10

Writing Procedures and Writing Programs

The aim of Part 1 of this book was to equip you with the skills to write procedures that are declaratively correct and have a sound procedural interpretation. The core of these skills is the programmer's toolkit, which we review in Figure 10.1.

Technique	Reference	Illustrative Programs	Case Study
Progressive Substitution	2.4	sentence/1 line_of_promotion/2	Problem-Solver
Case Analysis	3.4	conc/3 soundex/2	Problem-Solver
Ingoing Recursion	3.4	reverse/2 flatten/2	Problem-Solver
Selector Predicates	3.6	population/2	Electronic Diary
Utility Predicates	4.3	greater_or_equal/2 in_range_integer/3 subordinate/2	Electronic Diary
Operator Definition	5.2.1	truth_table/2	Problem-Solver
Hollow Terms	5.2.1	assign/4	Problem-Solver
Forced Backtracking	6.2	truth_table/1 get_users_move/2	Electronic Diary
Database Modification	7.1.3	add_member/1 count_members/2 reachable/2	Problem-Solver Electronic Diary

Figure 10.1 Summary of the Prolog programmers' toolkit

Mastery of the techniques in the toolkit is supported by an understanding of the issues of program termination and efficiency and a grasp of testing and debugging methods.

Part 2 is concerned with the application of these skills to programming in the large. The issue of large-scale program design, which we did not address in Part 1 is, therefore, of central concern. In the two case studies, we seek to demonstrate the practical consequences of the principles of the Prolog language for program design methods. Chief among these principles are:

- That a procedure has a declarative interpretation which enables it to be checked as a statement of logical relationships independently of its behaviour as an executable program.

- That the procedural semantics of a syntactically correct program is totally defined by the mechanism of matching between terms and Prolog's deterministic search strategy. In Prolog, it is impossible for an error condition to arise or for an undefined operation to be performed. A totally defined semantics ensures that faults in a program result only in failure of a match or of a goal to be satisfied and not in bizarre program behaviour or incomprehensible error messages.

Of course, these principles are diluted by compromises with the world of practical programming. Efficiency of execution, indeed the very question of program termination, must be considered together with a declarative view of a procedure. Some useful built-in predicates achieve actions by side-effects, which complicates the procedural semantics of a program. Others prescribe constraints on the types of their arguments, and errors do occur if these constraints are not respected. Nonetheless, the principles of Prolog do shine through the murky waters of these pragmatic considerations, and they form the basis for approaches to the design and implementation of large progams which are not available in other languages. Each of our case studies illustrates one approach.

If a Prolog procedure has a declarative interpretation, we ought to be able to carry out the translation of a given algorithm into a Prolog procedure, which is really the design phase, independently of procedural considerations. When we are satisfied that our translation is a correct one, we can study the procedural properties of what is also an executable program. Our first case study shows that this approach is indeed feasible. The basis of our problem-solving system is a recursive algorithm, and it can readily be expressed as a Prolog procedure. Indeed, the bulk of Chapter 11 is concerned with the procedural characteristics of the algorithm in Prolog and not with its declarative aspects.

If the procedural semantics of a program is totally defined, we expect to be able to combine programs developed as independent components without encountering problems arising from the interaction between these components in the whole system. Our second case study illustrates that this too is a feasible approach to program development. Through an analysis of the requirements for the electronic diary, we identify a number of functions it must support, and we design it as a set of interacting components. However, after describing the interactions informally, we implement the system by developing and testing the components entirely separately from each other. It is a development which proceeds neither strictly top-down nor bottom-up, and we emphasise that the success of this approach depends on the thoroughness of the analysis of requirements, the soundness of the resulting design, which is the guide to implementation, and on the rigour of the testing.

Each case study illustrates one option for the development of a large program: the first top-down development and the second functional decomposition, with implementation bottom-up. Both are, of course, independent of the programming language to be used. But we consider that the scope for *incremental program development* is particular to Prolog, is a consequence of the two principles of the language and really does make the task of implementation easier.

Chapter 11

A Problem-Solving System

This case study shows the development of a program which formulates plans of action to solve problems. The program is independent of any domain of application and suitable for use in diverse problem situations.

The case study illustrates the application of the following techniques from the programmers' toolkit:

- Progressive substitution, for building up a structure to represent a plan of action.

- Operator definition, for describing a problem domain.

- Database modification, for representing the effect of executing a plan of action.

- Hollow terms, as a possible way of recording the steps used in a plan.

Section 11.1 describes the requirements for the system. In section 11.2, we describe the problem-solving algorithm and the example problem to which we apply it. In section 11.3, the algorithm is implemented. The algorithm is a recursive one, and the ease with which it can be expressed as a procedure enables us quickly to obtain an executable program. This is characteristic of software development in Prolog and makes possible a prototyping approach: the procedural characteristics of a declaratively sound algorithm can be investigated by testing an implementation at a very early stage of program development. Section 11.4 shows the progress of that investigation as the declaratively sound algorithm is applied to a planning problem. The section shows the difficult process whereby the procedural weaknesses of an algorithm are identified and gradually overcome. Eventually, the program is capable of solving quite complex problems involving a long sequence of plan steps. In section 11.5, we draw attention to its remaining limitations and suggest further refinements as programming exercises for you.

11.1   System   Requirements

The system must be able to:

- Accept a description of a problem domain.   A problem domain is
  described in terms of an initial state and a set of problem-solving
  methods which are available in planning.   The system should allow the
  user the greatest possible flexibility in the form of this description.

- Accept a description of a problem to be solved.   The problem is
  expressed as a new state, into which the initial state is to be
  transformed.

- Produce plans to solve the problem.   The solution to a problem is the
  sequence of steps which achieves the required transformation.   The
  first plan is displayed at the user's terminal.   The user has the option
  of accepting or rejecting the proposed plan.   If he rejects it, the system
  is required to seek other ways of solving the problem.

- Maintain a description of the current problem state.   When the user
  accepts a proposed plan, the system must update its representation of
  the problem state to reflect the plan having been carried out.

- Display the current problem state.   We want this to be in exactly the
  form in which the user had described the initial state.

11.2   The   Problem-Solving   Algorithm

The algorithm used in our program is a version of one which was first published in 1971 and which was the stimulus for much research in problem-
solving methods (Fikes & Nilsson, 1971).   To illustrate it, we use the example
of a robot in a world of three connected rooms which contain some boxes.
In this example, plans are formulated to guide the robot in manoeuvring
about its world in response to commands.   The initial problem state is shown
in Figure 11.1.

11.2.1   Representing   a   problem   state

A requirement of the system is that it should allow the user the greatest
possible freedom in the representation of a problem.   The only restriction is
that the user must distinguish between features of the problem state which
are unvarying and features which could change as a result of the execution
of a plan.   We represent the first type by clauses for always/1 and the
second by clauses for presently/1.   We define always and presently as
prefix operators:

:- op(250, fx, [always, presently]).

In this representation, the problem state of Figure 11.1 is described as in Figure 11.2.

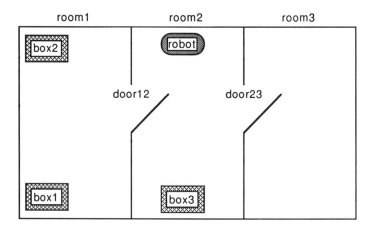

Figure 11.1 The initial problem state

:- op(210, xfy, [is_a, with, stands, is_in, is_at, is_next_to, connects]).

always room1 is_a room.
always room2 is_a room.
always room3 is_a room.
always door12 is_a door.
always door23 is_a door.
always box1 is_a object.
always box2 is_a object.
always box3 is_a object.
always door12 connects room2 with room1.
always door12 connects room1 with room2.
always door23 connects room2 with room3.
always door23 connects room3 with room2.

presently door12 stands opened.
presently door23 stands opened.
presently box1 is_in room1.
presently box2 is_in room1.
presently box3 is_in room2.
presently robot is_in room2.

Figure 11.2 Representation of the initial problem state

Every fact is of the form always X or presently Y, but the system allows the user complete freedom as to the form of the structures X and Y. Here, we use the operator definition technique to make the task of creating a problem description easier for a user and to make the display of a problem state more readable.

The operators is_next_to and is_at would denote that the robot or a box is next to another box or is at a door. In the initial state, there are no facts of this form.

We interpret a structure of the form D connects R1 with R2 as meaning:

"It is possible to use the door D to go from the room R1 to the room R2."

Under this interpretation, we need two structures to represent a two-way door. The interpretation of other structures is straightforward.

11.2.2   Representing problem-solving methods

The problem-solving methods available are described in terms of actions, the job of the planning program being to construct a complete plan from a collection of possible actions. An action is defined by when it can be carried out and what its effects are.

For each action, the first part of the definition is given by a clause for requires/2. The planning system defines operators:

```
:- op(240, xfx, [requires, removes, adds]).
:- op(230, xfy, and).
```

For the action of closing a door, we have the following clause:

```
:- op(220, fx, close).
```

```
close Door requires
     Door is_a door and        % The thing to be closed must be a door!
     Door stands opened and     % It must be open.
     robot is_at Door.          % The robot must be at the door.
```

The effects of an action could be defined by a description of the problem state after the action had been carried out, but because an action can usually be carried out in many different situations, it is difficult to give a complete description. However, as any action affects only a small part of the problem state, we can overcome the difficulty by describing just those features of a problem state which an action does change, with the assumption that all other aspects of the state are unchanged. For example, the action of closing a door alters the problem state only in that a door which was previously open is now closed. The changes are of two types:

- Some facts which were true in the previous state no longer hold true.

- Some facts hold true which did not apply in the previous state.

Defining changes of the first type by a clause for removes/2 and of the second type by a clause for adds/2, we have:

close Door removes
    Door stands opened.

close Door adds
    Door stands closed.

Problem-solving system

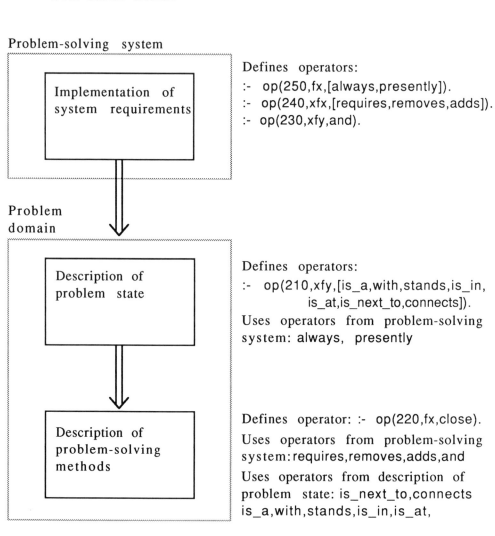

Defines operators:
:- op(250,fx,[always,presently]).
:- op(240,xfx,[requires,removes,adds]).
:- op(230,xfy,and).

Problem domain

Defines operators:
:- op(210,xfy,[is_a,with,stands,is_in,
                is_at,is_next_to,connects]).
Uses operators from problem-solving system: always, presently

Defines operator: :- op(220,fx,close).
Uses operators from problem-solving system: requires,removes,adds,and
Uses operators from description of problem state: is_next_to,connects
is_a,with,stands,is_in,is_at,

Figure 11.3 Hierarchy of operator definition and use

We have described, independently of what doors actually exist in a particular environment, a general class of action which is applicable in any state in which the set of requirements is satisfied. Such a description is called an *action schema*. A plan includes instances of this action schema, with a particular door substituted for the variable Door in the schema.

The definition and use of operators in this system is quite elaborate. The planning program defines some; the user defines more in the description of the problem state and in the description of actions. As we explained in section 5.2.1, safe use of the operator definition technique depends on paying careful attention to the interaction between operators. The situation in the present program is illustrated in Figures 11.3 and 11.4. Figure 11.3 shows the hierarchy of operator definitions in the system. Each component of the system can make use of operators which it defines and of those defined at higher levels.

This hierarchy implies that if the components of the system are held in separate files, these files must be read by Prolog from the top of the hierarchy down.

Figure 11.4 illustrates the structure of the clause for requires/2 which defines the close Door schema. It uses operators defined at each level of the hierarchy.

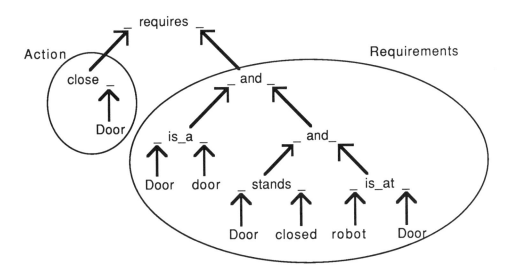

Figure 11.4 Form of a structure Action requires Requirements

Initially, the set of problem solving methods comprises the five action schemas in Figure 11.5. These do not include any actions to move the boxes. We add more later.

```
:- op(210, xfy, [through, to]).
:- op(220, fx, [open, close]).
```

```
go through Door to R1 requires
    R1 is_a room and
    Door is_a door and
    R2 is_a room and
    Door connects R2 with R1 and
    robot is_in R2 and
    robot is_at Door and
    Door stands opened.
go through Door to Room removes
    robot is_at Any_door and
    robot is_next_to Anything and
    robot is_in Any_room.
go through Door to Room adds
    robot is_in Room.
```

```
move to Object requires
    Object is_a object and
    Object is_in Room and
    robot is_in Room.
move to Object removes
    robot is_at Any_door and
    robot is_next_to Anything.
move to Object adds
    robot is_next_to Object.
```

```
go to Door requires
    Door is_a door and
    Door connects Room with R2 and
    robot is_in Room.
go to Door removes
    robot is_at Any_door and
    robot is_next_to Anything.
go to Door adds
    robot is_at Door.
```

```
open Door requires
    Door is_a door and
    Door stands closed and
    robot is_at Door.
open Door removes
    Door stands closed.
open Door adds
    Door stands opened.
```

```
close Door requires
    Door is_a door and
    Door stands opened and
    robot is_at Door
close Door removes
    Door stands opened.
close Door adds
    Door stands closed.
```

Figure 11.5 A set of action schemas

11.2.3   The planning algorithm

A problem to be solved is expressed as a fact or a conjunction of facts which partially specify a state. The problem is solved when a state is reached in which the facts hold true.   Given a problem statement, the algorithm proceeds as follows:

Algorithm 'planner'

For each of the facts in turn, test whether the fact is true in the present state. If it is, do nothing. If it is not, do the following:

- Find an action schema whose add clause includes an effect which matches the fact.   An instance of the action brings about a state in which the fact holds true.

- Find the requirements for the action, and satisfy them as a sub-problem using algorithm 'planner'.

- Include the action as a step in the plan after any actions needed to satisfy its requirements.

- Change the problem state by:

    - removing from it all facts which match an effect in the **remove** clause of the action, and then

    - adding to the description of the problem state all the effects in the **add** clause of the action.

Figure 11.6 shows the progress of the algorithm, where state S1 is that of Figure 11.2, given the problem: door23 stands closed

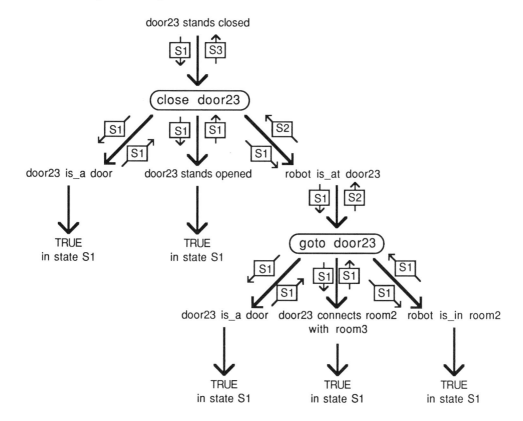

Figure 11.6 Solving the problem door23 stands closed

As each problem and sub-problem is encountered, the current problem state is examined to determine whether the problem is trivial, in the sense of describing a fact which holds true in the current state. The problem state changes during the process of planning, as each action in the plan is selected. The selection of the action go to door23 as the solution to the sub-problem robot is_at door23 changes state S1 to state S2; in state S2, the fact robot is_at door23 holds true. The result is a new state in which the problem is solved (state S3 in the figure), and a sequence of actions to transform the initial state into the new state.

11.3 A Program to Meet the System Requirements

We use a top-down method in designing a program to meet the requirements for the system. At the top level, the procedure for plan/1 is:

```
plan(Problem) :-
    initial_state_is(Si),
    devise_plan(Problem, Si, Plan, Sf),
    confirm_plan(Plan),
    update_state(Sf).
```

Problem is the problem to be solved. Si is the initial problem state. The procedure for devise_plan/4 implements algorithm 'planner'. Plan is a plan which solves Problem, from state Si, producing the final state Sf. The user is asked to confirm the plan, which is displayed at the terminal, and state Si is replaced by state Sf.

Before we proceed to the next stage, we must consider procedural aspects of the program so far. It is essential to be clear about the controlling logic under which the parts of the program interact before proceeding to design each part. As the control component is provided by Prolog's search strategy, the interaction is described very simply, by specifying, for each sub-goal:

* Whether the goal is always satisfiable, or whether it may fail.

* Whether the goal is re-satisfiable on backtracking.

For this program, we prescribe the following behaviour:

* ?- initial_state_is(Si) is always satisfiable. It is not re-satisfiable on backtracking.

* ?- devise_plan(Problem, Si, Plan, Sf) is satisfied if a plan can be found to solve the given problem and fails otherwise. It is re-satisfiable if an alternative plan can be found.

* ?- confirm_plan(Plan) is satisfied if the user confirms the proposed plan as acceptable and fails otherwise. It is not re-satisfiable on backtracking.

- ?- update_state(Sf) replaces state Si by state Sf using database modification. It is always satisfiable, and is not re-satisfiable on backtracking.

As Problem is expected to be a ground term, the user cannot force backtracking once the call to plan/1 has succeeded. We examine the implications for our design of Problem not being ground in section 11.5.1.

We are using database modification to manage the database of facts which describes the problem state. The design meets the criteria for use of the technique. Firstly, the database modification is confined to one part of the program. Secondly, the procedure within which the database is modified always succeeds when called as a goal, so the actions to retract a previous state and those to assert a new state will both be safely completed. There should be no possibility of just one phase happening.

At the top level of a design, one should as far as possible avoid decisions about the form which arguments passed between the sub-goals are to take. Such decisions should be taken at lower levels where they can be made on the basis of an understanding of the details of how the arguments are to be processed. At the top level of our program, we specify only that the argument Problem is an arbitrary structure to represent a single fact or a structure with functor and and arity 2 to represent a conjunction of facts.

11.3.1 Refinement of sub-goal: ?- initial_state_is(Si)

A plan can change any aspect of the problem state which is represented by a clause for presently/1. The following clause substitutes for Si a list of all such clauses:

```
initial_state_is(Si)  :-
      bag(Fact, presently Fact, Si).
```

A check on the controlling logic at the top level of the program makes clear that the clauses cannot be retracted from the database at this stage: later top-level goals might fail, causing backtracking over this sub-goal and loss of the description of the problem state.

The refinement of this sub-goal shows that Si is a list. This has implications for the refinement of the procedure for devise_plan/4.

11.3.2 Refinement of sub-goal:
?- devise_plan(Problem, Si, Plan, Sf)

Given the decision about the form of the argument Problem, two cases can be identified: either the problem is a conjunction of facts or it is a single fact. If we assume that a procedure for plan_step/4 produces a plan to solve a single problem, we can handle the first case by a clause which recursively reduces a conjunction of problems to a sequence of single problems and the second case by a call to plan_step/4:

```
devise_plan(P and Ps, Si, Plan and Plans, Sf) :-
    plan_step(P, Si, Plan, Sj),
    devise_plan(Ps, Sj, Plans, Sf).
devise_plan(P, Si, Plan, Sf) :-
    plan_step(P, Si, Plan, Sf).
```

There are two points to note about the first clause:

- Solving problem P changes the initial state, and problems Ps have to be solved from this changed state. The changed state is represented by Sj, returned as output from the call to plan_step/4 and given as input, in place of Si, to the recursive call to devise a plan for problems Ps.

- The complete plan is being built up in the third argument by progressive substitution. A match with this clause substitutes the structure Plan and Plans for the variable Plan in the call. The two components of the structure are passed to sub-goals, in which further substitutions are made. Notice also that the structure Plan and Plans expresses the linear ordering of actions in the final plan. The actions in Plan are carried out first, followed by those in Plans.

Refinement of: ?- plan_step(P, Si, Plan, Sf)

The algorithm 'planner' suggests two cases here: either the fact P, representing the problem, holds true in state Si, or it does not hold in state Si. Each case is handled by one clause:

```
plan_step(P, S, none, S) :-
    true_in_state(P, S).
plan_step(P, Si, Actions and Action, Sf) :-
    Action adds Effects,                          % Find an action
    relevant_action(P, Effects),                  %  which is relevant to P.
    Action requires Requirements,                 % Find its requirements
    devise_plan(Requirements,Si, Actions, Sj),    %  and devise a plan
                                                  %  to satisfy them.
    change_state(Sj, Action, Sf).                 % Change the problem state.
```

The head of the first clause expresses, for the first case, that the final problem state is identical to the initial state S and that the atom none denotes a plan which contains no steps.

In the second clause, progressive substitution continues to be used to build up the complete plan. The clause specifies the third argument to be a structure with functor and and arity 2 and also substitutes a value for the second component of the structure: it is the action which solves the problem. Actions to satisfy its requirements come before it in the plan.

The non-deterministic instruction in algorithm 'planner' to "Find an action schema whose add clause includes an effect which matches the fact" is implemented as a non-deterministic search through the clauses in the database for adds/2.

Again, an additional variable Sj is used for the state resulting from the satisfaction of all the requirements for carrying out the action Action.

Refinement of: ?- true_in_state(P, S), relevant_action(P,Effects) and change_state(Sj, Action, Sf)

The procedures for these predicates simply:

- find an item in a list;

- delete an item from a list;

- join two lists.

The procedures differ from those for the list-processing predicates present-ed in section 3.4 only because in this application some lists are represented by structures with functor and and do not have a distinguished atom to represent the empty list:

```
true_in_state(P, _) :-
    always(P).                      % P always holds.
true_in_state(P, State) :-
    member(P, State).               % P is part of the current state.
member(H, [H|_]).
member(H,[_|T]) :-
    member(H,T).
```

% Find an effect in a conjunction of effects

```
relevant_action(Effect, Effect).
relevant_action(Effect, Effect and _).
relevant_action(Effect, _ and Effects) :-
    relevant_action(Effect, Effects).
```

```
change_state(Si, Action, Sf) :-
    Action removes Removed,         % Find the facts to be removed
    remove(Si, Removed, Sj),        %  and remove them, giving Sj.
    Action adds Effects,            % Find the facts to be added
    add(Sj, Effects, Sf).           %  and add them, giving Sf.
```

```
% Remove a fact or a conjunction of facts from a list of facts.
remove(Si, Fact and Facts, Sf) :- !,    % There is a conjunction of facts.
    remove_first(Si, Fact, Sj),
    remove(Sj, Facts, Sf).
remove(Si, Fact, Sf) :-                  % There is a single fact only.
    remove_first(Si, Fact, Sf).


% Remove the first occurrence of a fact from a list of facts.
remove_first([ ], _, [ ]).
remove_first([Fact|Facts], Fact, Facts) :- !
remove_first([F1|Facts], Fact, [F1|Fs]) :-
    remove_first(Facts, Fact, Fs).


% Add an effect or a conjunction of effects to a list of facts.
add(Si, Fact and Facts, [Fact|F1]) :- !, % A conjunction of facts
    add(Si, Facts, F1).
add(Si, Fact, [Fact|Si]).                % A single fact only.
```

11.3.3   Refinement of sub-goal: ?- confirm_plan(Plan)

This component of the system simply displays the plan steps and seeks confirmation of whether the plan is acceptable:

```
confirm_plan(Plan)  :-
    write('The steps to be taken are:'),
    nl,
    show_steps(Plan),
    nl,
    write('Is this ok? (y/n): '),
    get(121).            % Succeeds if next printing character is "y"
```

The procedure for show_steps/1 is always satisfied when first called.   It is not re-satisfiable on backtracking.   The processing required is dictated by the form of the structure that represents the plan, which was described in section 11.3.2.   There are three clauses corresponding to the three cases. Mutual exclusion between the cases must be enforced to ensure that the procedure is not re-satisfiable on backtracking:

```
show_steps(none) :- !.                % There are no steps.
show_steps(Steps1 and Steps2) :- !,   % There is a series of steps.
    show_steps(Steps1),
    show_steps(Steps2).
show_steps(Step)  :-                  % There is a single step.
    tab(4),
    write(Step),
    nl.
```

11.3.4   Refinement of sub-goal: ?- update_state(Sf).

We first retract from the database all clauses for presently/1, and then assert as new clauses the facts in the list Sf. We also report the new state to the user:

```
update_state(Sf)  :-
    retractall(presently  _),    % First,  remove the existing state from
    nl,                                   % the database.
    write(' The  situation  now  is:'),     % Then display the new facts
    nl,
    show_facts(Sf).                  % and add them to the database.

show_facts([  ]).
show_facts([Fact|Facts])  :-
    tab(4),
    write(Fact),
    nl,
    assert(presently  Fact),
    show_facts(Facts).
```

11.4 Testing and Improving the Program

The first step in testing the program is to check each action. The initial state is:

```
?-  listing(presently).
presently  door12  stands  opened.
presently  door23  stands  opened.
presently  box1  is_in  room1.
presently  box2  is_in  room1.
presently  box3  is_in  room2.
presently  robot  is_in  room2.
yes
```

The test produces the following results:

```
?-  plan(door12  stands  closed).
The  steps  to  be  taken  are:
    go  to  door12
    close  door12

Is  this  ok?  (y/n):  y

  The  situation  now  is:
    door12  stands  closed
```

```
            robot  is_at  door12
            door23  stands  opened
            box1  is_in  room1
            box2  is_in  room1
            box3  is_in  room2
            robot  is_in  room2
    yes


    ?-  plan(robot  is_in  room3).
    The  steps  to  be  taken  are:
            go  to  door23
            go  through  door23  to  room3


    Is  this  ok?  (y/n):  y


      The  situation  now  is:
            robot  is_in  room3
            door12  stands  closed
            door23  stands  opened
            box1  is_in  room1
            box2  is_in  room1
            box3  is_in  room2
    yes


    ?-  plan(robot  is_in  room2).
```

At this point, Prolog paused and then responded sadly with:

```
    !  more  core  needed    [  execution  aborted  ]
```

The gory details vary between implementations of the language, but a message of this type is, for anything other than a very large program, a sure sign that the program is stuck in a loop, generating identical sub-goals to an ever greater depth. The system can formulate a plan to move the robot from room2 to room3 but not to send it back! In the remainder of section 11.4, we show how to detect and correct the faults which cause this failure.

11.4.1 Fault finding

With a program of this size, it is important to think carefully before using the debugging mode of Prolog operation to find faults. Section 9.2 showed that it is hard to prevent the debugging system generating too much detailed information about a program's procedural behaviour, and in the present problem we have the additional difficulty that several arguments to sub-goals have substituted for them large structures whose form would be difficult to discern if they were displayed at the terminal.

If we consider the program to be a declaratively correct statement of algorithm 'planner', the fault must lie in the way the algorithm is transformed procedurally. As we mentioned in section 11.3.2, the algorithm has a non-deterministic element which is rendered by a search through the Prolog database. This search, though non-deterministic in the sense of possibly yielding several relevant action schemas through backtracking, nonetheless follows the fixed Prolog search strategy. To examine the consequences of implementing a non-deterministic algorithm by a fixed search strategy, we set a spy-point on the sub-goal: ?- Action requires Requirements, in which the selection of a relevant action is made, and we set the leashing mode to loose:

```
?- debug.
Debug mode switched on
yes

?- spy(requires/2).
Spy-points set on:
    requires/2
yes

?- leash(loose).
Leashing set to loose (call)
yes

?- listing(presently).
presently robot is_in room3.          Robot is still in room3
presently door12 stands closed.
presently door23 stands opened.
presently box1 is_in room1.
presently box2 is_in room1.
presently box3 is_in room2.
yes

?- plan(robot is_in room2).
(22) 13 Call:  go through _52 to room2 requires _65683  s
(22) 13 Exit:  go through _52 to room2 requires room2 is_a room
               and _52 is_a door and _60 is_a room and _52
               connects _60 with room2 and robot is_in _60 and
               robot is_at _52 and _52 stands opened
(23) 13 Call:  devise_plan(room2 is_a room and _52 is_a door and
               _60 is_a room and _52 connects _60 with room2 and
               robot is_in _60 and robot is_at _52 and _52 stands
               opened,[robot is_in room3,door12 stands
               closed,door23 stands opened,box1 is_in room1,box2
               is_in room1,box3 is_in room2],_48,_65684) q
(55) 28 Call:  go through _117 to room1 requires _65884 s
(55) 28 Exit:  go through _117 to room1 requires room1 is_a room
```

213

and _117 is_a door and _125 is_a room and _117
connects _125 with room1 and robot is_in _125 and
robot is_at _117 and _117 stands opened

(56) 28 Call: devise_plan(room1 is_a room and _117 is_a door and
_125 is_a room and _117 connects _125 with room1
and robot is_in _125 and robot is_at _117 and _117
stands opened,[robot is_in room3,door12 stands
closed,door23 stands opened,box1 is_in room1,box2
is_in room1,box3 is_in room2],_113,_65885) q

(121) 43 Call: go through _182 to room2 requires _66085 s

(121) 43 Exit: go through _182 to room2 requires room2 is_a room
and _182 is_a door and _190 is_a room and _182
connects _190 with room2 and robot is_in _190 and
robot is_at _182 and _182 stands opened

(122) 43 Call: devise_plan(room2 is_a room and _182 is_a door and
_190 is_a room and _182 connects _190 with room2
and robot is_in _190 and robot is_at _182 and _182
stands opened,[robot is_in room3,door12 stands
closed,door23 stands opened,box1 is_in room1,box2
is_in room1,box3 is_in room2],_178,_66086) q

(154) 58 Call: go through _247 to room1 requires _66286 a

execution aborted
no

This glimpse at the execution of the program has produced a deluge of
output. The key point, which you might well have missed, is that invocation
121 is a duplicate of invocation 22, as is invocation 154 of invocation 55.
This reveals that the system has somehow got stuck in a loop going between
room1 and room2. However, what the debugging mode cannot reveal is the
cause of this failure; as we observed in section 9.2, it can only provide more
information about the symptoms. To find causes, there is really no
substitute for a careful analysis by hand of the progress of a program. We
now show how to analyse a failure of this type without mechanical aids.
The key to success is: be methodical, use a notation you can understand and
be sure not to depart from the search strategy which Prolog applies.
Execution with a spy-point has provided clues about what to look out for.

We can readily see that, given the substitution Problem ← robot is_in
room2 in the top-level goal: ?- plan(Problem), the call to devise_plan/4 has
the form: ?- devise_plan(robot is_in room2, Si, Plan, Sf) and the second
clause for the procedure is used. At the next level, the sub-goal is: ?-
plan_step(robot is_in room2, Si, Plan, Sj). Though this call matches the
first clause for plan_step/4, the sub-goal: ?- true_in_state(robot is_in
room2, Si) fails. The match with the second clause gives the substitution
Plan ← Actions and Action. The first relevant_action is go through Door to
room2, giving the substitution Action ← go through Door to room2. Finding
the requirements for the chosen action gives the substitution:

Requirements ← room2 is_a room and
      Door is_a door and
      R2 is_a room and
      Door connects R2 with room2 and
      robot is_in R2 and
      robot is_at Door and
      Door stands opened

At this stage, the variables in the structure which was substituted for Plan are Actions, R2 and Door. R2 and Door are wrapped up in the structure Requirements. Both are passed to the sub-goal: ?- devise_plan(Requirements, Si, Actions, Sj).

The attempt to satisfy each requirement in the sub-goal proceeds thus:

room2 is_a room   true in Si
Door is_a door   true in Si, with the substitution Door ← door12
R2 is_a room   true in Si, with the substitution R2 ← room1
door12 connects room1 with room2
          true in Si
robot is_in room1   false in Si. A plan has to be devised to satisfy
          this requirement

Because of the substitution Door ← door12, the last step in the plan has become go through door12 to room2, and to carry out this action robot is_in room1 must be true.

The relevant action to make this true is go through Door to room1, producing Plan ← Actions and go through Door1 to room1. The next sub-goal is: ?- devise_plan(Requirements, Si, Actions, Sj), where:

Requirements ← room1 is_a room and
      Door is_a door and
      R2 is_a room and
      Door connects R2 with room1 and
      robot is_in R2 and
      robot is_at Door and
      Door stands opened.

The attempt to satisfy each requirement in the sub-goal proceeds thus:

room1 is_a room   true in Si
Door is_a door   true in Si, with the substitution Door ←door12
R2 is_a room   true in Si, with the substitution R2 ← room1
door12 connects room1 with room1
          false in Si, and no plan can be devised to solve
          this as a sub-problem.

The failure to solve this sub-problem causes the system to backtrack to the previous sub-problem, undoing the substitution R2 ← room1. That sub-problem can be solved in a different way:

R2 is_a room   true in Si, with the substitution R2 ← room2
door12 connects room2 with room1
                               true in Si
robot is_in room2   false in Si. A plan has to be devised to satisfy this requirement

At this point, alerted by the results of our execution with a spy-point, we recognise the occurrence of a loop and the cause of it. The system decided that to get to room2 the robot would have to be in room1. To get to room1, it must be in room2, and so on. The cause of the problem is that in satisfying the requirements for the last step in the plan: go through Door to room2, the system, searching for a fact true_in_state to satisfy the requirement Door connects R2 with room2, finds a match with door12 connects **room1** with room2, but never backtracks to find the alternative, correct, match with door23 connects **room3** with room2.

11.4.2   Correcting the program

Figure 11.7 shows how a sequence of repeated steps builds up and suggests that the solution to the problem is to include a check that, when an action is selected, it does not duplicate another plan step.

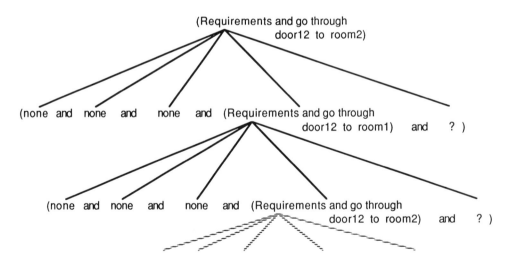

Figure 11.7 An endless sequence of sub-problems is generated

We could use a list to carry the information about the sequence of steps used in a plan. Then, whenever a relevant action was identified, we would check the list to ensure that the action had not already been used in the plan. If it had not, we would add it to the list. We might build the list up by ingoing recursion, but if we maintained it as a hollow term, we would need only one extra argument to the procedures for devise_plan/4 and plan_step/4. This approach is shown in Figure 11.8, given a problem in which a b c d and e are possible actions.

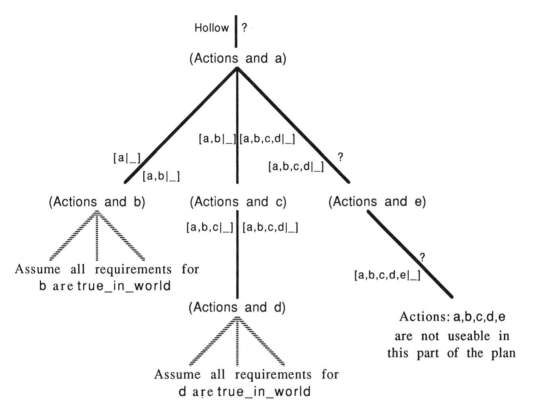

Figure 11.8 Repeated steps are precluded

This check seems appropriate at first sight, but is in fact too strict a test. There are circumstances in which a sound plan may be expected to include duplicate steps. Consider, for instance, the problem:

?- plan(box1 is_in room3 and box2 is_in room3)

We introduce action schemas to describe how boxes can be moved in section 11.4.4, but given that the robot can move only one box at a time, it is obvious that, in the initial state of Figure 11.1, the sequence of steps go to door12, go through door12 to room1 occurs first in the branch of the plan to solve the problem box1 is_in room3 and is needed again to solve the problem box2 is_in room3. The point is that the program should reject a relevant action only if it duplicates another action chosen for solving the same sub-problem. With this approach, the process illustrated in Figure 11.8 is simplified to that shown in Figure 11.9.

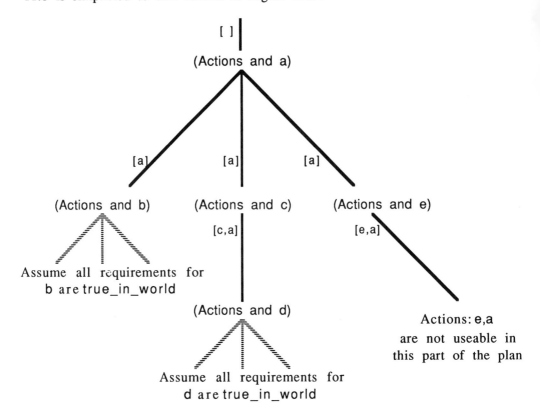

Figure 11.9 Repeated steps are precluded in the solution of a single sub-problem

Now, the argument which is given as input and which holds the record of actions used at higher levels in a single branch of the plan does not have to return an output, so we do not need a hollow term.

This refinement is implemented by the following clauses, which replace those for devise_plan/4 and plan_step/4:

```
devise_plan(P and Ps, Si, Steps, Plan and Plans, Sf) :-
    plan_step(P, Si, Steps, Plan, Sj),
    devise_plan(Ps, Sj, Steps, Plans, Sf).
devise_plan(P, Si, Steps, Plan, Sf) :-
    plan_step(P, Si, Steps, Plan, Sf).

plan_step(P, S, _, none, S) :-
    true_in_state(P, S).
plan_step(P, Si, Steps, Actions and Action, Sf) :-
    Action adds Effects,
    relevant_action(P, Effects),
```

```
fail_if(member(Action,   Steps)), % Check for duplicates.
Action requires Requirements,
devise_plan(Requirements, Si, [Action|Steps], Actions, Sj),
change_state(Sj, Action, Sf).
```

At the top level, the procedure for plan/1 also has to be altered to include the extra argument in the call to devise_plan, which now is a five argument predicate. In the call, the extra argument is the empty list:

```
plan(Problem) :-
        initial_state_is(Si),
        devise_plan(Problem, Si, [ ], Plan, Sf),
        confirm_plan(Plan),
        update_state(Sf).
```

With this refinement, the program solves the problem which had previously baffled it:

```
?- nodebug.
Debug mode switched off
All spy points removed
yes
```

We check that the robot is still in room3:

```
?-  listing(presently).
presently  robot is_in  room3.
presently  door12 stands closed.
presently  door23 stands opened.
presently  box1 is_in  room1.
presently  box2 is_in  room1.
presently  box3 is_in  room2.
yes
?- plan(robot is_in  room2).
The steps to be taken are:
      go to door23
      go through door23 to room2

Is this ok? (y/n): y

  The situation now is:
      robot is_in  room2
      door12 stands opened
      door23 stands opened
      box1 is_in  room1
      box2 is_in  room1
      box3 is_in  room2
yes
```

11.4.3 Refining the knowledge representation

In the example which we worked through in the previous section, the program tried to formulate a plan to solve the problem door12 connects room1 with room1 which the user would recognise as insoluble. We can eliminate such attempts to achieve the impossible by distinguishing between two types of requirement in the representation of an action schema. The first type is requirements which are set up as sub-problems if they are not satisfied in a problem state. Physical constraints of the problem domain which can never be altered are requirements of the second type. If these, which we call the assumptions for an action schema, are not satisfied, they should not be set up as sub-problems. If assumptions are not satisfied, the action schema is not relevant to the problem. In Figure 11.10, the set of actions is described in this richer representation.

```
:- op(210, xfy, [through, to, from, in]).
:- op(220, fx, [open, close]).
```

```
go from Room1 through Door to Room2 assumes
    Room1 is_a room and
    Door is_a door and
    Room2 is_a room and
    Door connects Room1 with Room2.
go from Room1 through Door to Room2 requires
    robot is_in Room1 and
    robot is_at Door and
    Door stands opened.
go from Room1 through Door to Room2 removes
    robot is_at Any_door and
    robot is_next_to Anything and
    robot is_in Room1.
go from Room1 through Door to Room2 adds
    robot is_in Room2.
```

```
move to Object in Room assumes
    Object is_a object and
    Object is_in Room.
move to Object in Room requires
    robot is_in Room.
move to Object in Room removes
    robot is_at Any_door and
    robot is_next_to Anything.
move to Object in Room adds
    robot is_next_to Object.
```

```
go to Door in Room assumes
    Door is_a door and
    Room is_a room and
    Door connects Room with Another_room.
go to Door in Room requires
    robot is_in Room.
go to Door in Room removes
    robot is_at Any_door and
    robot is_next_to Anything.
go to Door in Room adds
    robot is_at Door.
```

```
open Door assumes
    Door is_a door and
    Door stands closed.
open Door requires
    robot is_at Door.
open Door removes
    Door stands closed.
open Door adds
    Door stands opened.
```

```
close Door assumes
    Door is_a door and
    Door stands opened.
close Door requires
    robot is_at Door.
close Door removes
    Door stands opened.
close Door adds
    Door stands closed.
```

Figure 11.10 A set of action schemas, showing assumptions and requirements

Notice that this refinement has made our representation more perspicuous in a number of respects:

- By listing Object is_in Room as an assumption for the action move to Object in Room, we have made explicit that the robot is to move to wherever the object is, and that the position of the object does not alter.

- In the case of move to Object in Room and go to Door in Room, we now include the room within which the action takes place. This is necessary to ensure that the room in which the robot is required to be is the same as that in which the object is assumed to be.

Alterations to the planning program are limited to the extension of the operator definitions:

```
:- op(240, xfx, [requires, removes, adds, assumes]).
```

the introduction of two new sub-goals in the second clause for plan_step/5:

```
plan_step(P, Si, Steps, Actions and Action, Sf) :-
    Action adds Effects,
    relevant_action(P, Effects),
    fail_if(member(Action, Steps)),
    Action assumes Assumptions,     % Identify the assumptions
    satisfied(Assumptions, Si),     % and check they are satisfied.
    Action requires Requirements,
    devise_plan(Requirements, Si, [Action|Steps], Actions, Sj),
    change_state(Sj, Action, Sf).
```

and the addition of a procedure for the new predicate:

```
satisfied(Fact and Facts, S) :-     %There are several assumptions.
    true_in_state(Fact, S),
    satisfied(Facts, S).
satisfied(Fact, S) :-               % There is a single assumption.
    true_in_state(Fact, S).
```

It is characteristic of programs which manipulate a knowledge base describing a complex real-world situation that improvements in program performance are obtained by refinements to the knowledge representation framework, as well as by refinements to the reasoning process. In the next section, where we increase the number of actions available to the robot, both these aspects of our knowledge-based program have to be further refined.

11.4.4 Adding new actions

The new actions define how the robot can move the boxes about in its world. The first, shown in Figure 11.11, describes the action of moving a box so that it is_next_to another. By listing Obj2 is_in Room as an assumption for the action, we make clear that only the first object is to be moved.

```
:- op(220, fx, push).
```

```
push Obj1 to Obj2 in Room assumes
    Obj1 is_a object and
    Obj2 is_a object and
    Room is_a room and
    Obj2 is_in Room.
```

```
push Obj1 to Obj2 in Room requires
    robot is_next_to Obj1 and
    Obj1 is_in Room.
```

```
push Obj1 to Obj2 in Room removes
    robot is_at Door and
    robot is_next_to Thing1 and
    Obj1 is_next_to Thing2 and
    Thing3 is_next_to Obj1 and
    Obj1 is_at Door.
```

```
push Obj1 to Obj2 in Room adds
    Obj1 is_next_to Obj2 and
    robot is_next_to Obj1 and
    robot is_next_to Obj2.
```

Figure 11.11 An action schema for moving one box to another

```
:- op(220, fx, shift).
```

```
shift Object to Door in Room assumes
    Object is_a object and
    Door is_a door and
    Room is_a room and
    Door connects Room with Another_room.
```

```
shift Object to Door in Room requires
    robot is_next_to Object and
    Object is_in Room.
```

```
shift Object to Door in Room removes
    Object is_at Any_door and
    robot is_next_to Thing1 and
    Object is_next_to Thing2 and
    Thing3 is_next_to Object.
```

```
shift Object to Door in Room adds
    Object is_at Door and
    robot is_next_to Object and
    robot is_at Door.
```

```
push Object from R1 through Door to R2 assumes
    R1 is_a room and
    Door is_a door and
    R2 is_a room and
    Door connects R1 with R2.
```

```
push Object from R1 through Door to R2 requires
    Door stands opened and
    robot is_next_to Object and
    Object is_in R1 and
    Object is_at Door.
```

```
push Object from R1 through Door to R2 removes
    robot is_at Door and
    Object is_at Door and
    robot is_next_to Thing1 and
    Object is_next_to Thing2 and
    Thing3 is_next_to Object and
    robot is_in Any_room and
    Object is_in Any_other_room.
```

```
push Object from R1 through Door to R2 adds
    Object is_in R2 and
    robot is_in R2 and
    robot is_next_to Object.
```

Figure 11.12 Action schemas for moving boxes between rooms

Two more actions together enable a box to be moved between rooms. The first defines the action of shifting the box to a door, the second that of moving it through a door from one room to another. They are shown in Figure 11.12. Because the second of these actions alters the room which the robot and the object are in, the list of facts removed is quite lengthy. We must not only record that the object moved ceases to be next to anything which it might previously have been adjacent to, but we must also state explicitly the converse: anything previously next to the object named is now no longer so.

There is a more serious problem, however, than that of defining the effect of these new actions. It emerges that the system is no longer able to solve the problems which were previously within its grasp! We left the robot in room2. It can still find its way to room3:

```
?- plan(robot is_in room3).
The steps to be taken are:
    go to door23 in room2
    go from room2 through door23 to room3

Is this ok? (y/n): y

    The situation now is:
        robot is_in room3
        door12 stands opened
        door23 stands opened
        box1 is_in room1
        box2 is_in room1
        box3 is_in room2
yes
```

but it can no longer get back:

```
?- plan(robot is_in room2).
```

The only response to this request is a very long silence from the system!

We recommend that for programs of this size, the process of fault-finding should be carried out at a high level, by the programmer using pencil and paper, rather than at the low level that the debugging mode of Prolog operation allows. However, this approach can only be successful if the programmer is sufficiently experienced to be sure that he will not make false assumptions about the behaviour of his program at lower levels of detail. At this high level, tree diagrams, in the style of Figure 11.9, are useful.

Given the sub-goal:

```
?- plan_step(Si, P, Steps, Plan, Sf)
```

223

where: P ← robot is_in room2, the first level of the tree is as in Figure 11.13.

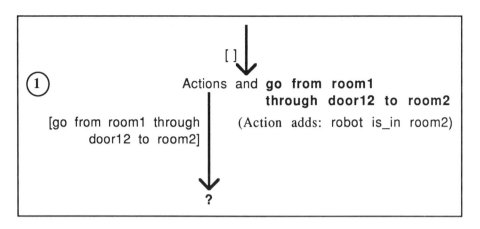

Figure 11.13 The top level of the search tree for the goal: ?- plan(robot is_in room2)

The action chosen to get the robot into room2 is inappropriate. The reason for it being chosen was investigated in section 11.4.1. As we refined the algorithm precisely to forestall the problems caused by this erroneous choice, it is all the more puzzling that the refinement is not now adequate. Continuing to work through the system's attempts to satisfy requirements, we have Figure 11.14.

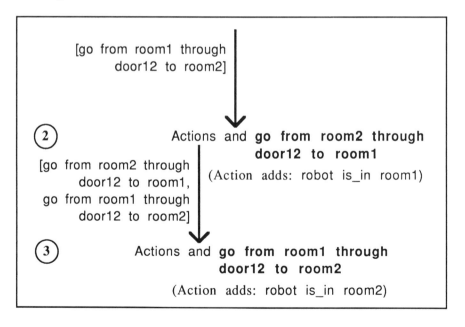

Figure 11.14 A relevant action at level 3 duplicates a previous action

At level 3, the system selects go from room1 through door12 to room2 as a relevant action to solve the problem: robot is_in room2, but this action is rejected as a duplicate. We intended the rejection of this action to make the system abandon the incorrect plan steps at levels 2 and 1. Following the addition of new action schemas, however, detection of the duplicated step at level 3 no longer forces backtracking all the way to level 1 because one of the new actions is relevant to achieving the goal robot is_in room2 at level 3. The relevant action is push Obj1 from R1 through Door to room2.

The assumptions for this action are satisfied and produce the substitutions:

Obj1 ← box1 (the first object in the problem state)
R1 ← room1
Door ← door12.

The system, instead of abandoning the attempt to get to room2 from room1, has discovered that the robot can get to room2 from room1 by pushing a box from the one room into the other! From this point onwards, the system is lost in a fruitless search in which there are so many alternative choices of action, all involving problem steps which differ slightly from one another, that it does not, within any acceptable time, get back to reconsider the incorrect choice at level 1. The impasse is represented in Figure 11.15.

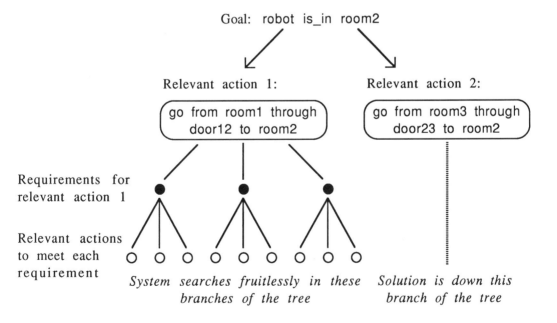

Figure 11.15 The effect of an incorrect choice at an early stage in a large search tree

The search in the wrong branch of the tree continues for a prohibitively long time because the check on duplicate actions is insufficient by itself to limit the length of a sequence of plan steps and because at each level of the tree there are liable to be many instances of a relevant action schema, each with different substitutions of values for the variables in the schema. We tackle the first problem by a refinement of the planning algorithm, the second by a refinement of the method of representing action schemas.

The depth of the search tree can be constrained by a depth count. Its effect is illustrated in Figure 11.16.

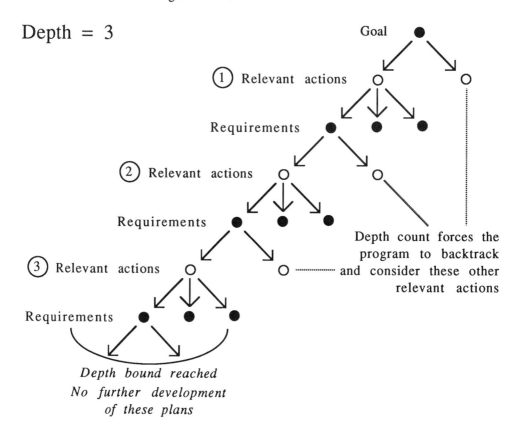

Depth = 3

Goal

① Relevant actions

Requirements

② Relevant actions

Requirements

③ Relevant actions

Requirements

Depth bound reached
No further development
of these plans

Depth count forces the program to backtrack and consider these other relevant actions

Figure 11.16 Using a depth count to force backtracking

The difficulty is that there is no single value for the depth count appropriate in all cases. We adopt the solution of requiring the user to supply a value for the count as an estimate of the length of the longest sequence of plan steps to solve any single sub-problem.

We can reduce the number of relevant actions at each level by distinguishing, in the representation of an action schema, between the main effects and the side-effects of carrying out an action and by prescribing that an action is only relevant if one of its main effects matches the current goal. For instance, the action push Object from R1 through Door to R2 has the effect of moving both the robot and Object to R2, but we would not wish it to be chosen unless the goal was Object is_in R2. The movement of the robot is just a side-effect of carrying out the action, and if the goal was to get the robot to R2, we would wish to use an action such as go through Door to Room. In a representation in which every action achieves one or more main effects and may produce one or more side-effects, the action schema push Object from R1 through Door to R2 is defined as in Figure 11.17.

```
push Object from Room1 through Door to Room2 assumes
    Object is_a object and
    Room1 is_a room and
    Door is_a door and
    Room2 is_a room and
    Door connects Room1 with Room2.

push Object from Room1 through Door to Room2 requires
    Door stands opened and
    robot is_next_to Object and
    Object is_in Room1 and
    Object is_at Door.

push Object from Room1 through Door to Room2 removes
    robot is_at Door1 and
    Object is_at Door2 and
    robot is_next_to Thing1 and
    Object is_next_to Thing2 and
    Thing3 is_next_to Object and
    robot is_in Any_room and
    Object is_in Any_other_room.

push Object from Room1 through Door to Room2 achieves
    Object is_in Room2.

push Object from Room1 through Door to Room2 produces
    robot is_in Room2 and
    robot is_next_to Object.
    robot is_next_to Object.
```

Figure 11.17 Distinguishing between main effects and side-effects in the representation of an action schema

A description in this representation of all the action schemas used in this case study is given in Appendix 1.

The changes to the planning program are to extend the list of operators:

```
:- op(240, xfx, [requires, removes, achieves, produces, assumes]).
```

to alter the procedures for devise_plan/5 and plan_step/5 to include as an extra argument the depth count, which is decremented as each action is chosen:

```
devise_plan(P and Ps, Si, Steps, Depth, Plan and Plans, Sf) :-
    plan_step(P, Si, Steps, Depth, Plan, Sj),
    devise_plan(Ps, Sj, Steps, Depth, Plans, Sf).
devise_plan(P, Si, Steps, Depth, Plan, Sf) :-
    plan_step(P, Si, Steps, Depth, Plan, Sf).

plan_step(P, S, _, _, none, S) :-
    true_in_state(P, S).
plan_step(P, Si, Steps, Depth, Actions and Action, Sf) :-
    Depth > 0,                       % Hit depth bound?
    Reduced is Depth - 1,            % If not, decrement count.
    Action achieves Effects,         % Find main effects of Action.
    relevant_action(P, Effects),
    fail_if(member(Action, Steps)),
    Action assumes Assumptions,
    satisfied(Assumptions, Si),
    Action requires Requirements,
    devise_plan(Requirements, Si, [Action|Steps], Reduced, Actions, Sj),
    change_state(Sj, Action, Sf).
```

and to alter the procedure for change_state/3 to take account of the
separation of main effects and side-effects:

```
change_state(Si, Action, Sf) :-
    Action removes Removed,
    remove(Si, Removed, Sj),
    Action achieves Main_effects,
    add(Sj, Main_effects, Sk),
    add_side_effects(Sk, Action, Sf).

add_side_effects(Si, Action, Sj) :-
    Action produces Side_effects, !, % There are side-effects.
    add(Si, Side_effects, Sj).
add_side_effects(S, _, S).            % There are no side-effects.
```

In the revised form, the predicate plan has two arguments and is defined
by the following procedure:

```
plan(Problem, Depth) :-
    initial_state_is(Si),
    devise_plan(Problem, Si, [ ], Depth, Plan, Sf),
    confirm_plan(Plan),
    update_state(Sf).
```

With these refinements, the performance of the program improves
markedly. Its capabilities are illustrated in the following interactions. The
robot gets safely back from room3:

```
?- plan(robot is_in room2, 3).
The steps to be taken are:
      go to door23 in room3
      go from room3 through door23 to room2

Is this ok? (y/n): y

  The situation now is:
      robot is_in room2
      door12 stands opened
      door23 stands opened
      box1 is_in room1
      box2 is_in room1
      box3 is_in room2
yes
```

The boxes can be moved:

```
?- plan(box3 is_next_to box2, 3).
The steps to be taken are:
      move to box3 in room2
      shift box3 to door12 in room2
      push box3 from room2 through door12 to room1
      push box3 to box2 in room1

Is this ok? (y/n): y

  The situation now is:
      robot is_next_to box3
      robot is_next_to box2
      box3 is_next_to box2
      robot is_in room1
      box3 is_in room1
      door12 stands opened
      door23 stands opened
      box1 is_in room1
      box2 is_in room1
yes
```

The depth count has to be adequate:

```
?- plan(door23 stands closed and door12 stands closed, 3).
no
```

A depth count of 4 is adequate:

```
?- plan(door23 stands closed and door12 stands closed, 4).
```

The steps to be taken are:
    go to door12 in room1
    go from room1 through door12 to room2
    go to door23 in room2
    close door23
    go to door12 in room2
    close door12

Is this ok? (y/n): y

  The situation now is:
    door12 stands closed
    robot is_at door12
    door23 stands closed
    robot is_in room2
    box3 is_next_to box2
    box3 is_in room1
    box1 is_in room1
    box2 is_in room1
yes

Conjunctions of problems can be solved. The depth count limits search in solving any single problem:

    ?- plan(box1 is_in room3 and box2 is_in room3 and box3 is_in room3, 5).
    The steps to be taken are:
        go to door23 in room2
        open door23
        go to door12 in room2
        open door12
        go from room2 through door12 to room1
        move to box1 in room1
        shift box1 to door12 in room1
        push box1 from room1 through door12 to room2
        shift box1 to door23 in room2
        push box1 from room2 through door23 to room3
        go to door23 in room3
        go from room3 through door23 to room2
        go to door12 in room2
        go from room2 through door12 to room1
        move to box2 in room1
        shift box2 to door12 in room1
        push box2 from room1 through door12 to room2
        shift box2 to door23 in room2
        push box2 from room2 through door23 to room3
        go to door23 in room3
        go from room3 through door23 to room2
        go to door12 in room2

```
        go from room2 through door12 to room1
        move to box3 in room1
        shift box3 to door12 in room1
        push box3 from room1 through door12 to room2
        shift box3 to door23 in room2
        push box3 from room2 through door23 to room3
```

  Is this ok? (y/n): y

```
  The situation now is:
        robot is_in room3
        robot is_next_to box3
        box3 is_in room3
        box2 is_in room3
        box1 is_in room3
        door12 stands opened
        door23 stands opened
yes
```

What rooms can the robot move to?

```
    ?- plan(robot is_in Some_room, 3).
    The steps to be taken are:
```

  Is this ok? (y/n): n

We don't want it to stay in the same room . . .

```
    The steps to be taken are:
        go to door23 in room3
        go from room3 through door23 to room2
        go to door12 in room2
        go from room2 through door12 to room1
```

  Is this ok? (y/n): n

or go to room1 . . .

```
    The steps to be taken are:
        go to door23 in room3
        go from room3 through door23 to room2
        go to door23 in room2
        go from room2 through door23 to room3
```

  Is this ok? (y/n): n

or out of room3 and back . . .

The steps to be taken are:
    go to door23 in room3
    go from room3 through door23 to room2

Is this ok? (y/n): n

or to room2 . . .

    no

and there are no other possibilities within the specified depth count.

    ?- plan(Some_door stands closed, 3).
    The steps to be taken are:
        go to door23 in room3
        close door23

Is this ok? (y/n): y

The situation now is:
    door23 stands closed
    robot is_at door23
    robot is_in room3
    door12 stands opened
    box1 is_in room1
    box2 is_in room1
    box3 is_in room2

    Some_door = door23

This is the substitution for the variable in the goal.

11.5 Further Development of the Program

The code for the program which produced the behaviour shown in the previous section is given in Appendix 1. In this section, we consider the scope for further improvements and the lessons to be drawn from from the development of the program thus far.

11.5.1 Variables in goals

The last two examples of the previous section showed a hollow goal term. As we specifically excluded this possibility when discussing the program design in section 11.3, we must examine the program's behaviour when the goal term does include variables.

If the user accepts a proposed plan but then rejects the substitutions for variables that it produces, Prolog backtracks over the goal which modified the problem state. The sub-goal: ?- update_state(Sf) succeeded by removing from the database all clauses for presently/1, which defined the initial problem state, and adding a new set of clauses recording the final state. This database modification does not interfere with the generation of alternative plans from state Si, and if one of the alternatives is eventually accepted by the user, the final set of clauses for presently/1 correctly defines the state resulting from execution of the plan. Problems arise, however, if the user after accepting a plan rejects all substitutions of values for variables in the goal and forces the top-level goal to fail. In this situation, the final state Sf, which the sub-goal: ?- update_state(Sf) had recorded, would remain in the Prolog database, as though the plan had been accepted and executed. The problem is illustrated in Figure 11.18.

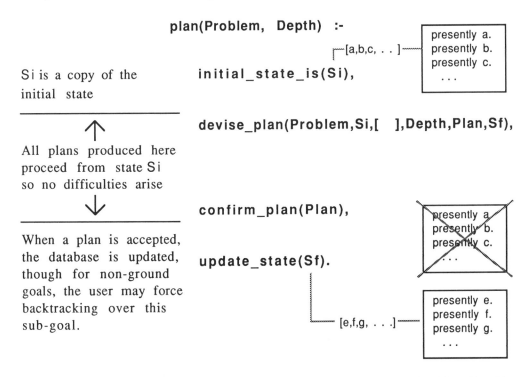

Figure 11.18 State Sf may replace state Si, even when the goal: ?- plan(Problem, Depth) fails

The simplest solution would be to put a cut at the end of the top-level goal, in effect saying to the user: "Once you have accepted a plan, it is carried out." Alternative solutions would involve adding a second clause to the procedure for initial_state/1 to ensure that on backtracking the procedure restored the problem description to its initial state before failing. The modifications to achieve this would be more extensive.

11.5.2   Limitations of the planning algorithm

Redundant steps in a plan

A top-level goal may be achieved as a side-effect of a step at a lower level in the plan. When this occurs, the plan step chosen to solve the top-level problem becomes redundant, but because the algorithm does not keep a record, when planning for a sub-goal, of what higher level goals it is working towards, it does not recognise redundant steps and proposes a sub-optimal plan.

Plans which do not meet the specified goal

In section 11.2.3, we stated that the planning algorithm should produce plans to transform an initial state into one in which a fact or a conjunction of facts held true. The program we have developed produces a plan for each fact in turn, and this approach is based on the important assumption that later steps in a plan do not undo the effects of earlier steps. If this assumption does not hold, the program produces a plan in which not all facts in the goal are true in the final state, as for instance after planning to meet the goal:

   ?- plan(robot is_in room2 and box3 is_in room1, 6).

This goal is treated as a request first to move the robot to room2 and then to move box3 to room1.

More sophisticated planning systems do treat a conjunction of goals as a description of facts to be made true simultaneously and include strategies to detect unrealisable goals. To such a system, the goal:

   ?- plan(robot is_in room2 and robot is_in room3, 6).

is an unrealisable goal, whereas in our system it simply means:

   "Move the robot to room2, and then move it to room3."

The advantage of our approach is its simplicity; its disadvantage is that it puts the burden of correctly ordering the requirements in each action schema firmly on the user. Some recent research has sought to automate the process of identifying these requirements (Silver, 1986).

Extending the program to overcome either of these limitations would be a substantial undertaking, but not one beyond the scope of the reader who has mastered the techniques and skills taught in Part 1 of this book.

11.6   Concluding Observations

The development of the planning program illustrated both the power of Prolog and the constraints which the language imposes. Its chief advantage is that the recursive algorithm 'planner' could be transformed quite easily into a procedure for a Prolog predicate which was an executable program.

However, the search strategy which the programmer is given for free was also the source of difficulties. We discovered that it did not enforce quite the behaviour which was required. This experience is a common one, indicating that the search strategy is both a help and a hindrance in program development. We adopted two techniques to make that strategy more useful: checks for duplication and a restriction on search depth. The further refinements to the program which we suggested in section 11.5.2 would be implemented by devising more elaborate mechanisms to constrain search.

But besides a search strategy, Prolog also makes available a very general-purpose data type for representing knowledge: the term. By using the operator definition technique, the programmer has in this data type a powerful representation for capturing the important characteristics of a problem in a readable notation. The development of the program showed that refining representations to capture more of the semantics of the planning problem was an important way of improving program performance. Development of representations proceeds in parallel with development of algorithms.

Chapter 12

An Electronic Diary

This case study is about the design and implementation of an electronic diary to manage staff commitments in a business organisation. We have chosen to use an academic institution as our example organisation. It has two features common to most business enterprises, which influence the design of the diary system:

- It has a hierarchical staffing structure.

- The commitments of the staff are a mixture of activities which recur at regular intervals, typically weekly or monthly, and engagements which are booked for just a single date.

The case study illustrates the application of the following techniques from the programmers' toolkit:

- Utility predicates, to check the validity of input values and to generate valid values in specified ranges.

- Database modification, to manage a body of stored data about the institution and to manage global variables in the input data validation phase of the program.

- Selector predicates, for accessing components of structures while hiding the form of the structures.

- Forced backtracking, to make procedures for utility predicates generate all valid values and to print the entries in a teacher's diary.

It also illustrates on a larger scale than was possible in section 7.2.1 the use of a meta-program for program structuring.

Section 12.1 describes the requirements for the electronic diary. In section 12.2, we present a system design: it makes clear how the requirements are to be met and identifies the functional components of the program. Section 12.3 shows the implementation of each component. In section 12.4, we consider how to extend the diary system, and we suggest some programming exercises for you.

12.1 System Requirements

The electronic diary must store a description of the institution. The description comprises the following information:

- The working pattern at the institution, for example the earliest and latest working hours of the day and which days of the week are working days.

- The departments into which it is divided.

- The teachers employed in it, each of whom is a member of one department.

- The courses offered by it, each being taught by one department.

- The days and times when classes in a course take place.

- Which teachers are teaching which courses during each academic term.

- The dates of terms.

- The commitments of each teacher. Some commitments, such as giving classes in a course, are recurring ones. Others are non-recurring, such as meetings, interviews and the like. The set of commitments for a teacher constitutes that teacher's diary. We assume that all commitments begin on the hour and are booked in one hour blocks.

We assume that the working pattern is the same for all staff, is unchanging and is known when the program is written. A representation of it forms part of the program. All other aspects of the description are to be provided by the program's user. This implies both the need to accept and validate input data and the requirement for a permanent record of the data external to Prolog. The validation of the input data includes various checks, for example that each department, teacher and course has a unique name and whether a new commitment for a teacher conflicts with existing ones.

In reality, provision of information about the departments into which the institution is divided, the teachers employed in those departments and the courses offered by them would probably be the responsibility of a senior member of staff. The ability of other personnel to view or modify this information would be controlled, their access to the system being limited to viewing and modifying their own diaries. However, issues of data protection and the vetting of the system's users are not considered in this case study. Similarly, the problems of shared concurrent access to the diary are beyond the scope of this chapter. We view the system from the standpoint of a single user with access to all its facilities and all the institution's data.

The system must provide access to the record of teachers' commitments in convenient ways. It must be able to display a teacher's engagements for a given date, for a given purpose or at a given time of day or of a given duration. In each case, the display must be in date order and chronological order within a day.

Finally, the system must be able to find free times in users' diaries for new appointments. The user indicates the duration of the booking and the earliest date for it, and the system must report on available slots and book an acceptable one. The user must be able either to input the list of teachers for whom the booking is to be made or to specify some distinguishing characteristic and have the system make the booking for all teachers who share the characteristic. For instance, if the user wishes to arrange a meeting for all staff in the "Financial Studies" department, he must be able to instruct the system to make the booking for all teachers T for whom teacher(T, financial_studies) is true.

12.2   System Design

In problems where the requirement is for a set of disparate functions, the most difficult part of writing a program is settling on a suitable design which ties the functions together and serves as the framework within which implementation can proceed. The best starting point is to analyse the information which the system manages: how it is obtained, how it is stored and how, in its stored form, it supports the required functions of the system.

We identified in the previous section that some basic information about the institution is included as part of the program. We can represent it as facts, thus:

```
earliest_hour(9).              % Nothing starts before 9.00am
latest_hour(21).               % Everything finishes by 9.00pm

working_day(mon).
working_day(tue).
working_day(wed).
working_day(thu).
working_day(fri).
```

We can also express some basic information in terms of rules. The following rule defines the number of hours in the working day:

```
working_hours(H) :-
    earliest_hour(E),
    latest_hour(L),
    H is L - E.
```

It is wise to express information as rules, derived from a small set of facts, because rules make the description more flexible. Using this rule for working_hours/1 is better than using a fact:

```
working_hours(12).
```

because the rule would not have to be changed if teachers agreed to work until midnight, i.e. latest_hour(24), whereas the fact would.

Information which the program user is to supply can most simply be represented as facts which are added to the Prolog database. We use facts as follows:

- department/1
  To record the departments at the institution.

- teacher/2
  To record the teachers in the institution, the first component giving the teacher's name, the second the department to which the teacher belongs.

- course/2
  To record the courses offered by the institution, the two components giving the title of the course and the department offering it.

- class/3
  To record the classes in a course. The three components are the title of the course, the day of the week and the starting time of the class. We assume that all classes are one hour long.

- teaches/3
  To record the period when a teacher is teaching a course. The three components give the name of the teacher, the title of the course and the period when the teacher is teaching the course.

At this stage, we do not consider the form of components within these structures.

It is not so obvious what is the most suitable representation for the information about term dates. Clearly, the system must be able to establish, for any date in the calendar, whether the date falls within a term, but it is equally clear that we must not require the user to state this for every date in the calendar. We can only reasonably expect him to provide the starting and finishing dates for each term. We might choose to store just these dates, perhaps as clause for start_and_finish/5:

```
start_and_finish(start, autumn, 26, sep, 1988).
start_and_finish(finish, autumn, 16, dec, 1988).
```

These clauses would say that the Autumn term 1988 ran from 26 September to 16 December.

This representation would have the merit of economy, but the disadvantage that a non-trivial calculation would have to be carried out each time we wished to know whether a date occurred in term time or to generate dates which did fall in a term. At the other extreme, we could store a fact for term_date/4 for every date of a term:

```
term_date(autumn, 26, sep, 1988).
    . . .
```

and each date down to:

```
    . .·.
term_date(autumn, 16, dec, 1988).
```

The initial calculation would be considerable and the redundancy in the data representation could be costly, but it would then be trivial to find or generate dates of terms.

The trade-off between economy of representation and efficiency of computation is a familiar one in Prolog programming, and in isolation from the rest of a system it is hard to know whether one has made a sensible choice. You can be reassured, however, by the knowledge that a choice can readily be revised without having any impact on procedures in a program which are to use the information represented.

In the present problem, we choose a method between the two extremes, storing the dates of a term as clauses for term_dates/5, one for each month in the term. Each records:

- Whether the term is the autumn, spring or summer term (first component).

- The month and year (second and third components).

- For the month of the year, the first and last dates which fall within the stated term (fourth and fifth components).

These facts are added to the Prolog database when the user calls add_term_dates/3 to input the start and finish dates of a term and are read by the procedure for in_term_time/2. The design is illustrated in Figure 12.1.

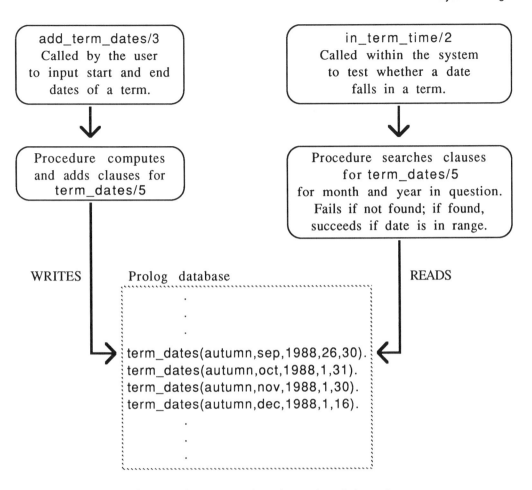

Figure 12.1 Representation of term dates information

For teachers' commitments, we must record the date of the commitment and the purpose of it, its start time and duration. However, the use of a fact for every engagement would be unsatisfactory because of the redundancy which would arise in the representation of recurring commitments. For instance, if there is a clause for teaches/3 recording that Miss Beak teaches "Physiology of British Birds" in the present term and a clause for class/3 recording a class in this subject on Wednesday at 10.00am, then it is implicit that Miss Beak has a one hour engagement at 10.00am every Wednesday of term. Much better than to record each class as a separate engagement for her is to write a rule to express the connection between teaching, classes and a teacher's engagements. This rule is one clause for appointment/4, in which:

- The first component gives the teacher's name.

- The second component gives the date of the engagement.

- The third component gives the start time and duration of the engagement.

- The fourth component gives the purpose of the engagement.

There is a clause for each type of commitment, including one for the non-recurring engagements.   When the user inputs details of a non-recurring engagement, we add a fact for single_booking/4 to the Prolog database.   Its components have the same use as those for appointment/4.

How is this information to be used in supporting the functions of the diary system?   Well, as it does not constitute part of the system, we must provide the user with predicates to save it permanently at the end of a program run and to reload it at the start of a run.   The system has a file-handling component.

Next, the information is used in the process of validating user commands. We have already mentioned some integrity constraints: one was that each teacher's name be unique.   Some of the constraints we enforce are simplifications of a real-world situation, but we design and implement a general-purpose framework for the data entry component of the system which you can use in your own programming.

Besides validating new information against existing data in the diary, we must check that all dates are in the required format and are meaningful. We must forestall attempts to book appointments for 31 November, for example, and for dates which do not fall on working days.   Another component of the system, therefore, manages a calendar, providing a range of operations on structures representing dates.   Components of these structures are days, weeks, months and years, and we provide selector predicates to access them.

The management of the record of teachers' commitments is handled by another component of the system.   It provides predicates to display parts of the diary and to find free slots in it.   Though the predicates which the user calls as goals provide quite complex functions, the procedures defining them should not be especially complex.   For we envisage that routines which check the validity of given dates and times in the data entry component of the system, are utility procedures and serve equally to generate valid dates and times, for example when the system seeks a free slot for a new appointment.

Putting these components together gives us the system design shown in Figure 12.2, where the dependency of all the components on the data managed by the system is clear.   The sections referred to in the figure are the sections of this chapter in which the implementation is described.

The importance of a sound design is crucial to Prolog programming, for it is not a language with a block structure and scope rules to restrict the visibility of procedures, and if we tried to implement without the framework which the design provides, the problem of system structure, or rather of its absence, would become acute.

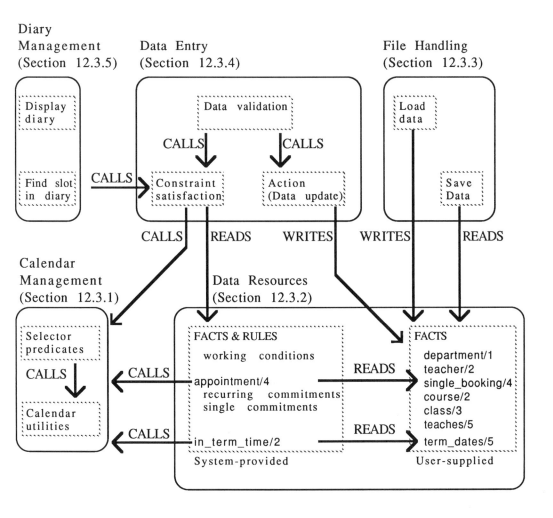

Figure 12.2 System design

12.3   Implementation

We begin the implementation by developing a representation for the calendar and a set of calendar utilities and selector predicates. We then examine how data about teachers' commitments can be represented as rules which use these utilities, and when we have a complete picture of how the system's data resources are held we implement the file handling component of the system. We then write the data entry component. We have called the checking part of this component "constraint satisfaction" to emphasise that procedures within it do not just check the validity of users' input but also generate valid data. It is in the latter way that they are used by the diary manager, the last component of the system.

12.3.1   The calendar

The basis of the calendar is a definition, using facts and rules, of the order of days and months and the lengths of months:

```
next_day(sun, mon).
next_day(mon, tue).
next_day(tue, wed).
next_day(wed, thu).
next_day(thu, fri).
next_day(fri, sat).
next_day(sat, sun).

next_month(jan, feb).
next_month(feb, mar).
next_month(mar, apr).
next_month(apr, may).
next_month(may, jun).
next_month(jun, jul).
next_month(jul, aug).
next_month(aug, sep).
next_month(sep, oct).
next_month(oct, nov).
next_month(nov, dec).
next_month(dec, jan).


month_length(M, _, 30) :-
    ( M = apr; M = jun; M = sep; M = nov ).
month_length(M, _, 31) :-
    ( M = jan; M = mar; M = may; M =jul; M = aug; M = oct; M = dec ).
month_length(feb, Year, 29) :-
    leap_year(Year), !.
month_length(feb, _, 28).

leap_year(Y) :-
    0 is Y mod 400, !.
leap_year(Y) :-
    0 is Y mod 4,
    fail_if(0 is Y mod 100).
```

We must be clear how we intend month_length/3 to be used. Given a month and a year, it is to tell us how many days are in that month of that year:

```
?- month_length(feb, 1900, L).
L = 28
```

```
?- month_length(feb, 2000, L).
L = 29
```

It is not designed to check whether a given month has a given number of days, and it cannot safely be used in this way:

```
?- month_length(feb, 1900, 28).
yes
```

```
?- month_length(feb, 2000, 28).
yes
```

The answer to the second question is wrong for exactly the same reason that the procedure for max/3 with the cut, which we showed in section 6.1.2, sometimes gave the wrong answer.

You will have noticed that we call ;/2 in the procedure for month_length/3, though we advised you against using it. In our experience, the predicate can be used without detriment to program readability in procedures which are simply using =/2 to test an argument against a series of values. However, as always, ;/2 could be replaced by an equivalent formulation using separate clauses:

```
month_length(apr, _ 30).
month_length(jun, _ 30).
etc.
```

The calendar must also provide a means of establishing the correspondence between dates and days of the week, so that when the user seeks to book an appointment, for instance, the program can check that the date given is a working_day. To do this, we require the user to indicate the day of the week on which the 1st. of the starting month falls when he initialises the diary with the month and year from which it is to start and the year to which it is to run. It runs to the end of this year. However, if we recorded in the Prolog database just the information which the user gave, we would have to recalculate from this starting point every time we wanted the day of a later date. As with the record of term dates, we prefer a method which trades an increase in the data stored for a substantial reduction in the processing required in using the data. The method is to record the day on which the first of each month in the currency of the diary falls, and compute the day of the week for other dates from that for the 1st. The procedure for find_days/3 does this:

```
% find_days(Day_of_first_in_month, Date, Day_of_date)
find_days(D, 1, D).                    % Given day is 1st. of month.
find_days(D1, N, D2) :-                % Given day is after 1st.
    next_day(D1, D3),
    M is N - 1,
    find_days(D3, M ,D2).
```

The procedure gives the correct answer when it is used in the way we have described:

```
?- find_days(mon, 1, D).
D = mon

?- find_days(tue, 10, D).
D = thu
```

The system design of Figure 12.2 indicates that the calendar utilities are a low-level component and may be expected to be called with different patterns of argument. find_days/3 is a utility predicate, and the procedure for it must be designed accordingly.

One use for such a utility would be to answer the question:

"For a month beginning on a Monday, on what dates do the Fridays fall?"

The question would be formulated as the goal:

```
?- find_days(mon, N, fri)
```

In this call, execution would produce a Prolog error because when the second sub-goal was called: ?- M is N - 1, N would be a variable and Prolog would not be able to evaluate the expression N - 1. To prevent this, the variable N must always have a substitution applied to it before the arithmetic expression is evaluated. The substitution is made when the base case is reached. Therefore, the arithmetic must come after the recursive call. This reasoning leads us to an improved procedure for find_days/3:

```
find_days(D, 1, D).
find_days(D1, N, D2) :-
     find_days(D1, N1, D3),
     next_day(D3, D2),
     N is N1 + 1.
```

Now we get:

```
?- find_days(mon, N, fri)
N =  5;

N =  12;

N =  19;

N = 26
```

The predicate has other uses. The question:

"When the first of the month is a Sunday, what days of the week do other dates in the month fall on?"

is answered by:

```
?-find_days(sun, N, D)
N = 1
D = sun;

N = 2
D = mon;

N = 3
D = tue;
etc.
```

In fact, the procedure would behave correctly whenever the second argument in the goal was a variable. To make the utility completely all-purpose, we must enclose the call to find_days/3 in a predicate which tests the status of this argument. This is what corresponding_day/3 does. The procedure is:

```
corresponding_day(Day1, N, Day2) :-
    var(N), !,
    find_days(Day1, N, Day2).
corresponding_day(Day1, N, Day2) :-
    0 is N mod 7, !,
    find_days(Day1, 7, Temp), !,
    Day2 = Temp.
corresponding_day(Day1, N, Day2) :-
    Min is N mod 7,
    find_days(Day1, Min, Temp), !,
    Day2 = Temp.
```

To make the procedure efficient, we take advantage of the weekly cycle of days and in the second and third clauses reduce the second argument to an integer in the range 1 to 7 before calling find_days/3. The case of a date exactly divisible by 7 must be distinguished from that of other dates because find_days/3 cannot be called with 0 as its second argument. Mutual exclusion between the three clauses is enforced by the cuts after the guards: ?- var(N) in the first clause and: ?- 0 is N mod 7 in the second. In the second and third clauses, we use the sub-goals: ?- find_days(Day1, 7, Temp), !, Day2 = Temp instead of the single sub-goal: ?- find_days(Day1, Min, Day2) to ensure correct behaviour when all arguments in a call are ground terms. For instance, to answer the question:

"For a month which starts on a Tuesday, does the 24th. fall on a Sunday?"

the call is:

```
?- corresponding_day(tue, 24, sun).
```

The answer is: no, but formulating these clauses with the single sub-goal would cause the procedure to continue indefinitely generating ever-larger dates and finding none matching 24. To prevent this, we use the variable Temp as the third argument in the call to find_days/3, and after the call has succeeded, test whether the value substituted for it matches the given Day2. The cut prevents backtracking if it does not. The two formulations are declaratively identical. Procedurally, we have to separate the attempt to satisfy the sub-goal find_days from the attempt to match the third argument in this sub-goal with the given date, and put a cut between the two. This is a situation in which the programmer must use =/2, rather than Prolog's matching mechanism, and it exemplifies the point we made in section 4.5 about the differences between the two under the procedural interpretation of a program.

We emphasised in section 4.3 that the programmer must test a utility under all patterns of argument and document any restrictions on the patterns which may be used. In the case of corresponding_day/3, there are no restrictions.

The procedure for set_up_diary/4 adds the information about the 1st. of each month to the Prolog database as a clause for first_of_month/3:

```
% set_up_diary(Start_year, Start_month, First_of_start_year, End_year)

% Clause 1: Reached Dec. in the year to which the diary is to run.
set_up_diary(Year, dec, S, Year) :- !,
    assert(first_of_month(dec, Year, S)).

% Clause 2: Reached Dec. in a different year:
% Set up diary from start of following year.
set_up_diary(Current_year, dec, S, End_year) :- !,
    assert(first_of_month(dec, Current_year, S)),
    corresponding_day(S, 32, S2),
    Next_year is Current_year + 1,
    set_up_diary(Next_year, jan, S2, End_year).

% Clause 3: set up diary from start of following month.
set_up_diary(Current_year, Current_month, S, End_year) :-
    assert(first_of_month(Current_month, Current_year, S)),
    month_length(Current_month, Current_year, L),
    corresponding_day(S, L, S2),
    next_day(S2, S3),
```

```
next_month(Current_month, Next_month),
set_up_diary(Current_year, Next_month, S3, End_year).
```

We also provide todays_date/1 to obtain the current date. There may be a built-in predicate in your Prolog system which enables you to get this information from the computer system's clock. If there is not, the procedure for get_date/1, which is used as a directive, prompts the user to supply the current date and stores it in the Prolog database as a clause for todays_date/1:

```
get_date :-
    write('Please enter the date in the form:'),
    nl,
    write('date(1, jan, 1999).'),
    nl,
    write('The month must be abbreviated'),
    nl,
    write('to its first three characters'),
    nl,
    seeing(F),                   % Record current input stream.
    see(user),                   % Take input from terminal.
    read(Date),
    assert(todays_date(Date)),
    see(F).                      % Revert to taking input from file
                                 % being consulted.
:- get_date.
```

The date is recorded as a structure with functor date and arity 3, in which:

- The first component is an integer and gives the date in the month.

- The second component is the month, abbreviated to the first three letters.

- The third component is an integer, giving the year.

We provide selector predicates same_or_later/2, date_falls_on/2, in_term_time/2 and teaching/3 to access components of such structures. The procedures for them follow.

A call to same_or_later/2, takes dates D1 and D2 and succeeds if D2 is the same date as D1 or is a later date than D1:

```
% Clause 1: D2 falls in a later year.

same_or_later(date(_, _, Y1), date(_, _, Y2)) :-
    Y2 > Y1, !.
```

% Clause 2: D2 falls in a later month of the same year.

```
same_or_later(date(_, M1, Y), date(_, M2, Y)) :-
    after_month(M1, M2), !.
```

% Clause 3: D2 falls on the same or a later day of the same month
% of the same year.

```
same_or_later(date(D1, M, Y), date(D2, M, Y)) :-
    D2 >= D1.
```

We gave a procedure for after_month/2 in section 6.3.2.

A call to date_falls_on/2 succeeds if the first argument is a date and the second argument is the day of the week on which the date falls:

```
date_falls_on(date(D, M, Y), Day1) :-
    first_of_month(M, Y, Day2),
    month_length(M, Y, L),
    in_range_integer(1, D, L),
    corresponding_day(Day2, D, Day1).
```

A call to in_term_time/2 succeeds if the first argument is a term and the second is a date which falls in that term:

```
in_term_time(Term, date(Date, Month, Year)) :-
    term_dates(Term, Month, Year, From, To),
    in_range_integer(From, Date, To).
```

A call to teaching/3 succeeds if the first argument is the name of a teacher, the second is a subject and the third is a date which falls within the period for which the teacher is recorded as teaching the subject:

```
teaching(T, S, date(Date, Month, Year)) :-
    teach(T, S, Term, Year),
    in_term_time(Term, date(Date, Month, Year)).
```

The last three are written as utilities which can be called with any pattern of arguments and generate alternatives through backtracking. The order of the last two sub-goals in the procedure for date_falls_on/2 is crucial in ensuring the correct behaviour on backtracking when the first argument in the call is a variable. The first two sub-goals identify the starting day and the length of a month. We then use in_range_integer/3, for which we gave a procedure in section 4.3, to generate a date in that month and corresponding_day/3 to test the day that the date falls on. When all dates in the month have been generated, the call to in_range_integer/3 fails, and Prolog backtracks to seek another month. Eventually, the call fails. This would not be so if we reversed the last two sub-goals, using corresponding_day/3 to generate a date which did fall on the given day of the week and `in_range_integer` to test whether the date existed in the month. The call to `corresponding_day/3` would always be re-satisfiable on backtracking, generating progressively larger dates, all of which would fail the test of being an in_range_integer.

We use this example to emphasise the importance of testing utilities exhaustively before they are used in a large program. To test `date_falls_on/2`, we temporarily add to the Prolog database two clauses for `first_of_month/3`:

```
first_of_month(oct,  1987,  thu).
first_of_month(nov,  1987,  sun).
```

There are now not too many alternatives when we test the procedure with the goal:

```
?- date_falls_on(Date, tue).
Date  =  date(6,oct,1987);

Date  =  date(13,oct,1987);

Date  =  date(20,oct,1987);

Date  =  date(27,oct,1987);

Date  =  date(3,nov,1987);

Date  =  date(10,nov,1987);

Date  =  date(17,nov,1987);

Date  =  date(24,nov,1987);
no
```

12.3.2   Representing data by rules

We obtain details of teachers' commitments by calling appointment/4 as a goal. In section 12.1, we mentioned two types of commitment, and each is defined by one clause:

```
appointment(Name, Date, period(T, 1), teaching(S)) :-
        teaching(Name, S, Date),
        class(S, D, T),
        date_falls_on(Date,  D).

appointment(Teacher, Date, Period, Purpose) :-
        single_booking(Teacher, Date, Period, Purpose).
```

The first clause handles classes. They recur at the same time on the same day of the week in every week of term and are one hour long. The start time and duration are represented in the third argument as the two compnents of a structure with functor period. The rule states that for any subject S which teacher Name is teaching on a date Date and for which there is a class at time T on day D, Name has an appointment on Date starting at T and of one hour's duration for the purpose of teaching S if the date Date falls on the day D. The second clause handles one-off appointments, booked for a specific teacher on a specific date and for a specific period and purpose.

By using rules to capture the structure of the database, we enhance the clarity of the representation and prevent redundancy in it. We also conceal from the rest of the system that teachers' commitments are represented in several different ways. Other components see nothing of these rules, but simply call appointment/4, as though the information were stored as facts.

We use the same technique to deal with the different periods for which teachers teach courses. In section 12.2, we wrote that this information would be recorded as clauses for teaches/3, with the third component recording the period covered by the course. This component is a structure, having one of two forms:

* in(Y1/Y2)
  To represent that the course continues throughout the academic year denoted by the integers Y1 and Y2.

* in(T, Y)
  To represent that the course is taught only in term T of academic year Y.

To conceal the different representations from other components of the system, we provide teach/4. A call succeeds by giving a term in which a teacher is teaching a course. When the course is given for a whole academic year, the call generates each of the three terms on backtracking. The procedure is:

```
teach(Teacher, Subject, autumn, Year) :-
    teaches(Teacher, Subject, in(Year/_)).
teach(Teacher, Subject, spring, Year) :-
    teaches(Teacher, Subject, in(_/Year)).
teach(Teacher, Subject, summer, Year) :-
    teaches(Teacher, Subject, in(_/Year)).
teach(Teacher, Subject, Term, Year) :-
    teaches(Teacher, Subject, in(Term, Year)).
```

We also provide term_of/3 as a selector predicate for getting at components of structures with functor in and arity 2. The procedure is:

```
term_of(in(Y/_), autumn, Y).
term_of(in(_/Y), spring, Y).
term_of(in(_/Y), summer, Y).
term_of(in(Term, Year), Term, Year).
```

12.3.3   File handling

Having defined how all information relating to the institution is recorded, we can write procedures for save_diary/1 and load_diary/1 to save data in, and load data from, the file which is given as argument in the call:

```
save_diary(File) :-
    write_file_of_terms(File).
```

The procedure for write_file_of_terms/1 was given in section 5.3. In this case, the procedure for next/1 is:

```
next(Entry) :-
    diary_entry_type(Functor/Arity),
    functor(Entry, Functor, Arity),
    call(Entry).

diary_entry_type(first_of_month/3).
diary_entry_type(term_dates/5).
diary_entry_type(teacher/2).
diary_entry_type(course/2).
diary_entry_type(single_booking/4).
diary_entry_type(teaches/3).
diary_entry_type(class/3).
diary_entry_type(department/1).
```

We could also use the procedure for read_file_of_terms/1 from section 5.3, but as the processing required for each term read is just to add it to the Prolog database, we use a simpler procedure:

```
load_diary(File) :-
    consult(File).
```

12.3.4   Data entry

The structure of this component is based on that of the meta-program for data input validation which we gave in section 7.2.1. The meta-program is extended to handle a common situation in data validation problems, that in which the user's input contains an error which is to be reported to him but which does not necessarily invalidate the command. For instance, when the user adds a new commitment to a teacher's diary which conflicts with exising engagements, we must warn the user of the conflict, but it is for him to decide whether to cancel the new commitment. The teacher might want to preserve both in the diary as a reminder to fulfil the second engagement if the first is cancelled.

The first part of the meta-program becomes:

```
validate(warning(Check_clash), none) :- !,
    arg(1, Check_clash, Details),
    bag(Details, Check_clash, Result),
    check_result(Result).
validate(Check, _) :-
    call(Check), !.
validate(_, Error_message) :-
    assert(error(Error_message)).

check_result([ ]) :- !.
check_result(L) :-
    assert(warning(L)).
```

A call from the object program to check for clashes between existing engagements and those implied by a new commitment has the form validate(warning(Check), none). Check is a term which identifies the procedure in the object program to be called to apply the check. The procedure may have any form, but its first argument must be a structure with functor appointment and arity 4, and it must be defined so that when a call succeeds, it returns in the components of this structure details of an existing engagement with which the new one clashes. By passing Details and the whole structure represented by Check as the first two arguments in a call to bag/3, we obtain in the third argument a list of all the existing engagements with which the new commitment clashes. If this list is not empty, the procedure for check_result/1 adds it to the Prolog database as a clause for warning/1. To make clear that in this type of call to validate/2 the second argument has no significance, we use the atom none, rather than the anonymous variable

The second part of the meta-program, that which defines how a command in the object program is executed, has an extra clause to handle the case where a warning has been recorded:

```
do_action(Action) :-
    retract(warning(Message)), !,
    write_out(['New commitment clashes with:'|Message]),
    write('Should it be added? (y/n): '),
    get(Answer),
    act_on(Answer, Action).
do_action(_) :-
    retract(error(Message)), !,
    report_error(Message).
```

```
do_action(Action) :-
    call(Action).

act_on(121, Action) :- !,                    % Character entered was "y"
    call(Action).
act_on(_, _).

report_error(Message) :-
    write_out(Message),
    nl,
    retract(error(Next_message)), !,
    report_error(Next_message).
report_error(_).

write_out([ ]).
write_out([H|T]) :-
    write(H),
    nl,
    write_out(T).
```

We give first the procedures for those data input predicates which do not imply new commitments for a teacher: add_term_dates/3, add_dept/1, add_teacher/2 and add_course/2:

```
add_term_dates(Term, From, To) :-
    validate(is_term(Term), [Term,' is not a term']),
    validate(same_or_later(From, To),
        ['finish date must not be before start date']),
    do_action(record_term_dates(Term, From, To)).

is_term(autumn).
is_term(spring).
is_term(summer).

record_term_dates(Term, date(D1, M, Y), date(D2, M, Y)) :- !,
    assert(term_dates(Term, M, Y, D1, D2)).
record_term_dates(Term, date(D, dec, Y), To) :- !,
    assert(term_dates(Term, dec, Y, D, 31)),
    Y2 is Y + 1,
    record_term_dates(Term, date(1, jan, Y2), To).
record_term_dates(Term, date(D, M, Y), To) :-
    month_length(M, Y, L),
    assert(term_dates(Term, M, Y, D, L)),
    next_month(M, Next_m),
    record_term_dates(Term, date(1, Next_m, Y), To).

add_dept(Dept) :-
    do_action(add_fact(department(Dept))).
```

```
add_teacher(Teacher, Dept) :-
    validate(fail_if(teacher(Teacher, _)), [Teacher,'already exists']),
    validate(department(Dept), [Dept,'is not a department']),
    do_action(add_fact(teacher(Teacher, Dept))).

add_course(Course, Dept) :-
    validate(fail_if(course(Course,_)), [Course,'already exists']),
    validate(department(Dept), [Dept,'is not a department']),
    do_action(add_fact(course(Course, Dept))).

add_fact(Fact) :-
    clause(Fact, true), !,
    write('This information is already stored in the database'),
    nl.
add_fact(Fact) :-
    assert(Fact).
```

Notice that the procedure for add_dept/1 does not call validate/2. This is because a department can have any name at all. The only constraint is that its name must not duplicate that of an existing department, and this is checked within the procedure for add_fact/1.

The procedures for add_appointment/4, add_teaches/3 and add_class/3 include checks for clashes between a new appointment, a new teaching commitment or a new class for a course and existing engagements in the diaries of the teachers concerned. It is in the rule which determines whether there is a clash that we make use of warnings. The procedure for add_appointment/4 is:

```
add_appointment(Teacher, Date, Period, Purpose) :-
    validate(teacher(Teacher, _),[Teacher,'is not a teacher']),
    validate(bookable_date(Date), [Date,'is not a bookable date']),
    validate(bookable_hours(Period), [Period, 'is not within working
                                       hours']),
    validate(warning(appointment_clashes(appointment(Teacher, Date,
                                       _, _), Period)), none),
    do_action(assert(single_booking(Teacher, Date, Period, Purpose))).

bookable_date(Date) :-
    date_falls_on(Date, Day),
    working_day(Day),
    todays_date(Today),
    same_or_later(Today, Date).

bookable_hours(period(Start, Duration)) :-
    earliest_hour(E),
    latest_hour(L),
```

```
Last_start is L - 1,
in_range_integer(E,  Start,  Last_start),
Max_duration is L - Start,
in_range_integer(1,  Duration,  Max_duration).
```

appointment_clashes/2 checks for conflicts between existing commit-ments and the proposed new appointment.   The procedure is:

```
appointment_clashes(Present_commitment,  Period)  :-
    call(Present_commitment),
    arg(3,  Present_commitment,  P),
    overlapping(P,  Period).

overlapping(period(S,D),  period(NewS,  NewD))  :-
    NewS < S + D,
    NewS + NewD > S.
```

The logic of appointment_clashes/2 is that a conflict occurs if there is a Present_commitment for period P, and P overlaps with the Period of the new commitment.   And the procedure for overlapping/2 says that a new commitment overlaps with an existing one if its start time is before the end time of the existing commitment and its end time is after the start time of the existing commitment.

The procedures for add_teaches/3 and add_class/3 are:

```
add_teaches(Teacher,  Subject,  When)  :-
    validate(teacher(Teacher,  _),  [Teacher,'is  not  a  teacher']),
    validate(course(Subject,  _),  [Subject,'is  not  a  subject']),
    validate(unit_of_teaching(When),  [When,  'is  not  a  unit  of  teaching']),
    validate(warning(teaching_clashes(appointment(Teacher,  _,  _,  _),
                                  Subject,  When)),  none),
    do_action(add_fact(teaches(Teacher,  Subject,  When))).

unit_of_teaching(in(Term,  Year))  :-
    term_dates(Term,  _,  Year,  _,  _).
unit_of_teaching(in(Y1/Y2))  :-
    Y2 is Y1 + 1,
    term_dates(autumn,  _,  Y1,  _,  _),
    term_dates(spring,  _,  Y2,  _,  _),
    term_dates(summer,  _,  Y2,  _,  _).

teaching_clashes(appointment(T,  date(Date,  Month,  Year),  P,  W),
        S,  When)  :-
    class(S,  Day,  Time),                  % For any class in the subject S
    term_of(When,  Term,  Year),            % and, in the period when T is
    in_term_time(Term,  date(Date,  Month,  Year)),        % to teach S,
    date_falls_on(date(Date,  Month,  Year),  Day),      % any date which
                                            % falls on the day of the class,
```

```
        appointment(T, date(Date, Month, Year), P, W),    % does T have an
                                                           % appointment
        overlapping(P, period(Time, 1)). % which overlaps with the class?

    add_class(Subject, Day, Time) :-
        validate(course(Subject, _), [Subject,'is not a subject']),
        validate(working_day(Day), [Day,'is not a working day']),
        validate(bookable_hours(period(Time, 1)),
             [Time, 'is not a valid time for the start of a class']),
        validate(warning(class_clashes(appointment(_, _, _, _), Subject,
             Day, Time)), none),
        do_action(assert(class(Subject, Day, Time))).

    class_clashes(appointment(T, Date, P, Why), Subject, Day, Time) :-
        teaching(T, Subject, Date),    % For any teacher T who is teaching
                                       % the subject on a date
        date_falls_on(Date, Day),      % which falls on the day of a class,
        appointment(T, Date, P, Why),  % does T have an appointment
        overlapping(P, period(Time, 1)). % which overlaps with the class?
```

When the user inputs the information that a teacher is to teach a subject in a particular period, the system checks for clashes between any timetabled classes in the subject and existing engagements for the teacher. When the user inputs details of a new class in an existing course, the system checks for clashes with existing engagements for any teacher who is to teach the course. Identifying such rules as these is difficult, but the use of the meta-program does lessen the difficulty of correctly expressing them. It reduces the problem to that of stating statically the conditions for a clash. The procedural problem of collecting a list of all engagements which satisfy the conditions is handled in the meta-program by the call to bag/3.

Meta-programming, in which terms that are variables in the text of a program are called as goals after substitutions have been applied to them, introduces a level of indirection in the execution of the program, and if several levels are used, the program can become confusing for a reader. It is easy to lose track of the substitutions that have been applied to a variable, which makes the program very hard to understand when that variable is then called as a goal. The manipulation of variables and the calls involved in satisfying the sub-goal: ?- validate(warning(class_clashes(appointment(_, _, _, _), Subject, Day,Time)), none) are illustrated in Figure 12.3.

At the object program level, the variable Check stands for a structure which is the goal in the object program that detects a clash between an existing engagement and commitments implied by the new class for a course. At level 2, the first level of the meta-program, the variable Details has substituted for it the first component of this structure. At level 3, the meta-program calls bag/3, giving Details and Check as the first two arguments.

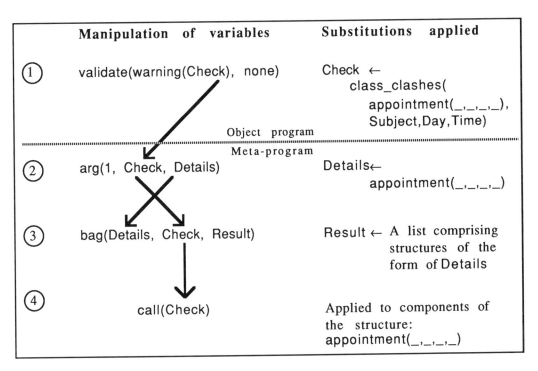

Manipulation of variables	Substitutions applied
① validate(warning(Check), none)	Check ← class_clashes(appointment(_,_,_,_), Subject,Day,Time)
Object program	
Meta-program	
② arg(1, Check, Details)	Details← appointment(_,_,_,_)
③ bag(Details, Check, Result)	Result ← A list comprising structures of the form of Details
④ call(Check)	Applied to components of the structure: appointment(_,_,_,_)

Figure 12.3 Relationship of object program and meta-program calls

The point here is that the structure substituted for Details also occurs in that which was substituted for Check, and though in the object program we used the anonymous variable for components of this structure, those variables share with corresponding ones in the first component of the structure that Check stands for. When, at level 4, the built-in predicate bag exhaustively satisfies the goal represented by Check, values substituted each time for the variables that were anonymous are preserved in the list which Result stands for.

We can now test all the procedures for the data entry predicates. The fact that we have not yet written procedures for the predicates which display the diary entries does not prevent us from checking that new information is being correctly added to the Prolog database. We can use lower-level mechanisms for examining the diary. After we enter the information that today's date is: date(7, oct, 1987), the program behaves as follows:

```
?- set_up_diary(1987, sep, tue, 1988).
yes
```

Check that the correct clauses have been added:

```
?- listing(first_of_month).
first_of_month(sep,1987,tue).
first_of_month(oct,1987,thu).
```

```
first_of_month(nov,1987,sun).
first_of_month(dec,1987,tue).
first_of_month(jan,1988,fri).
first_of_month(feb,1988,mon).
first_of_month(mar,1988,tue).
first_of_month(apr,1988,fri).
first_of_month(may,1988,sun).
first_of_month(jun,1988,wed).
first_of_month(jul,1988,fri).
first_of_month(aug,1988,mon).
first_of_month(sep,1988,thu).
first_of_month(oct,1988,sat).
first_of_month(nov,1988,tue).
first_of_month(dec,1988,thu).
yes
```

Check the validation routines:

```
?- add_term_dates(autum,date(11,dec,1987),date(5,oct,1987)).
autum
is not a term

finish date must not be before start date
yes

?- add_term_dates(autumn,date(5,oct,1987),date(11,dec,1987)).
yes

?- add_term_dates(spring,date(25,jan,1988),date(18,mar,1988)).
yes

?- add_term_dates(summer,  date(18,apr,1988),date(17,jun,1988)).
yes
```

Check the correct clauses have been added:

```
?-  listing(term_dates).
term_dates(autumn,oct,1987,5,31).
term_dates(autumn,nov,1987,1,30).
term_dates(autumn,dec,1987,1,11).
term_dates(spring,jan,1988,25,31).
term_dates(spring,feb,1988,1,29).
term_dates(spring,mar,1988,1,18).
term_dates(summer,apr,1988,18,30).
term_dates(summer,may,1988,1,31).
term_dates(summer,jun,1988,1,17).
yes
```

```
?- add_dept(financial_studies).
yes
```

Check the general-purpose validation routine:

```
?- add_dept(financial_studies).
This information is already stored in the database
yes

?- add_teacher(sterling,financial_studies).
yes
```

Check some validation routines:

```
?- add_teacher(sterling,ornithology).
sterling
already exists

ornithology
is not a department
yes

?- add_teacher(ledger,financial_studies).
yes

?- add_course(tax_evasion,financial_studies).
yes

?- add_course(vat_frauds,financial_studies).
yes

?- add_course(asset_stripping,financial_studies).
yes
```

Check the correct clauses have been added:

```
?- listing(course).
course(tax_evasion,financial_studies).
course(vat_frauds,financial_studies).
course(asset_stripping,financial_studies).
yes
```

Check more validation routines:

```
?-add_appointment(ledger,date(17,oct,1987),period(8,3),
    seeing_solicitor).
date(17,oct,1987)
is not a bookable date
```

```
period(8,3)
is not within working hours
yes
```

```
?- add_appointment(ledger,date(16,oct,1987),period(10,3),
    seeing_solicitor).
yes
```

The next check is that the system does detect an overlap of a new appointment with the beginning of an existing engagement:

```
?- add_appointment(ledger,date(16,oct,1987),period(9,2),
    seeing_bank_manager).
```

```
New commitment clashes with:
appointment(ledger,date(16,oct,1987),period(10,3),seeing_solicitor)
Should it be added? (y/n): n
yes
```

Now we check that it detects an overlap with the end of an existing engagement, though we add the new one anyway:

```
?- add_appointment(ledger,date(16,oct,1987),period(12,1),
    seeing_bank_manager).
New commitment clashes with:
appointment(ledger,date(16,oct,1987),period(10,3),seeing_solicitor)
Should it be added? (y/n): y
yes
```

Check that the correct clauses have been added:

```
?- listing(single_booking).
single_booking(ledger,date(16,oct,1987),period(10,3),seeing_solicitor).
single_booking(ledger,date(16,oct,1987),period(12,1),
    seeing_bank_manager).
yes
```

```
?- add_teaches(ledger,vat_frauds,in(autumn,  1987)).
yes
```

Check that the correct clause was added:

```
?- listing(teaches).
teaches(ledger,vat_frauds,in(autumn,  1987))
yes
```

Check the behaviour of the procedure for class_clashes/4:

```
?- add_class(vat_frauds,fri,10).
New commitment clashes with:
appointment(ledger,date(16,oct,1987),period(10,3),seeing_solicitor)
Should it be added? (y/n): n
yes

?- add_class(vat_frauds,fri,18).
yes
```

Check the correct clause was added:

```
?- listing(class).
class(vat_frauds,fri,18).
yes

?- add_appointment(sterling,date(16,oct,1987),period(18,2),
    cocktail_party).
yes
```

Check the behaviour of the procedure for teaching_clashes/3:

```
?- add_teaches(sterling,vat_frauds,in(autumn,1987)).
New commitment clashes with:
appointment(sterling,date(16,oct,1987),period(18,2),cocktail_party)
Should it be added? (y/n): y
yes

?- save_diary(diary).
yes
```

Progressive testing of constituent procedures as they are written must be a part of program development in Prolog. We allow ourselves great flexibility in the approach to implementation of a large system because we consider the language is powerful enough for it to be safe to do so. However, the incremental approach is only valid as an alternative to the discipline of conventional top-down program development if it is applied within the framework of its own discipline. Incremental testing is an essential part of that discipline.

12.3.5 Diary management

Procedures in this component of the system make extensive use of utilities already written. For this reason, the programming is relatively straight-forward, despite the rather complex requirements in respect of the display and management of the diary entries.

Firstly, print_entries/2 provides the display of diary entries in the required form. The procedure is:

```
print_entries(Teacher, Commitment) :-
    validate(teacher(Teacher, _), [Teacher, ' is not a teacher']),
    do_action(list_entries(Teacher, Commitment)).

list_entries(T, date(D, M, Y)) :-              % Entries on a given date.
    show_entries(T, date(D, M, Y), _, _).
list_entries(T,subject(S))  :-            % Entries about a given subject.
    show_entries(T, _, _, S).
list_entries(T, period(S, D)) :-    % Entries at given time and/or of a
    show_entries(T, _, period(S, D), _).          % given duration.

show_entries(T, Date, period(S, D), Purpose) :-
    bookable_date(Date),
    earliest_hour(E),
    latest_hour(L),
    in_range_integer(E, S, L),
    appointment(T, Date, period(S, D), Purpose),
    write('Date: '),
    write(Date),
    write(' Time: '),
    write(S),
    write(' Duration: '),
    write(D),
    write(' Purpose: '),
    write(Purpose),
    nl,
    fail.
show_entries(_, _, _, _).
```

In the procedure for show_entries/4, the utilities bookable_date/1 and in_range_integer/3 generate valid dates and starting times if Date or S is a variable when the goal is called, and we use forced backtracking to generate all valid values. The utilities generate alternative values in chronological order, as is required.

The same utilities are used in the procedure for book_soonest/4 which the user calls to find the earliest free slot in the diary on or after a given date:

```
book_soonest(For, Duration, Purpose, Not_before) :-
    validate(bookable_hours(period(_, Duration)),
        [Duration,'is longer than working day']),
    validate(bookable_date(Not_before),
        [Not_before, 'is not a bookable date']).
    do_action((
        make_list(For, [First|Others]),
```

```
        find_soonest(First, Duration, Not_before, When),
        check_others(Others, When),
        confirm_time(When),
        record_group_booking([First|Others], When, Purpose)
        )).

make_list([H|T], [H|T]).
make_list(people(People, Condition), List_of_people) :-
    bag(People, Condition, List_of_people).

find_soonest(Teacher, Duration, Not_before,
        slot(Date, period(Start, Duration))) :-
    date_falls_on(Date, Day),
    working_day(Day),
    same_or_later(Not_before , Date),
    bookable_hours(period(Start, Duration)),
    fail_if(appointment_clashes(appointment(Teacher, Date, _, _),
        period(Start, Duration))).

check_others([ ], _).
check_others([First|Others], slot(Date, Period)) :-
    fail_if(appointment_clashes(appointment(First, Date, _, _), Period)),
    check_others(Others, slot(Date, Period)).

confirm_time(slot(Date,Period))  :-
    write('Appointment could be booked for: '),
    write(Date),
    nl,
    write('At:  '),
    write(Period),
    nl,
    write('Is this ok (y/n)? '),
    get(121).                              % succeeds if user types "y"

record_group_booking([First|Others], slot(Date, Period), P) :-
    teacher(First, _), !,
    write('Booked for: '),
    write(First),
    nl,
    assert(single_booking(First, Date, Period, P)),
    record_group_booking(Others, slot(Date, Period), P).
record_group_booking([First|Others], When, Purpose) :-
    write('Ignored: '),
    write(First),
    nl,
    record_group_booking(Others, When, Purpose).
record_group_booking([ ], _, _).
```

The structure is that used for all procedures which validate data input by the user. In this case, a conjunction of actions is given as the argument in the call to do_action/1. These actions are:

- To make a list of all the teachers for whom the booking is to be made.

- For the first teacher in the list, to find the earliest time when the teacher is free for an appointment of the given length.

- To check that at this time all other teachers in the list are free. If any is not free, the goal fails, and Prolog backtracks to find the next time when the first teacher is free.

- To obtain confirmation from the user that the time found is suitable. If it is not, the goal fails, and Prolog seeks another time.

- To record the confirmed time as a booking for all those in the list. Before adding the new booking, we check that each name is indeed that of a teacher at the institution.

The diary display and management components can now be tested. First, we restore the previous diary entries:

```
?- load_diary(diary).
yes
```

Check the display of entries for a date:

```
?- print_entries(ledger,date(23,oct,1987)).
Date: date(23,oct,1987) Time: 18 Duration: 1 Purpose:
    teaching(vat_frauds)
yes
```

and on a subject:

```
?- print_entries(sterling,subject(teaching(vat_frauds))).
Date: date(9,oct,1987) Time: 18 Duration: 1 Purpose:
    teaching(vat_frauds)
Date: date(16,oct,1987) Time: 18 Duration: 1 Purpose:
    teaching(vat_frauds)
Date: date(23,oct,1987) Time: 18 Duration: 1 Purpose:
    teaching(vat_frauds)
Date: date(30,oct,1987) Time: 18 Duration: 1 Purpose:
    teaching(vat_frauds)
Date: date(6,nov,1987) Time: 18 Duration: 1 Purpose:
    teaching(vat_frauds)
Date: date(13,nov,1987) Time: 18 Duration: 1 Purpose:
```

```
        teaching(vat_frauds)
Date: date(20,nov,1987) Time: 18 Duration: 1 Purpose:
        teaching(vat_frauds)
Date: date(27,nov,1987) Time: 18 Duration: 1 Purpose:
        teaching(vat_frauds)
Date: date(4,dec,1987) Time: 18 Duration: 1 Purpose:
        teaching(vat_frauds)
Date: date(11,dec,1987) Time: 18 Duration: 1 Purpose:
        teaching(vat_frauds)
yes
```

and at a time:

```
?- print_entries(ledger,period(10,_)).
Date: date(16,oct,1987) Time: 10 Duration: 3 Purpose: seeing_solicitor
yes
```

Check that the system does not double-book:

```
?- book_soonest([ledger], 3, city_visit, date(16,oct,1987)).
Appointment could be booked for: date(16,oct,1987)
At: period(13,3)
Is this ok (y/n)? y
Booked for: ledger
yes
```

Check that the correct clause has been added:

```
?- print_entries(ledger,date(16,oct,1987)).
Date: date(16,oct,1987) Time: 10 Duration: 3 Purpose: seeing_solicitor
Date: date(16,oct,1987) Time: 12 Duration: 1 Purpose:
        seeing_bank_manager
Date: date(16,oct,1987) Time: 13 Duration: 3 Purpose: city_visit
Date: date(16,oct,1987) Time: 18 Duration: 1 Purpose:
        teaching(vat_frauds)
yes
```

Check that a booking can be made for a group:

```
?- book_soonest(people(P,teaches(P,vat_frauds,_)),4,
        remand_appearance, date(16,oct,1987)).
Appointment could be booked for: date(19,oct,1987)
At: period(9,4)
Is this ok (y/n)? y
Booked for: ledger
Booked for: sterling
P = _31.
```

Check that it has been made:

```
?- print_entries(ledger,date(19,oct,1987)).
Date: date(19,oct,1987) Time: 9 Duration: 4 Purpose: remand_appearance
yes
```

```
?- print_entries(sterling, date(19,oct,1987)).
Date: date(19,oct,1987) Time: 9 Duration: 4 Purpose: remand_appearance
yes
```

Check that the system treats correctly a booking for a group which includes an unknown name:

```
?- book_soonest([ledger, sterling, nemo], 2, directors_meeting,
      date(16, oct, 1987)).
Appointment could be booked for: date(19,oct,1987)
At: period(13,2)
Is this ok (y/n)? y
Booked for: ledger
Booked for: sterling
Ignored: nemo
```

```
?- save_diary(diary).
yes
```

12.4 Extensions to the System

In this section, we suggest some extensions to the electronic diary as programming exercises for you.

12.4.1 Other types of commitment

It is a simple matter to extend the system to handle other types of recurring commitment. For each, the programmer has to make three additions:

- A validation predicate to accept details of a commitment of the new type and record it in the Prolog database. The procedure for the predicate should conform to the structure of existing validation routines. It should include a check, like that in the procedures for add_appointment/4, add_teaches/3 and add_class/3, to identify conflicts between existing appointments for teachers and engagements implied by the new commitment.

- A new clause for appointment/4, defining the commitment.

- A new clause for diary_entry_type/1, so that commitments of the new type are saved when save_diary/1 is called.

Using this method, you should be able to write an extension to incorporate departmental meetings into the diary system, assuming:

- A department holds a departmental meeting once a month in term.

- The meeting is held on the corresponding day each month.

- The meeting is always scheduled for the same period.

When you have written the code, test it by entering the information that the Financial Studies department meets on the third Monday of the month at 10.00am for 3 hours. If the diary includes the information which we have used for illustration in this chapter, the program should give some warnings about clashes between existing commitments and departmental meetings. Does it do so? If you override these warnings, does the program correctly record the information in the representation you have chosen?

12.4.2 Other operations on the diary

Many other questions about activities in the institution can be answered by calling lower-level procedures as goals. Some examples are:

> "Which teachers in the Financial Studies department have to make remand appearances and when?"

The question is posed as the goal:

```
?- teacher(T, financial_studies), appointment(T, Date, Period,
      remand_appearance).
```

> "Mr. Sterling has to make an all-day visit away from the institution. On what dates might he make it?"

The question is posed as the goal:

```
?- bookable_date(Date), fail_if(appointment(sterling, Date, _, _)).
```

If Mr. Sterling were definitely going to book the visit for one of the available dates, the question could be posed as the goal:

```
?- working_day(W),
      todays_date(T),
      book_soonest([sterling], W, all_day_visit, T).
```

"Mr. Sterling has had enough of teaching VAT frauds. How many more classes has he got to take before the end of term?"

Using length/2 from section 4.1, the question is posed as the goal:

```
?- todays_date(T),
   bag(class(Date, P),
       (appointment(sterling, Date, P, teaching(vat_frauds)),
        same_or_later(T,Date)), List),
   length(List, L).
```

With these examples to guide you, try formulating goals for the following questions:

"Mr Sterling wishes to arrange for his classes in VAT frauds to be held in the computer laboratory in November. What are the dates and times for which he has to book this laboratory?"

"The head of the department of Financial Studies wishes to arrange a three hour meeting of the staff in the department for 4th December 1987 at 4.00pm. What other commitments do they have at this time?"

Unfortunately, diary users cannot be expected to use conjunctions of procedures defined within the diary system in asking questions. They would not know of their existence, and any who did would have difficulty in formulating queries correctly, as you will have discovered if you tried to answer our example questions. The diary system would be easier to use if it did not require input to be formulated as Prolog goals. However, it is very hard to design an interface which conceals the syntax of the implementation language while being flexible enough to accept ad hoc queries. The simplest method of shielding users from the syntax of Prolog would be to provide a menu of commands and to prompt for the required input according to the command selected. The system would then convert the user's input into arguments to a goal which would be called to execute the command. A program to provide a menu-driven interface which repeatedly prompted the user to enter a command could be implemented using either forced backtracking or recursion, as described in section 6.2. It should be within your scope to write such a program.

The disadvantage of a menu-driven system is its inflexibility. As the most flexible language for query formulation is natural language, researchers in databases have devoted much effort to investigating the feasibility of using natural language as a query language. They have encountered many problems, not the least of which is that once users have an unrestricted language in which to formulate their questions, they either ask complicated questions that require an extended clarification dialogue or conceive unrealistic expectations of the system's power to answer questions of a philosophical nature. Nonetheless, progress has been made. A good summary of recent work is given in the early chapters of Wallace, 1985. The later chapters describe Wallace's own design for a natural language interface. He used Prolog as the implementation language. If you wish to try writing a natural language interface to the diary system, that book is a good source of ideas on how to set about it.

Code for the Final Version
of the Problem-Solving System

This appendix gives the program text for the problem-solving system developed in Chapter 11. It also includes the description of the problem domain used in problem solving in that chapter and the complete set of action schemas in the final representation, which distinguishes assumptions from requirements and main effects from side-effects.

```
:- op(850, xfx, [requires, removes, achieves, produces, assumes]).
:- op(900, fx, [always, presently]).
:- op(800, xfy, and).

plan(Problem, Depth) :-
      initial_state_is(Si),
      devise_plan(Problem, Si, [], Depth, Plan, Sf),
      confirm_plan(Plan),
      update_state(Sf).

initial_state_is(Si)  :-
      bagof(Fact, presently(Fact), Si).

devise_plan(P and Ps, Si, Steps, Depth, Plan and Plans, Sf) :-
      plan_step(P, Si, Steps, Depth, Plan, Sj),
      devise_plan(Ps, Sj, Steps, Depth, Plans, Sf).
devise_plan(P, Si, Steps, Depth, Plan, Sf) :-
      plan_step(P, Si, Steps, Depth, Plan, Sf).

plan_step(P, Si, _, _, none, Si) :-
      true_in_state(P, Si).
plan_step(P, Si, Steps, Depth, Actions and Action, Sf) :-
      Depth > 0,
      Reduced is Depth - 1,
      Action achieves Effects,
      relevant_action(P, Effects),
      fail_if(member(Action, Steps)),
      Action assumes Assumptions,
      satisfied(Assumptions, Si),
      Action requires Requirements,
      devise_plan(Requirements, Si, [Action|Steps], Reduced, Actions, Sj),
      change_state(Sj, Action, Sf).
```

```
satisfied(Fact and Facts, S) :-
     true_in_state(Fact, S),
     satisfied(Facts, S).
satisfied(Fact, S) :-
     true_in_state(Fact, S).

true_in_state(P, _) :-
     always(P).
true_in_state(P, State) :-
     member(P, State).

member(H, [H|_]).
member(H,[_|T]) :-
     member(H,T).

relevant_action(Effect, Effect).
relevant_action(Effect, Effect and _).
relevant_action(Effect, _ and Effects) :-
     relevant_action(Effect, Effects).

change_state(Si, Action, Sf) :-
     Action removes Removed,
     remove(Si, Removed, Sj),
     Action achieves Main_effects,
     add(Sj, Main_effects, Sk),
     add_side_effects(Sk, Action, Sf).

add_side_effects(Si, Action, Sj) :-
     Action produces Side_effects, !,
     add(Si, Side_effects, Sj).
add_side_effects(S, _, S).

remove(Si, Fact and Facts, Sf) :- !,
     remove_first(Si, Fact, Sm),
     remove(Sm, Facts, Sf).
remove(Si, Fact, Sf) :-
     remove_first(Si, Fact, Sf).

remove_first([], _, []).
remove_first([Fact|Facts], Fact, Facts) :- !.
remove_first([F1|Facts], Fact, [F1|Fs]) :-
     remove_first(Facts, Fact, Fs).

add(Si, Fact and Facts, [Fact|F1]) :- !,
     add(Si, Facts, F1).
add(Si, Fact, [Fact|Si]).

confirm_plan(Plan) :-
     nl,
     write('The steps to be taken are:'),
     nl,
     show_steps(Plan),
     nl,
     write('Is this ok? (y/n)'),
     nl,
     get(121).


show_steps(none) :- !.
```

```
show_steps(Steps1 and Steps2) :- !,
    show_steps(Steps1),
    show_steps(Steps2).
show_steps(Step) :-
    tab(4),
    write(Step),
    nl.

update_state(_) :-
    retract(presently _),
    fail.
  update_state(Sf) :-
    nl,
    write(' The situation now is:'),
    nl,
    show_facts(Sf).

show_facts([]).
show_facts([Fact|Facts]) :-
    tab(4),
    write(Fact),
    nl,
    assert(presently Fact),
    show_facts(Facts).



:- op(700, xfy, [is_a, with, stands, is_in, is_at, is_next_to, connects]).

always room1 is_a room.
always room2 is_a room.
always room3 is_a room.
always door12 is_a door.
always door23 is_a door.
always box1 is_a object.
always box2 is_a object.
always box3 is_a object.
always door12 connects room2 with room1.
always door12 connects room1 with room2.
always door23 connects room2 with room3.
always door23 connects room3 with room2.

presently door12 stands opened.
presently door23 stands opened.
presently box1 is_in room1.
presently box2 is_in room1.
presently box3 is_in room2.
presently robot is_in room2.

:- op(700, xfy, [from, through, to, in]).
:- op(750, fx, [open, close, push, shift]).

go to Door in Room assumes
        Door is_a door and
        Room is_a room and
        Door connects Room with Another_room.

go to Door in Room requires
        robot is_in Room.
```

go to Door in Room removes
    robot is_at Any_door and
    robot is_next_to Anything.

go to Door in Room achieves
    robot is_at Door.

open Door assumes
    Door is_a door and
    Door stands closed.

open Door requires
    robot is_at Door.

open Door removes
    Door stands closed.

open Door achieves
    Door stands opened.

close Door assumes
    Door is_a door and
    Door stands opened.

close Door requires
    robot is_at Door.

close Door removes
    Door stands opened.

close Door achieves
    Door stands closed.

go from Room1 through Door to Room2 assumes
    Room1 is_a room and
    Door is_a door and
    Room2 is_a room and
    Door connects Room1 with Room2.

go from Room1 through Door to Room2 requires
    robot is_in Room1 and
    robot is_at Door and
    Door stands opened.

go from Room1 through Door to Room2 removes
    robot is_at Any_door and
    robot is_next_to Anything and
    robot is_in Room1.

go from Room1 through Door to Room2 achieves
    robot is_in Room2.

move to Object in Room assumes
    Object is_a object and
    Object is_in Room.

move to Object in Room requires
    robot is_in Room.

move to Object in Room removes

    robot is_at Any_door and
    robot is_next_to Anything.

move to Object in Room achieves
    robot is_next_to Object.

push Object1 to Object2 in Room assumes
    Object1 is_a object and
    Object2 is_a object and
    Room is_a room and
    Object2 is_in Room.

push Object1 to Object2 in Room requires
    robot is_next_to Object1 and
    Object1 is_in Room.

push Object1 to Object2 in Room removes
    robot is_at Door1 and
    robot is_next_to Thing1 and
    Object1 is_next_to Thing2 and
    Thing3 is_next_to Object1 and
    Object1 is_at Door2.

push Object1 to Object2 in Room achieves
    Object1 is_next_to Object2.

push Object1 to Object2 in Room produces
    robot is_next_to Object1 and
    robot is_next_to Object2.

shift Object to Door in Room assumes
    Object is_a object and
    Door is_a door and
    Room is_a room and
    Door connects Room with Another_room.

shift Object to Door in Room requires
    robot is_next_to Object and
    Object is_in Room.

shift Object to Door in Room removes
    Object is_at Door1 and
    robot is_next_to Thing1 and
    Object is_next_to Thing2 and
    Thing3 is_next_to Object.

shift Object to Door in Room achieves
    Object is_at Door.

shift Object to Door in Room produces
    robot is_next_to Object and
    robot is_at Door.

push Object from Room1 through Door to Room2 assumes
    Object is_a object and
    Room1 is_a room and
    Door is_a door and
    Room2 is_a room and
    Door connects Room1 with Room2.

push Object from Room1 through Door to Room2 requires
Door stands opened and
robot is_next_to Object and
Object is_in Room1 and
Object is_at Door.

push Object from Room1 through Door to Room2 removes
robot is_at Door1 and
Object is_at Door2 and
robot is_next_to Thing1 and
Object is_next_to Thing2 and
Thing3 is_next_to Object and
robot is_in Any_room and
Object is_in Any_other_room.

push Object from Room1 through Door to Room2 achieves
Object is_in Room2.

push Object from Room1 through Door to Room2 produces
robot is_in Room2 and
robot is_next_to Object.

Code for the Final Version
of the Electronic Diary System

This appendix gives the program text for the electronic diary developed in Chapter 12. The code is given in the order in which it was presented in that chapter.

```
earliest_hour(9).
latest_hour(21).

working_day(mon).
working_day(tue).
working_day(wed).
working_day(thu).
working_day(fri).

working_hours(H)  :-
    earliest_hour(E),
    latest_hour(L),
    H is L - E.

next_day(sun,  mon).
next_day(mon,  tue).
next_day(tue,  wed).
next_day(wed,  thu).
next_day(thu,  fri).
next_day(fri,  sat).
next_day(sat,  sun).

next_month(jan,  feb).
next_month(feb,  mar).
next_month(mar,  apr).
next_month(apr,  may).
next_month(may,  jun).
next_month(jun,  jul).
next_month(jul,  aug).
next_month(aug,  sep).
next_month(sep,  oct).
next_month(oct,  nov).
next_month(nov,  dec).
next_month(dec,  jan).
```

```
month_length(M, _, 30) :-
    ( M = apr; M = jun; M = sep; M = nov ).
month_length(M, _, 31) :-
    ( M = jan; M = mar; M = may; M =jul; M = aug; M = oct; M = dec ).
month_length(feb, Year, 29) :-
    leap_year(Year), !.
month_length(feb, _, 28).

leap_year(Y) :-
    0 is Y mod 400, !.
leap_year(Y) :-
    0 is Y mod 4,
    fail_if(0 is Y mod 100).

find_days(D, 1, D).
find_days(D1, N, D2) :-
    find_days(D1, N1, D3),
    next_day(D3, D2),
    N is N1 + 1.

corresponding_day(Day1, N, Day2) :-
    var(N), !,
    find_days(Day1, N, Day2).
corresponding_day(Day1, N, Day2) :-
    0 is N mod 7, !,
    find_days(Day1, 7, Temp), !,
    Day2 = Temp.
corresponding_day(Day1, N, Day2) :-
    Min is N mod 7,
    find_days(Day1, Min, Temp), !,
    Day2 = Temp.

set_up_diary(Year, dec, S, Year) :- !,
    assert(first_of_month(dec, Year, S)).
set_up_diary(Current_year, dec, S, End_year) :- !,
    assert(first_of_month(dec, Current_year, S)),
    corresponding_day(S, 32, S2),
    Next_year is Current_year + 1,
    set_up_diary(Next_year, jan, S2, End_year).
set_up_diary(Current_year, Current_month, S, End_year) :-
    assert(first_of_month(Current_month, Current_year, S)),
    month_length(Current_month, Current_year, L),
    corresponding_day(S, L, S2),
    next_day(S2, S3),
    next_month(Current_month, Next_month),
    set_up_diary(Current_year, Next_month, S3, End_year).

get_date :-
    write('Please enter the date in the form:'),
    nl,
    write('date(1, jan, 1999).'),
    nl,
    write('The month must be abbreviated'),
    nl,
    write('to its first three characters'),
    nl,
    seeing(F),
    see(user),
    read(Date),
```

```
        assert(todays_date(Date)),
        see(F).

:- get_date.

same_or_later(date(_, _, Y1), date(_, _, Y2)) :-
        Y2 > Y1, !.
same_or_later(date(_, M1, Y), date(_, M2, Y)) :-
        after_month(M1, M2), !.
same_or_later(date(D1, M, Y), date(D2, M, Y)) :-
        D2 >= D1.

after_month(dec, _) :- !,
        fail.
after_month(M1, M2) :-
        next_month(M1, M2).
after_month(M1, M2) :-
        next_month(M1, M3),
        after_month(M3, M2).

date_falls_on(date(D, M, Y), Day1) :-
        first_of_month(M, Y, Day2),
        month_length(M, Y, L),
        in_range_integer(1, D, L),
        corresponding_day(Day2, D, Day1).

in_term_time(Term, date(Date, Month, Year)) :-
        term_dates(Term, Month, Year, From, To),
        in_range_integer(From, Date, To).

teaching(T, S, date(Date, Month, Year)) :-
        teach(T, S, Term, Year),
        in_term_time(Term, date(Date, Month, Year)).

appointment(Name, Date, period(T, 1), teaching(S)) :-
        teaching(Name, S, Date),
        class(S, D, T),
        date_falls_on(Date, D).
appointment(Teacher, Date, Period, Purpose) :-
        single_booking(Teacher, Date, Period, Purpose).

teach(Teacher, Subject, autumn, Year) :-
        teaches(Teacher, Subject, in(Year/_)).
teach(Teacher, Subject, spring, Year) :-
        teaches(Teacher, Subject, in(_/Year)).
teach(Teacher, Subject, summer, Year) :-
        teaches(Teacher, Subject, in(_/Year)).
teach(Teacher, Subject, Term, Year) :-
        teaches(Teacher, Subject, in(Term, Year)).

term_of(in(Y/_), autumn, Y).
term_of(in(_/Y), spring, Y).
term_of(in(_/Y), summer, Y).
term_of(in(Term, Year), Term, Year).
save_diary(File) :-
        write_file_of_terms(File).

write_file_of_terms(To) :-
        telling(Currently),
        tell(To),
```

```
            write_each_term,
            tell(Currently).

    write_each_term :-
            next(Term),
            write(Term),
            write('.'),
            nl,
            fail.
    write_each_term :-
            told.

    next(Entry) :-
            diary_entry_type(Functor/Arity),
            functor(Entry, Functor, Arity),
            call(Entry).

    diary_entry_type(first_of_month/3).
    diary_entry_type(term_dates/5).
    diary_entry_type(teacher/2).
    diary_entry_type(course/2).
    diary_entry_type(single_booking/4).
    diary_entry_type(teaches/3).
    diary_entry_type(class/3).
    diary_entry_type(department/1).

    load_diary(File) :-
            consult(File).

    validate(warning(Check_clash), none) :- !,
            arg(1, Check_clash, Details),
            bag(Details, Check_clash, Result),
            check_result(Result).
    validate(Check, _) :-
            call(Check), !.
    validate(_, Error_message) :-
            assert(error(Error_message)).

    check_result([ ]) :- !.
    check_result(L) :-
            assert(warning(L)).

    do_action(Action) :-
            retract(warning(Message)), !,
            write_out(['New commitment clashes with:'|Message]),
            write('Should it be added? (y/n): '),
            get(Answer),
            act_on(Answer, Action).
    do_action(_) :-
            retract(error(Message)), !,
            report_error(Message).
    do_action(Action) :-
            call(Action).

    act_on(121, Action) :- !,
            call(Action).
    act_on(_, _).
```

```
report_error(Message) :-
    write_out(Message),
    nl,
    retract(error(Next_message)), !,
    report_error(Next_message).
report_error(_).

write_out([ ]).
write_out([H|T])  :-
    write(H),
    nl,
    write_out(T).

add_term_dates(Term, From, To) :-
    validate(is_term(Term), [Term,' is not a term']),
    validate(same_or_later(From, To), ['finish date must not be before start date']),
    do_action(record_term_dates(Term, From, To)).

is_term(autumn).
is_term(spring).
is_term(summer).

record_term_dates(Term, date(D1, M, Y), date(D2, M, Y)) :- !,
    assert(term_dates(Term, M, Y, D1, D2)).
record_term_dates(Term, date(D, dec, Y), To) :- !,
    assert(term_dates(Term, dec, Y, D, 31)),
    Y2 is Y + 1,
    record_term_dates(Term, date(1, jan, Y2), To).
record_term_dates(Term, date(D, M, Y), To) :-
    month_length(M, Y, L),
    assert(term_dates(Term, M, Y, D, L)),
    next_month(M, Next_m),
    record_term_dates(Term, date(1, Next_m, Y), To).

add_dept(Dept) :-
    do_action(add_fact(department(Dept))).

add_teacher(Teacher, Dept) :-
    validate(fail_if(teacher(Teacher, _)), [Teacher,'already exists']),
    validate(department(Dept), [Dept,'is not a department']),
    do_action(add_fact(teacher(Teacher, Dept))).

add_course(Course, Dept) :-
    validate(fail_if(course(Course,_)), [Course,'already exists']),
    validate(department(Dept), [Dept,'is not a department']),
    do_action(add_fact(course(Course, Dept))).

add_fact(Fact) :-
    clause(Fact, true), !,
    write('This information is already stored in the database'), nl.
add_fact(Fact) :-
    assert(Fact).

add_appointment(Teacher, Date, Period, Purpose) :-
    validate(teacher(Teacher, _),[Teacher,'is not a teacher']),
    validate(bookable_date(Date), [Date,'is not a bookable date']),
    validate(bookable_hours(Period), [Period, 'is not within working hours']),
    validate(warning(appointment_clashes(appointment(Teacher, Date, _, _), Period)),
                                none),
```

```
            do_action(assert(single_booking(Teacher, Date, Period, Purpose))).

    bookable_date(Date) :-
        date_falls_on(Date, Day),
        working_day(Day),
        todays_date(Today),
        same_or_later(Today, Date).

    bookable_hours(period(Start, Duration)) :-
        earliest_hour(E),
        latest_hour(L),
        Last_start is L - 1,
        in_range_integer(E, Start, Last_start),
        Max_duration is L - Start,
        in_range_integer(1, Duration, Max_duration).

    appointment_clashes(Present_commitment, Period) :-
        call(Present_commitment),
        arg(3, Present_commitment, P),
        overlapping(P, Period).

    overlapping(period(S,D), period(NewS, NewD)) :-
        NewS < S + D,
        NewS + NewD > S.

    add_teaches(Teacher, Subject, When) :-
        validate(teacher(Teacher, _), [Teacher,'is not a teacher']),
        validate(course(Subject, _), [Subject,'is not a subject']),
        validate(unit_of_teaching(When), [When, 'is not a unit of teaching']),
        validate(warning(teaching_clashes(appointment(Teacher, _, _, _), Subject, When)),
                                          none),
        do_action(add_fact(teaches(Teacher, Subject, When))).

    unit_of_teaching(in(Term, Year)) :-
        term_dates(Term, _, Year, _, _).
    unit_of_teaching(in(Y1/Y2)) :-
        Y2 is Y1 + 1,
        term_dates(autumn, _, Y1, _, _),
        term_dates(spring, _, Y2, _, _),
        term_dates(summer, _, Y2, _, _).

    teaching_clashes(appointment(T, date(Date, Month, Year), P, W), S, When) :-
        class(S, Day, Time),
        term_of(When, Term, Year),
        in_term_time(Term, date(Date, Month, Year)),
        date_falls_on(date(Date, Month, Year), Day),
        appointment(T, date(Date, Month, Year), P, W),
        overlapping(P, period(Time, 1)).

    add_class(Subject, Day, Time) :-
        validate(course(Subject, _), [Subject,'is not a subject']),
        validate(working_day(Day), [Day,'is not a working day']),
        validate(bookable_hours(period(Time, 1)), [Time,
                                        'is not a valid time for the start of a class']),
        validate(warning(class_clashes(appointment(_, _, _, _), Subject,Day, Time)), none),
        do_action(assert(class(Subject, Day, Time))).

    class_clashes(appointment(T, Date, P, Why), Subject, Day, Time) :-
        teaching(T, Subject, Date),
        date_falls_on(Date, Day),
```

```
        appointment(T, Date, P, Why),
        overlapping(P, period(Time, 1)).

print_entries(Teacher, Commitment) :-
        validate(teacher(Teacher, _), [Teacher, ' is not a teacher']),
        do_action(list_entries(Teacher, Commitment)).

list_entries(T, date(D, M, Y)) :-
        show_entries(T, date(D, M, Y), _, _).
list_entries(T,subject(S))   :-
        show_entries(T, _, _, S).
list_entries(T, period(S, D)) :-
        show_entries(T, _, period(S, D), _).

show_entries(T, Date, period(S, D), Purpose) :-
        bookable_date(Date),
        earliest_hour(E),
        latest_hour(L),
        in_range_integer(E, S, L),
        appointment(T, Date, period(S, D), Purpose),
        write('Date: '),
        write(Date),
        write(' Time: '),
        write(S),
        write(' Duration: '),
        write(D),
        write(' Purpose: '),
        write(Purpose),
        nl,
        fail.
show_entries(_, _, _, _).

book_soonest(For, Duration, Purpose, Not_before) :-
        validate(bookable_hours(period(_, Duration)),
            [Duration,'is longer than working day']),
        validate(bookable_date(Not_before),
            [Not_before, 'is not a bookable date']),
        do_action((
            make_list(For, [First|Others]),
            find_soonest(First, Duration, Not_before, When),
            check_others(Others, When),
            confirm_time(When),
            record_group_booking([First|Others], When, Purpose)
            )).

make_list([H|T], [H|T]).
make_list(people(People, Condition), List_of_people) :-
        bag(People, Condition, List_of_people).

find_soonest(Teacher, Duration, Not_before,
        slot(Date, period(Start, Duration))) :-
        date_falls_on(Date, Day),
        working_day(Day),
        same_or_later(Not_before , Date),
        bookable_hours(period(Start, Duration)),
        fail_if(appointment_clashes(appointment(Teacher, Date, _, _), period(Start,
                                            Duration))).

check_others([ ], _).
```

```
check_others([First|Others], slot(Date, Period)) :-
    fail_if(appointment_clashes(appointment(First, Date, _, _), Period)),
    check_others(Others, slot(Date, Period)).

confirm_time(slot(Date,Period))  :-
    write('Appointment could be booked for: '),
    write(Date),
    nl,
    write('At:  '),
    write(Period),
    nl,
    write('Is this ok (y/n)? '),
    get(121).

record_group_booking([First|Others], slot(Date, Period), P) :-
    teacher(First, _), !,
    write('Booked for: '),
    write(First),
    nl,
    assert(single_booking(First, Date, Period, P)),
    record_group_booking(Others, slot(Date, Period), P).
record_group_booking([First|Others], When, Purpose) :-
    write('Ignored: '),
    write(First),
    nl,
    record_group_booking(Others, When, Purpose).
record_group_booking([ ], _, _).
```

A Standard for the Prolog Language

There are many versions of Prolog available. In this book, we have used the syntax of Edinburgh Prolog, developed at the University of Edinburgh for the DECSystem-10 computer, but widely adopted by other suppliers for other machines. The set of built-in predicates we have described is also based on that of Edinburgh Prolog. However, we have taken account of some of the developments initiated by the British Standards Institute's Working Group on Prolog standardisation, indicating by footnotes in the text where the Working Group is diverging from commonly-available implementations. In this appendix, we mention some of the main proposals which seem likely to emerge as a result of the Working Group's efforts, though we should emphasise that its deliberations have not yet been completed.

Types of Term

The introduction of string as a type of term. Values of the type to be denoted by double quotes. So:

"abc"	is a string.
abc	is an atom.
""	is the empty string.

Another built-in predicate to test the type of a term. A call to string/1 would succeed if the argument was a string.

Built-in predicates to operate on strings:

strlength/2	to determine the length of a string.
concat/3	to concatenate two strings.
substring/4	to determine the substring starting at a given position in a string and of a given length.

Input and Output

The stream for input or output to be able to be specified in calls to the relevant built-in predicates and the format to be able to be specified in term I/O. So, in calls to write/3 and read/3 the first argument would be the stream for output or input, the second the format of the term and the third the term to be written or with which the term read was to be matched.

Term Ordering

A total ordering of all terms and a set of built-in predicates for testing term ordering:

@</2	less than, in the ordering of terms.
@=</2	less than or equal to, in the ordering of terms.
@>/2	greater than, in the ordering of terms
@>=/2	greater than or equal to, in the ordering of terms

For the types of terms, the following order:

var < real < integer < string < atom < compound

Within types, the order of variables remains to be defined, that of reals and integers is numeric and of strings and atoms is lexicographic. Structures are ordered:

- First, according to their arity;
- Second, according to the lexicographic order of their functors;
- Third, according to the order of corresponding components of each, starting with the first.

Arithmetic

An extension to the definition of is/2 to allow its second argument to be a call to a procedure. So, the goal:

?- X is length(Y).

would be satisfied if a procedure for length/2 was defined and the goal:

? length(Y, X).

was satisfied.

Appendix 4

Answers to Exercises

1.1　(a)
(i)　An atom
(ii)　Not an atom (in fact, a variable)
(iii)　An atom
(iv)　Not an atom (an integer)
(v)　Not an atom (a structure)
(vi)　An atom

1.3　(a)
(i)　Invalid: functor is not an atom
(ii)　Valid: arity 1, arity of the component: 0
(iii)　Valid: arity 0
(iv)　Valid: arity 4; arity of each component: 0
(v)　Valid: arity 1; arity of the component: 4; arity of its component: 0
(vi)　Valid: arity 1; arity of the component: 4; arity of its components: 1, 1, 0, 0
(vii)　Valid: arity 4; arity of the components: 1, 1, 0, 0
(viii)　Invalid: components not separated by ","
(ix)　Valid: arity 1; arity of the component: 0
(x)　Valid: arity 5; arity of each component: 0

(b)　?- soldier(name(towser), rank(sergeant)).
　　?- soldier(name(cathcart), rank(captain)).
　　?- soldier(name(dreedle), rank(general)).
　　?- soldier(name(aardvark), R).
　　?- soldier(S, rank(colonel)).
　　?- soldier(name(aardvaark), R), soldier(name(flume), R).

(c)　The instruments mentioned would be:

　　　　instrument(instrument(violin),　type(string)).
　　　　instrument(instrument(viola),　type(string)).
　　　　instrument(instrument(clarinet),　type(woodwind)).
　　　　instrument(instrument(bassoon),　type(woodwind)).
　　　　instrument(instrument(trumpet),　type(brass)).
　　　　instrument(instrument(trombone),　type(brass)).
　　　　instrument(instrument(horn),　type(brass)).

1.4　(a)
(i)　Match: T ← 'animal farm', Author ← author('george orwell')
(ii)　Match: Day ← day(wednesday), Date ← date(21), Month ← month(M), Year ← year(1986), M: no substitution made
(iii)　Match: H ← christmas, Day ← day(25), Month ← month(december), Y ← 1986
(iv)　Not a match: different arity

2.1

(a)
```
same_rank(First_soldier, Second_soldier, Rank) :-
    soldier(First_soldier, Rank),
    soldier(Second_soldier, Rank).
```

(b) See section 2.2.

2.3

(a)
```
Who = player(hermann)
Who = player(klaus)
Who = player(wilfrid)
```

(b)
```
What = instrument(clarinet)
What = instrument(bassoon)
What = instrument(trumpet)
What = instrument(trombone)
What = instrument(horn)
```

If the clauses were reversed, the brass instruments would be listed before the woodwind.

2.4

(a)
```
S = s(np(d(the), n(woman)), vp(v(sees), np(d(the), n(woman))))
S = s(np(d(the), n(woman)), vp(v(sees), np(d(the), n(girl))))
S = s(np(d(the), n(woman)), vp(v(sees), np(d(a), n(woman))))
S = s(np(d(the), n(woman)), vp(v(sees), np(d(a), n(girl))))
S = s(np(d(the), n(woman)), vp(v(calls), np(d(the), n(woman))))
S = s(np(d(the), n(woman)), vp(v(calls), np(d(the), n(girl))))
S = s(np(d(the), n(woman)), vp(v(calls), np(d(a), n(woman))))
S = s(np(d(the), n(woman)), vp(v(calls), np(d(a), n(girl))))
```

and this sequence of vp structures repeated for each of the subject np structures:

```
np(d(the), n(girl))        np(d(a), n(woman))        np(d(a), n(girl))
```

(b)
```
verb_phrase(vp(Vb)) :-
    verb(Vb).
```

3.2

(a) See section 3.3

(b)
```
commands(S, L) :-
    soldier(name(S), rank(R)),
    ranks_commanded(R, L).

ranks_commanded(private, none).
ranks_commanded(R1, rank(R2, Ranks)) :-
    next_rank(R2, R1),
    ranks_commanded(R2, Ranks).
```

(c)
```
relative_ranks(S1, S2, L) :-
    soldier(name(S1), rank(R1)),
    soldier(name(S2), rank(R2)),
    ranks_from(R1, R2, L).

ranks_from(R, R, none).
ranks_from(R1, R2, next(R3, Others)) :-
    next_rank(R1, R3),
    ranks_from(R3, R2, Others).
```

(d)
```
commands(S, L) :-
```

```
                    ranks_commanded(R, none, L).

            ranks_commanded(private, L, L).
            ranks_commanded(R1, L, Ranks) :-
                    next_rank(R2, R1),
                    ranks_commanded(R2, rank(R2, L), Ranks).
```

3.3   (a)
(i)   Match: H ← [grey, green], T ← [black, blue]
(ii)   Match: H ← [george, millicent]
(iii)   Match: First ← [william, mary], Others ← [Second], Second: no substitution
(iv)   No match
(v)   A ← [married(george, millicent)]
(vi)   Match: A ← 1805, B ← [ ], C ← 1815, D ← [ ]
(vii)   [A|B, C|D] is syntactically incorrect.
(viii) Match: A ← jack, B ← jill, C ← []
(ix)   No match

3.4
(a)   permute([ ], [ ]).
        permute([H|T], [I|L]) :-
                remove(I, [H|T], L2),
                permute(L2, L).

(b)   remove_all(_, [ ], [ ]).
        remove_all(H, [H|T], L) :-
                remove_all(H, T, L).
        remove_all(I, [H|T], [I|L]) :-
                different(I, H),
                remove_all(I, T, L).

(c)   no_duplicates([ ], [ ]).
        no_duplicates([H|T], [H|L]) :-
                remove_all(H, T, L1),
                no_duplicates(L1, L).

3.5
(a)   The sub-goal: ?- conc(Front, Back, List) is re-satisfiable with Front containing
        from 0 to n of the n items in List.   Each time this goal is satisfied, the second sub-
        goal: ?- conc(F, Sub, Front) is re-satisfiable with Sub containing from m to 0 of
        the m items in Front.   The empty list is generated n + 1 times.

(b)   sublist(Any, [ ]).
        sublist(L, [H|T]) :-
                split(H, L, Back),
                front_of(T, Back).

        split(H, [H|T], T).
        split(I, [H|L1], L2) :-
                split(I, L1, L2).

        front_of([ ], Any).
        front_of([H|L1], [H|L2]) :-
                front_of(L1, L2).

The call:

        ?- sublist([1, 2, 3], Sub)

produces:
```
```

```
                Sub = [ ];
                Sub = [1];
                Sub = [1, 2];
                Sub = [1, 2, 3];
                Sub = [2];
                Sub = [2, 3];
                Sub = [3];
                no
```

4.1

(a)   The call produces infinite recursion as the procedure generates ever longer lists, testing each to see if it is of length 3.

(b)
```
        length([ ], 0).
        length([ [H|T] | L], N) :-              % First element in list is a list.
            length([H|T], P),
            length(L, Q),
            N is P + Q.
        length([H|T], N) :-
            different(H, [_|_]),               % First element is not a list.
            length(T, M),
            length(N is M + 1.
```

(c)
```
        sum_of_elements([ ], 0).
        sum_of_elements([H|T], M) :-
            sum_of_elements(T, N),
            M is N + H.
```

4.2   (a)

(i)   Succeeds, substituting N ← 8*9. Though the expression is evaluated in the subgoal, the value substituted is that of the expression given as argument.

(ii)   Fails: the arguments do not match either clause.

(b)
```
        split([ ], _, [ ], [ ]).                 % Empty list splits into two empty lists.
        split([H|L1], N, [H|L2], L3) :-          % Head belongs in list of less if
            H < N,                               %   it is less than N
            split(L1, N, L2, L3).
        split([H|L1], N, L2, [H|L3]) :-          % Otherwise head belongs in list of greater
            H >= N,
            split(L1, N, L2, L3).
```

(c)
```
        position_of_max([N], N, 1).
        position_of_max([H, L|M], Max_num, Max_pos) :-
            position_of_max([L|M], Tail_max, Tail_pos),
            max_of_positions(H, Tail_max, Tail_pos, Max_num, Max_pos).

        max_of_positions(First, Tail_max, _, First, 1) :-
            max(First, Tail_max, First).
        max_of_positions(First, Tail_max, Tail_pos, Tail_max, Pos) :-
            max(First, Tail_max, Tail_max),
            Pos is Tail_pos + 1.
```

On backtracking, this procedure gives each position of the highest in the list, though with some duplication!

4.3

(a)
```
        greater_or_equal(N1, N2) :-              % Both integers
            integer(N1),
            integer(N2),
            N2 >= N1.
```

292

```
            greater_or_equal(N1, N2) :-        % N2 a variable
                integer(N1),
                var(N2),
                next_integer(N1, N2).
            greater_or_equal(N1, N2) :-        % N1 a variable
                var(N1),
                integer(N2),
                previous_integer(N1, N2).

            previous_integer(N, N).
            previous_integer(N1, N2) :-
                N3 is N2 - 1,
                previous_integer(N1, N3).
```

4.4
(a)
```
            plural_form(Singular, Plural) :-        % Clause for special plural forms of nouns
                name(Singular, Chs1),
                conc(Begins, [Last_but_one, Last], Chs1),
                special_form([Last_but_one, Last], Special_plural),
                conc(Begins, Special_plural, Chs2),
                name(Plural, Chs2).
            plural_form(Singular, Plural) :-        % Clause for ordinary forms
                name(Singular, Chs1),
                conc(Chs1, [115], Plural_chs),   % Add "s"
                name(Plural, Plural_chs).

            special_form([Ch, 121], [Ch, 105, 101, 115]) :- % Consonant + "y"
                consonant(Ch).
            special_form([Ch, 111], [Ch, 111, 101, 115]) :- % Consonant + "o"
                consonant(Ch).

            consonant(Ch) :-                   % "b" to "d"
                Ch > 97,
                Ch < 101.
            consonant(Ch) :-                   % "f" to "h"
                Ch > 101,
                Ch < 105.
            consonant(Ch) :-                   % "j" to "n"
                Ch > 105,
                Ch < 111.
            consonant(Ch) :-                   % "p" to "t"
                Ch > 111,
                Ch < 117.
            consonant(Ch) :-                   % "v" to "z"
                Ch > 117,
                Ch < 123.
```

Note that this program produces incorrect alternatives on backtracking because the case of a special_form does not exclude the second case.

(b)
```
            cifer(Plain, Shift, Code) :-
                name(Plain, Plain_chars),
                convert_chars(Plain_chars, Shift, Code_chars),
                name(Code, Code_chars).

            convert_chars([ ], _, [ ]).
            convert_chars([Plain|L1], Shift, [Code|L2]) :-
                Code is (Plain - 97 + Shift) mod 26 + 97,
                convert_chars(L1, Shift, L2).
```
(c)
```
            select_a_move(Board, Move) :-
                test_next_square(1, Board, Move).
```

```
test_next_square(Move, Board, Move) :-
    arg(Move, Board, Square),
    var(Square).
test_next_square(Possible_square, Board, Move) :-
    arg(Possible_square, Board, Square),
    nonvar(Square),
    Next is Possible_square + 1,
    Next < 10,
    test_next_square(Next, Board, Move).
```

5.1
(a)
```
display_position(Board) :-
    write('Position  is:'),
    nl,
    display_squares(Board, 1).

display_squares(_, Pos) :-
    Pos > 9.
display_squares(Board, Pos) :-
    Pos =< 9,
    arg(Pos, Board, Square),
    display_a_square(Square),
    align_output(Pos),
    Next_pos is Pos + 1,
    display_squares(Board, Next_pos).

display_a_square(Square) :-
    var(Square),
    write('_').
display_a_Square(Square) :-
    Square == o,
    write(o).
display_a_square(Square) :-
    Square == x,
    write(x).

align_output(P)  :-
    P mod 3 =:= 0,
    nl.
align_output(P)  :-
    P mod 3 > 0,
    tab(2).
```

5.2.1
(a)
```
:- op(80, fx, [a, the]).
:- op(90, fx, [by, on, under]).
:- op(100, xfx, stands).
```

(b)
```
:- op(91, xfy, '->').

t -> t gives t.
t -> f gives f.
f -> t gives t.
f -> f gives t.
```

A new clause for assign/4:

```
assign(E1 -> E2, L, C1 -> C2, V) :-
    assign(E1, L, C1, V1),
    assign(E2, L, C2, V2),
    V1 -> V2 gives V.
```

5.2.2

(a)   First, we must distinguish a punctuation mark and a letter in the procedure for form_a_list/3:

```
form_a_list(C, [C], C1) :-
    punctuation_mark(C),
    get0(C1).
form_a_list(C, [C|Cs], C2) :-
    letter(C),
    get0(C1),
    form_a_list(C1, Cs, C2).
```

These clauses replace the existing third clause.   Procedures for the guards are:

```
punctuation_mark(40).            % "("
punctuation_mark(41).            % ")"
punctuation_mark(44).            % ","
punctuation_mark(58).            % ":"
punctuation_mark(59).            % ";"

letter(C)  :-
    C > 64,                      % "A" to "Z"
    C < 91.
letter(C)  :-
    C > 96,                      % "a" to "z"
    C < 123.
```

Then, replace the call to occurs_in_word/1 in the third clause of the procedure for form_words/2 with a new guard:

```
form_words(C, [W|Ws]) :-
    first_of_word(C).

first_of_word(C)  :-
    punctuation_mark(C).
first_of_word(C)  :-
    letter(C).
```

Finally, remove the procedure for occurs_in_word/1, which is no longer called.

5.3

(a)   The following procedure for change/2 performs the conversion:

```
change(C, C) :-
    C < 65.
change(C, C) :-
    C > 90.
change(C, C1) :-
    C > 64,
    C < 91,
    C1 is C + 32.
```

(b)   We require an extra clause in the procedure for change_char/1:

```
change_char(32)  :-                  % <space>
    get0(C1),
    compress_spaces(C1, C2),
    change_char(C2).

compress_spaces(32, C) :-
```

```
            get0(C1),
            compress_spaces(C1, C2).
        compress_spaces(C, C) :-
            C \= 32,
            put(32).                        % Output one <space>.
```

The guard on the second clause must also be changed:

```
        change_char(C) :-
            end_of_file_char(C1),
            C \= C1,
            C \= 32,
            put(C),
            get0(C2),
            change_char(C2).
```

6.1.2
(a)   intersection([ ], _, [ ]).
        intersection([H|T], S, [H|S1]) :-
            member(H, S), !,
            intersection(T, S, S1).
        intersection([_|T], S, S1) :-
            intersection(T, S, S1).

        subset(_, [ ]).
        subset(S, [H|T]) :-
            member(H, S),
            subset(S, T).

        difference([ ], _, [ ]).
        difference([H|T], S, S1) :-
            member(H, S), !,
            difference(T, S, S1).
        difference([H|T], S, [H|S1]) :-
            difference(T, S, S1).

        equal_sets([ ], [ ]).
        equal_sets([H|T], S) :-
            remove(H, S, S1),
            equal_sets(T, S1).

        disjoint(S1, S2) :-
            fail_if(member(E, S1) , member(E, S2)).

(b)   game_over(Board, winner_is(P1)) :-
            winning_line(S1, S2, S3),
            arg(S1, Board, P1),
            arg(S2, Board, P2),
            arg(S3, Board, P3),
            P1 == P2,
            P2 == P3, !.
        game_over(Board, 'The game is drawn') :-
            ground(Board).

        winning_line(1, 2, 3).
        winning_line(4, 5, 6).
        winning_line(7, 8, 9).
        winning_line(1, 4, 7).
        winning_line(2, 5, 8).
        winning_line(3, 6, 9).
        winning_line(1, 5, 9).
```
```

```
                winning_line(3, 5, 7).

(c)             greater_integer(N1, N2) :-        % Both integers
                    integer(N1),
                    integer(N2), !,
                    N2 > N1
                greater_integer(N1, N2) :-        % Just N1 an integer
                    integer(N1), !,
                    next_integer(N1, N2).
                greater_integer(N1, N2) :-        % just N2 an integer
                    integer(N2),
                    previous_integer(N1, N2).
```

6.2

(a) See section 6.3.1

(b)
```
        get_users_move(Board, Move) :-
            write('Type in a number between 1 and 9'),
            nl,
            write(' for the square you want to occupy: '),
            read(Possible_move),
            verify_move(Board, Possible_move, Move).

        verify_move(Board, Move, Move) :-    % Possible_move is valid if . . .
            integer(Move),                   % it is an integer . . .
            Move >= 1,                        % which represents a square . . .
            Move =< 9,
            empty_square(Move, Board), !.    % that is empty.
        verify_move(Board, Invalid, Move) :-
            write(Invalid is impossible),
            nl,
            get_users_move(Board, Move).
```

6.3.1

(a) When the call to sub1 fails and the call to sub3 succeeds.

(b)
```
        proc2 :-
            sub1,
            sub2.
        proc2 :-
            sub3.

        proc3 :-
            sub1,
            proc4.

        proc4 :-
            sub2.
        proc4 :-
            sub3.
```

6.3.2 Because it matches the first clause. The problem is overcome by having a new clause as the first:

```
        after_month(M1, M2) :-
            var(M1),
            next_month(M1, M3), !,
            after_month(M1, M2).
```

7.1.1.

(a)
```
        actions_on(Member) :-
            assert(Member).
```

```
        next(member(Name, Age, Status)) :-
            member(Name, Age, Status).
```

7.1.2

(a)   In each case, the nodes would be in reverse order in the list.

8.2.1

(a)   To distinguish subject noun phrases from object noun phrases, we make
noun_phrase a five argument predicate. The calls to it become:

```
        sentence(s(Np, Vp)) -->
            noun_phrase(Np, F, subject),
            verb_phrase(Vp, F).

        verb_phrase(vp(V, Np), F) -->
            verb(V, F),
            noun_phrase(Np, _, object).
```

In the existing clause, the extra argument is the anonymous variable:

```
        noun_phrase(np(D, N), form(third, Number), _) -->
            determiner(D, Number),
            noun(N, Number).
```

The clause to recognise pronouns is:

```
        noun_phrase(np(pn(Person, Number)), form(Person, Number), Position) -->
            pronoun(Person, Number, Position).

        pronoun(first, singular, subject) --> [i].
        pronoun(second, _, _) --> [you].
        pronoun(third, singular, _) --> [it].
        pronoun(third, singular, subject) --> [he].
        pronoun(third, singular, subject) --> [she].
        pronoun(first, plural, subject) --> [we].
        pronoun(third, plural, subject) --> [they].
        pronoun(first, singular, object) --> [me].
        pronoun(third, singular, object) --> [him].
        pronoun(third, singular, object) --> [her].
        pronoun(first, plural, object) --> [us].
        pronoun(third, plural, object) --> [them].
```

8.2.2

(a)
```
        noun_phrase(np(none, N), form(third, plural), _) -->
            noun(N, plural).
```

8.3

(a)
```
        noun(n(Noun), Number) -->
            [N],
            {is_noun(N, Noun, Number)}.

        is_noun(N, N, singular) :-
            noun_entry(N, _).
        is_noun(Plural, Singular, plural) :-
            noun_entry(Singular, Plural).
```

A typical dictionary entry would be:

```
        noun_entry(woman, women).
```

(b)   Dictionary entries:

    verb_entry(see, sees, seen, subject(animate)).

    noun_entry(woman, women, type(animate)).

Other rules would have an extra argument to return the new information.   The
rule for sentence/3 would test for a match:

    sentence(s(Np, Vp)) -->
        noun_phrase(Np, F, subject, type(T)),
        verb_phrase(Vp, F, subject(T)).

8.4.
(a)   An extra clause is required for factor/3:

    factor(F) -->
        ['('],
        expression(F),
        [')'].

(b)   condition(C) -->
        boolean_term(T),
        other_condition(T, C).

    other_condition(T, expr(T, or, C)) -->
        [or],
        condition(C).
    other_condition(T, T) --> [ ].

    boolean_term(C) -->
        comparison(T),
        other_comparison(T, C).

    other_comparison(T, expr(T, and, C)) -->
        [and],
        boolean_term(C).
    other_comparison(T, T) --> [ ].

    comparison(rel_expr(E1, Op, E2)) -->
        expression(E1),
        [Op],
        {relational_operator(Op)},
        expression(E2).

    relational_operator('=').
    relational_operator('\=').
    relational_operator('>').
    relational_operator('<').
    relational_operator('>=').
    relational_operator('=<').

(c)   evaluate(rel_expr(E1, Op, E2), Value) :-
        Comparison =.. [Op, E1, E2],
        test(Comparison, Value).
    evaluate(expr(E1, Op, E2), Value) :-
        evaluate(E1, Sub_value),
        combined_value(Sub_value, Op, E2, Value).

    test(C, true) :-
        call(C), !.

```
test(false, _).

combined_value(true, or, _, true).
combined_value(false, or, E, Value) :-
    evaluate(E, Value).
combined_value(true, and, E, Value) :-
    evaluate(E, Value).
combined_value(false, and, _, false).
```

9.1

(a) The procedure cannot be used to generate alternatives in a call such as:

```
?- permute(L, [1, 2, 3]).
```

Written as:

```
permute([ ], [ ]).
permute([X|L], P) :-
    permute(L, L1),
    insert(X, L1, P).

insert(H, T, [H|T]).
insert(X, [H|T1], [H|T2]) :-
    insert(X, T1, T2).
```

the procedure does generate all alternatives for the call given, but when the user rejects the last answer, the procedure goes into endless recursion.

9.3

(a)
```
satisfy_goal(Goal) :-
    satisfy_the_goal(Goal).
satisfy_goal(_) :-
    retractall(succeeded(_)),
    retractall(failed(_)).

satisfy_the_goal(Goal) :-
    satisfy_and_display(Goal), !,
    fail.
```

(b) The final clause for satisfy/1 becomes:

```
satisfy(Goal, by(Goal, 'user intervention')) :-
    functor(Goal, Functor, Arity),
    suspect(Functor/Arity),
    satisfied(Goal).
```

9.4

(a) To document the predicate:

- The first argument is an atom representing a node on a directed graph.
- The second argument is a list representing the nodes reachable from it.
- Arcs on the graph are represented by facts which are clauses for arc/2.

To document the procedure:
- In calls, the first argument must be an atom; the second can be a variable.
- The procedure uses database modification to accumulate results through forced backtracking. The procedure for traverse_graph/1 is the adding phase; the collecting phase is that for collect_nodes/1.
- The clauses added in the first phase are facts for reached/1.

The Ascii Character Set

Code	Character
33	!
34	"
35	£
36	$
37	%
38	&
39	'
40	(
41	)
42	*
43	+
44	,
45	-
46	.
47	/
48 - 57	0 - 9
58	:
59	;
60	<
61	=
62	>
63	?
64	@
65 - 90	A - Z
91	[
92	\
93	]
94	^
95	_
96	`
97 - 122	a - z
123	{
124	|
125	}
126	~

References

Brna et al, 1987
>
> "Programming tools for Prolog environments"
> P. Brna, A. Bundy, H. Pain & L. Lynch
> in: "Advances in artificial intelligence" (Proceedings of AISB, 1987)
> J. Hallam & C. Mellish, eds.
> Wiley, 1987

Fikes & Nilsson, 1971
>
> "STRIPS: A new approach to the application of theorem proving to problem solving"
> R. E. Fikes & N. J. Nilsson
> Artificial Intelligence, Vol 2, pp 189 - 208

Pereira & Shieber, 1987
>
> "Prolog and natural language analysis"
> L. C. N. Pereira & S. M. Shieber
> CSLI, 1987

Silver, 1986
>
> "Pre-condition analysis: learning control information"
> B. Silver
> in "Machine Learning: an artificial intelligence approach, Volume 2"
> R. S. Mickalski et al, eds.
> Morgan Kaufmann, 1987

Index